MARKETS AND CONFLICT

Perspectives in Behavioral Economics and the Economics of Behavior

MARKETS AND CONFLICT

Economics of War and Peace

WILLIAM R. PATTERSON

DANIEL W. KUTHY
Brescia University

Series Editor
MORRIS ALTMAN

ELSEVIER

Elsevier
Radarweg 29, PO Box 211, 1000 AE Amsterdam, Netherlands
125 London Wall, London EC2Y 5AS, United Kingdom
50 Hampshire Street, 5th Floor, Cambridge, MA 02139, United States

Notices
Knowledge and best practice in this field are constantly changing. As new research and experience broaden our understanding, changes in research methods, professional practices, or medical treatment may become necessary.

Practitioners and researchers must always rely on their own experience and knowledge in evaluating and using any information, methods, compounds, or experiments described herein. In using such information or methods they should be mindful of their own safety and the safety of others, including parties for whom they have a professional responsibility.

To the fullest extent of the law, neither the Publisher nor the authors, contributors, or editors, assume any liability for any injury and/or damage to persons or property as a matter of products liability, negligence or otherwise, or from any use or operation of any methods, products, instructions, or ideas contained in the material herein.

ISBN: 978-0-323-85525-9

For information on all Elsevier publications
visit our website at https://www.elsevier.com/books-and-journals

Publisher: Mica H Haley
Acquisitions Editor: Kathryn Eryilmaz
Editorial Project Manager: Aleksandra Packowska
Production Project Manager: Gomathi Sugumar
Cover Designer: Miles Hitchen

Typeset by STRAIVE, India

Working together
to grow libraries in
developing countries

www.elsevier.com • www.bookaid.org

Contents

Acknowledgments

The conception of this book originated with Michael Taillard, an economist with expertise in the interaction between the economy and war and with a number of significant publications on this broad issue under his belt. In his 2019 book *Economics and Modern Warfare*, he recognized that there was a gap in the literature when it came to how various markets affect and are in turn affected by conflict. He conceived of this book as "compiling the most current information about market behaviors during conflicts of different types and severity, and details how markets actually respond as well as what readers can do to implement a proactive early-response strategy." Though for personal reasons Michael was not able to complete this project himself, he deserves the credit for launching it, and we hope that the final product meets with his approval. Though it would have been a better book with his contribution, we have endeavored to answer the important questions he laid out and hope we have done so with some degree of success.

One of the authors, William, is deeply grateful to his wife Jessica for her endless patience and her unerring editorial eye. Jessica spends considerable time and effort reading through everything I write. She always provides constructive comments, copyediting, and, most importantly, moral support and motivation. Jessica is at the bedrock of my accomplishments, not only with this book but also in every aspect of my life. Thank you, Jess.

Daniel extends immense gratitude to his parents, Bill and Susan Kuthy, for their unwavering love and support throughout his life. Thank you for your numerous sacrifices that supported my development as a human and an academic. Through your guidance and life lessons, you opened the breadth and richness of the world. You created a safe space for me to explore, learn, and fail without judgment, but with your acceptance and love.

Finally, the authors would also like to thank the editorial and production staff at Elsevier for their patience and guidance during the process of producing this book. A number of people have played a role in its fruition, including Andrae Akeh, Kathryn Eryilmaz, and most especially Aleksandra Packowska. Their patience and professionalism throughout a variety of obstacles and delays kept this book alive.

Though the authors owe much of whatever is good about this book to the aforementioned people, whatever deficiencies, omissions, or mistakes it may contain are of their own making and responsibility. We hope such mistakes are the exception and that this book makes an important contribution to the literature. Our final acknowledgments are to the reader. Thank you for considering the arguments we put forth here, and we hope that you profit from them.

CHAPTER 1

Introduction

"War," declared Gen. Smedley Butler, a veteran of several wars and two-time recipient of the Medal of Honor, "is a racket" (Smedley, 1935). According to Butler, war was propagated by the few who would profit from it at the expense of everyone else. It was a way for the rich and powerful to expand their riches and their power while the common soldier was maimed, ground into the mud and killed.

> War is a racket. It always has been. It is possibly the oldest, easily the most profitable, surely the most vicious. It is the only one international in scope. It is the only one in which the profits are reckoned in dollars and the losses in lives. A racket is best described, I believe, as something that is not what it seems to the majority of the people. Only a small 'inside' group knows what it is about. It is conducted for the benefit of the very few, at the expense of the very many. Out of war a few people make huge fortunes.
>
> **(Butler, 2010, pp. 1–2)**

World War I was infamous for the "war profiteers" that made millions producing weapons and other materiel that allowed them to profit from the misery of others. There is something distasteful, even ghoulish, about reaping profits—especially exorbitant profits—on suffering and death. And nothing, apart perhaps from pandemics, causes more concentrated suffering and death than war and armed conflict in general.

It is bad form to make too much money from war. While some earnings by private industry are understandable, too much profit is viewed as exploitative. In some cases, profiteering is downright treasonous as it may interfere with the state's ability to acquire the resources necessary for victory. As Eugene Meyer put it in 1917 as the United States was entering World War I, "Fairness in price *includes* a *profit*, as much as it *precludes profiteering*" (Meyer, 1917, p. 2). Fairness demands moderation in profit realization during times of war.

During most major wars, governments have done what they could to prevent excessive profit-making by the private sector. Price controls, nationalization of natural resources, factories, and other means of production

Markets and Conflict
https://doi.org/10.1016/B978-0-323-85525-9.00006-4

have been common during times of war. These measures have met with varying levels of success, sometimes meeting their goals and other times counterproductively resulting in black markets and other undesirable financial outcomes. In fact, belligerents' efforts to marshal material resources and direct them toward war-making often determine the winners and losers in war. Without a robust economy, combatants cannot arm or clothe their troops, transport them to the battlefield, or feed them. Economic power is at the heart of wars and can be the decisive determinant of which side wins them.

While wars are impacted substantially by economic capacity, the wars themselves can dramatically alter economies. During wartime, states invest substantial sums in technological developments that, while aimed at military purposes, often have substantial and far-reaching impacts on peacetime economies. Additionally, war and the risk of war play a role in shaping patterns of investment and trade. While wars are associated with economic growth due to increased government spending, they are tremendously destructive in the end. Economies are ruined, infrastructure and capital assets are destroyed, labor and capital are diverted to less productive or nonproductive purposes, and people are killed and permanently disabled. The human tragedy of war is immeasurable, but the economic toll of war is measurable and often heavy. Moreover, by understanding the complex economic impacts, individuals and societies can anticipate these impacts and respond to them more effectively.

So, studying the intersection of economics and war is necessary for understanding how wars are won and lost. But studying that intersection to understand how private individuals or corporations can profit is another matter. From a moral point of view, such study strikes some as indecent. That is likely one reason why there has been very little published in the scholarly literature to date about how conflict—war, terrorism, and other forms of armed conflict—interacts with various markets and market dynamics during conflict. Research has been conducted on the effects of conflict on particular aspects of markets, but there is little to nothing that takes a more holistic approach, especially in book format.

While this book is not a how-to book on market investment during conflict and should not be interpreted as providing investment advice, it does seek to fill a gap in the academic literature by providing an analysis of the existing literature and putting it together in one place. Through this compilation and critical analysis of the research, this book demonstrates how markets respond to the turmoil unleashed by conflict and offers clues as to how governments, corporations, and individuals can act to protect their own financial interests.

This book is not an encouragement to profiteering, but it does take the position that the making of fair profits during conflict is not morally reprehensible or even dubious. Economic devastation is one of the evils of war and the more that private markets can adjust to wartime in ways that avoid the worst outcomes and perhaps bring about some flourishing, the more that evil will be diminished. Economic prosperity is a positive good, even during times of conflict and war. Understanding how conflict alters markets and using that knowledge to produce more positive outcomes is not wrong. In fact, it is a powerful way to reduce one of the chief evils of war. Moreover, markets already respond to armed conflicts; therefore, understanding these responses can help governments, companies, and people make informed decisions in how to manage the disruptions that collective violence causes.

Today's international "order" is one characterized by instability and pervasive danger. Russia's invasion of Ukraine, escalating tension over the status of Taiwan, bellicosity from a nuclear-emboldened North Korea, and continued turmoil in the Middle East, including in Syria, Israel, and Iran, are only some examples of ongoing or potential trouble. Major and minor armed conflicts flare up, or threaten to, on a continual basis. Market responses to this instability are often irrational and short-sighted. Fear induces volatility in markets, based on panicked efforts to protect individual interests. This book aims, in part, to present a comprehensive understanding of conflict (as manifested in various ways, primarily in interstate war, but also in internal war, smaller armed conflicts, and terrorism) and market dynamics to enable informed judgments by market participants. Additionally, it provides lessons on the more macro-level dynamics that may be of use to governments and policy analysts.

Both economic activity and armed conflict have been with humanity since at least the dawn of civilization and have been mixed up with each other since the beginning. As the earliest agricultural communities began to form, they suffered a constant threat of raiding and invasion from their neighbors—and equally presented such a threat. Those unprepared to defend themselves were quickly overcome and disappeared. War-fighting became a necessary skill for sustained economic development and civilizational stability. Economics and warfare became further intertwined as enemies targeted each other's economic sustenance and as it became clear that economic power was the engine of military might. A strong military capability was necessary to protect economic advances from foreign depredations, and a vibrant economy was necessary to the establishment of a strong and innovative military.

This circle of interdependence between military and economic power has never dissipated and has only become more robust and complicated as civilization has advanced. The economy, both the economies of belligerents and also the global economy writ large, remains vulnerable to disruption by conflict. At the same time, militaries remain dependent on their economic underpinnings. In a world reliant upon natural resources—most especially oil—and enmeshed in complicated global resource, financial, and equity markets, the relationship between conflict and markets is more and more difficult to grasp, understand, and react to effectively. This book aims to make those dynamics more comprehensible by presenting the latest and best research on the various ways in which conflict and markets interact.

Before getting too far ahead of ourselves it is useful to lay out some key terms. Conflict has a very broad meaning and can refer to any sort of clash of interests between two or more parties. A workable definition is provided by Rubin et al as a "perceived divergence of interest, or a belief that the parties' current aspirations cannot be achieved simultaneously" (Rubin et al., 1994, p. 5). Conflicts also generally involve the taking of certain actions by each party against the other in order to advantage oneself. For the purposes of this book, the meaning is more specific to international conflicts, generally between states. Most of the conflicts we discuss involve the use of force and violence by organized groups, though we do cover some forms of non-violent conflict, such as trade wars. While much of this book focuses on conflicts among states, we also discuss two forms of conflict that do not involve two or more states, civil wars, which occur within one state, and terrorism.

For wars and civil wars, we accept the definition used by the Correlates of War Project. International wars involve sustained combat between the regular military forces of at least two states, resulting in at least 1000 battle-induced fatalities among combatants (not inclusive of civilians). In addition to wars between two or more states, international wars may also include armed conflicts resulting in similar casualty levels between an armed state and a nonstate political entity, such as a colony (Sarkees, 2010, p. 3). Civil wars are also constituted by armed conflicts resulting in at least 1000 battle deaths but are contained to one state. These conflicts involve military clashes between the official government and some other internal entity, both of which are providing effective resistance to the other (Sarkees, 2010, p. 5).

Terrorism is less easily defined, and in fact there is no internationally accepted definition of it. Efforts by the United Nations (UN) to reach consensus on a definition have failed. According to Martini and Njoku, writing in the *Palgrave Handbook of Global Counterterrorism Policy*, "Terrorism is a political term and, as other politically charged words, is the subject of a huge debate on its exact meaning, the nature of the specific elements its definition should focus on (causes, perpetrators, means of attack, etc.), and the specific violence this term should refer to" (Martini and Njoku, 2017, p. 73).

This definitional difficulty has not, however, prevented effective action against terrorism by either individual states or the international community, including the UN. For our purposes, the definition for international terrorism offered by the Federal Bureau of Investigation in the United States will suffice: "Violent, criminal acts committed by individuals and/or groups who are inspired by, or associated with, designated foreign terrorist organizations or nations (state-sponsored)" (Federal Bureau of Investigation Homepage (FBI), n.d.).

The next term to come to grips with is that of markets. Markets fundamentally have to do with the exchange of goods and services. We do not refer with the term "market" to merely a physical market, such as the farmer's market down the street, but rather the economic structures, processes, and institutions that allow for the regular exchange or purchase of commodities or services, though in this book we are generally referring to commodities. Markets facilitate the forces of supply and demand to reach equilibrium, thereby playing a large role in the setting of prices, and can be local, regional, or global in scope (or anywhere in-between). In this book we place particular focus on equity, agricultural, industrial, natural resource, and energy markets.

With these preliminary definitional tasks out of the way, we next provide a brief overview of the rest of the book's contents. Chapter 2 focuses on investment markets. It presents the basics of equity markets and then explains how they can be disrupted in times of conflict or even by the threat of conflict. Historical and statistical research provides an opportunity to understand, and potentially make rough predictions, about how investment markets are affected by conflict. Economic loss is not a foregone conclusion and is not inevitable. Wise and informed action can reduce risk and help investors avoid the worst economic outcomes created by conflict. The aim of this chapter is to explore how conflict directly and indirectly impacts investment markets and how investors can protect, and perhaps even improve, their interests during times of conflict.

Energy markets are fundamental to conflict. Without energy, militaries cannot function. Energy fuels conflict in two ways: in the literal way that it fuels the machinery of war and also in the sense that it may be the ultimate cause of conflict. Chapter 3 examines how energy markets, primarily the oil and gas markets, intersect with conflict. Under what conditions does oil increase the risk of conflict? How does conflict impact the price of oil and gas? How is access to energy seen as an objective of war? Can energy markets drive terrorism? These and other questions will be explored in this section.

If there is a market commodity more fundamental to war than energy, it is food. While oil fuels the machinery of war, food fuels the warriors themselves. From ancient times, agricultural production has been a target of war and often the deciding factor between victory and defeat. Combatants have sought to deprive each other of food, weakening their enemies to the point of surrender. Chapter 4 presents an overview of the fundamentals of agricultural markets. It then details the research on how agriculture can cause conflict and the effects that conflict can have on agricultural production. In addition to general findings, several examples from various conflicts and historical periods offer lessons for future application.

In Chapter 5, we analyze industrial markets. Conflict can have massive effects on industrial markets, especially in large wars. Civilian products may be repurposed to serve military purposes (and vice versa at the conclusion of the war), factories created to meet new military demands, and of course, industrial infrastructure will be targeted and destroyed by enemy combatants. Industrial markets may also be affected by a drain in available labor, as men are shipped off to fight and are no longer available on the factory floor. Disrupted trade relationships also distort normal industrial market behavior and may impact prices and availability of products and materials. War can completely upend entire industries, sometimes only for the duration of the conflict, but sometimes permanently. It can also create new industries or breathe new life into once struggling industries. This chapter examines all of these possibilities in order to identify historical trends and draw general lessons.

Chapter 6 examines issues related to trade and currency and how they intersect with both violent conflict and international nonviolent currency and trade wars. This chapter provides a general overview of currency and trade and describes how governments use currency and trade to accomplish other goals. It also analyzes the scholarship regarding the relationship between trade and the likelihood of war. While much of this scholarship supports the idea that increased trade reduces the probability of war as both sides have more to lose, trade relationships can act as a source of friction as well in some cases. In addition to international wars, this chapter also looks at how civil wars impact international trade and currencies. To make the discussion more concrete, two case studies are presented. The first study is of the trade and currency wars of the 1930s, which likely contributed to the onset of World War II. The second examines Russia's 2022 invasion of Ukraine.

In Chapter 7, we consider military contracting. This is an obvious way in which the economy and conflict interact as it involves the government paying private entities to provide support services, weapons and other equipment, and even direct fighting services in some cases. This has become particularly prevalent in the United States. Several large companies, such as Halliburton, Boeing, and Northrop Grumman, made massive amounts of money from providing support to the United States military during the War on Terror and for more conventional military purposes. This chapter will examine the extent of military contracting and its effect on conflict, what makes particular contractors successful or not, and how contracting has impacted modern conflict generally.

Chapter 8 discusses the historical and modern relationship between resources and war, along with analysis of how wars affect material prices and extraction. It also delves into the relationship between civil wars and raw materials and provides an overview of how terrorism and natural resources interact. This chapter provides two case studies to concretely demonstrate its points, World War II and the Russian invasion of Ukraine. It concludes by presenting lessons on the relationship between resource management and war for governments, companies, and investors.

In Michael Taillard's book *Economics and Modern Warfare*, he notes a lack of research at the intersection of war studies and economics (Taillard, 2018). Most experts on war, strategy, and conflict in general do not have significant expertise in economics. On the other hand, most economists do not focus on conflict but on how economic systems and phenomenon operate under normal conditions. He further notes that "through this neglected overlap... there is born the possibility to submit enemy combatants while reducing the risk of harm to one's own soldiers, neutral civilians, and even the opposition's soldiers" (p. 289). Here we argue that such knowledge can also help reduce the economic costs associated with war and other conflicts. Such costs can be massive and affect combatants and noncombatants alike.

Scarcity of food brought on by warfare, for example, either through direct interference with food production or through the disruption of trade routes, has the potential to affect not only access to food by soldiers but also civilians in combat areas and even people in other parts of the world who have nothing to do with the conflict by increasing global food prices. Conflict can cause famine and add immensely to the suffering and death created by the fighting itself. One horrific historical example of this is the famine in Bengal in 1943, which was exacerbated by wartime inflation and other economic impacts of World War II. It is estimated to have resulted in between two and three million deaths. Obtaining the knowledge to cope with the economic effects of conflict are central to not only limiting economic damage, but in saving lives.

Economics is an intrinsic part of war and other forms of conflict. It enables them, motivates them, drives them, and potentially ends them. Economic pain and damage are among the primary threats of conflict. Conflict can cause impoverishment and economic devastation. War threatens lives not only through bombs and bullets but also through scarcity. Knowledge of how the economy and conflict interact may enable the amelioration or alleviation of the worst economic effects of war—or allow us to prevent at least some armed conflicts altogether, as war often has economic roots. In some cases, such knowledge may even facilitate economic benefit for those who implement it wisely. Though it is certainly immoral to kill for economic gain, and armed conflict is not an acceptable method of economic advancement, when it does occur it is surely better to reduce its negative consequences and increase whatever positive outcomes can be derived.

The authors hope that this book will offer a step forward in understanding the complex interconnections between conflict and markets in a number of their key elements. It is further hoped that this knowledge will assist future policymakers, economists, businesspeople, and just plain ordinary folks in avoiding the greatest economic harms of conflict, and maybe even come out ahead.

References

Butler, S., 2010. War is a Racket, Kindle. Vantage Point University Press.
Federal Bureau of Investigation Homepage (FBI), What We Investigate: Terrorism. https://www.fbi.gov/investigate/terrorism.
Martini, A., Njoku, E.T., 2017. The challenges of defining terrorism for counter-terrorism policy. In: Romaniuk, S.N., Grice, F., Irrera, D., Webb, S. (Eds.), The Palgrave Handbook of Global Counterterrorism Policy. Palgrave MacMillan, pp. 73–89.
Meyer Jr., E., 1917. War Profiteering: Some Practical Aspects of its Control. Washington, DC.

Rubin, J.Z., Pruitt, D.G., Kim, S.H., 1994. Social Conflict: Escalation, Stalemate, and Settlement, second ed. McGraw-Hill.

Sarkees, M.R., 2010. The COW Typology of War: Defining and Categorizing Wars (version 4 of the data). https://correlatesofwar.org/wp-content/uploads/COW-Website-Typology-of-war.pdf.

Smedley, B., 1935. War Is a Racket. Round Table Press.

Taillard, M., 2018. Economics and Modern Warfare, second ed. Palgrave MacMillian.

CHAPTER 2

Equity markets

Introduction

Equity markets are markets comprised of stocks, issued by private companies to bring additional capital and funding into their businesses. This promotes business growth "by channeling funds from savers to firms" (Baker et al., 2020, pp. 1–2). There are a multitude of country-specific and regional stock exchanges through which equities are sold throughout the world. A weighted average of a group of stocks within a particular exchange is called a market index. Market indexes provide a snapshot of the overall health and trends of a market. Futures markets involve the agreement to purchase a specific commodity (such as oil or gold) or stock at a particular price at a specified point in the future. For example, one might contract to purchase a specified amount of oil 3 months in the future at the current price. If the price goes up during the ensuing 3 months, the buyer has insulated himself from that additional cost. If the price goes down, the supplier has protected himself from the loss. The purpose of this is to stabilize risk over time and to create stability for both suppliers and buyers. It can also be used to speculate.

Equity markets have become one of the key elements of modern economies over the 20th and into the 21st centuries as they have fueled business and corporate growth. Growth over the past 50 years has been expansive. World market capitalization rose from around $2.5 trillion in 1980 to slightly more than $79 trillion by 2017, though it fluctuated significantly during that period. Nearly half (41%) of global equity market capital is in North American exchanges, though there are 16 markets that have capitalization greater than $1 trillion (Baker et al., 2020, p. 1).

Though there has been a steady long-term increase in the value of equity markets across the globe, in the short run there is often considerable uncertainty and volatility. Large swings in the markets make or break fortunes. Taufiq Choudhry notes that there are two primary types of change in equity values: "'blips' that persist for only a day or so and 'turning points' that persist for much longer" (Choudhry, 2010, p. 1030). There are any number of events or catalysts for fluctuation in the markets. Political change,

Markets and Conflict
https://doi.org/10.1016/B978-0-323-85525-9.00004-0

technological innovation, and turmoil in other areas of the economy are some examples. Another is conflict. War, terrorism, armed rebellions, and even the threat of such events can have major impact on the economy in general and on equity markets in particular. Research by Wolfers and Zitzewitz determined that 30% of the volatility experienced in the S&P (Standard and Poor's) market between September 2002 and February was due to changing perceptions of the probability of the onset of war between the United States, its allies, and Iraq (Wolfers and Zitzewitz, 2009, p. 227).

The remainder of this chapter will explore how conflict directly and indirectly impacts equity markets and how investors can use that knowledge to protect themselves, and perhaps even come out ahead, during times of conflict.

Equity markets and conflict

The onset of war, terrorism, and other forms of violent conflict—or even the threat of such conflict—can introduce substantial volatility to equity markets and generate major shifts in valuation, usually, but not always, in the direction of devaluation. There are two primary ways in which equity markets are affected by conflict: a rise or fall in the price of shares and a shift in investor perceptions about the level of risk and future profitability of equities (Choudhry, 2010, p. 1030). Like war, terrorism, and conflict itself, their effects can be unpredictable and sometimes counterintuitive, though they are generally negative.

Unfortunately, there is not a single pattern that develops from all wars, terrorist events, or other forms of conflict, making prediction of their effects more difficult and unreliable. The same event can also have different results in different equity markets, depending upon a variety of factors, such as geographical location, alliance responsibilities, and perceived vulnerability. Research by economic historian Niall Ferguson highlights this variability:

> British equities performed poorly in the First World War but produced higher real returns in the Second World War and the Korean War. The U.S. market performed better than the British market in the First World War and much better in the Korean War but—surprisingly—worse in the Second World War. In short, there is no simple recurrent pattern. U.S. stocks and bonds produced the best returns in the First World War relative to British and German assets. U.K. stocks, followed by U.S. stocks, produced the best returns in the Second World War. But German stocks, which had been a disastrous investment in both world wars, ended up outperforming those of the other two countries in the wake of the Korean War.
>
> **(Ferguson, 2008, p. 441)**

The following sections will provide brief analyses on various major conflicts and terrorist events and their impacts on equity markets. After looking at specific events, we will identify some of the overall trends that have emerged from recent research efforts.

World Wars I and II

As noted before, British equities were hit hard by the onset of World War I, known contemporaneously as the Great War. Ferguson (on whose work the following analyses of World War I and II are dependent) notes that the Austrian ultimatum to the Serbians issued after the assassination of Archduke Franz Ferdinand in Sarajevo on June 28, 1914, began the downward trend. First, insurance premiums began to rise. Stock prices began to fall as wary investors sought greater liquidity. By the end of July, stock prices sank as investors panic-sold, driving stockbrokers into bankruptcy. Borrowers who had used stock as collateral suddenly could not repay their debts and defaulted. Lenders began calling in debts. The situation deteriorated so precipitously that some the world's major stock markets closed completely for up to 5 months (Ferguson, 2008, p. 446).

British government bonds proved to be the worst investment, losing nearly half their value (46%) by 1920. Meanwhile, the index of real returns on British equities lost more than a quarter of their value (27%) (Ferguson, 2008, p. 450). A superior strategy would have been switching to gold which increased in value 37% from 1913 to 1920 (Ferguson, 2008, p. 450). Investment in U.S. dollars, which was on the gold standard at the time, would have been equally sound, but free-floating German and French currencies were devastated by hyperinflation. Russian, Austrian, Hungarian, and Ottoman bonds—all ultimate losers in the conflict which saw the dissolution of their governments or empires—proved disastrous (Ferguson, 2008, p. 450).

Because the U.S. remained aloof from the fighting until it finally swooped in to deal the final blow to Germany and its Central Alliance partners, its stock market remained stable—and even profited. The American stock market certainly performed better than the British. "A British investor who had converted his entire portfolio into a selection of blue-chip American stocks on the eve of the war would have seen the index of real returns rise by, on average, 47 percent between 1914 and 1923" (Ferguson, 2008, pp. 450–451). The degree of direct involvement in the war had a major impact on equity market valuations during World War I, perhaps offering a valuable lesson to investors.

But Ferguson warns that lessons learned from one war may lead one astray in the next. During the next global conflict (World War II), British equities proved to be a superior investment to both gold and U.S. equities from 1939 to 1948. "In real terms, with dividends reinvested, the total return index for British equities was 50 percent above the 1938 level, on average, between 1939 and 1948, compared with a figure of 25 percent for American equities" (Ferguson, 2008, p. 464). Even the Blitz could not hold London equities back.

U.S. markets did not fare as well, and research by Taufiq Choudhry demonstrates that the war impacted stock prices and the volatility in American equity markets. His research also found that the markets were also sensitive to particular events throughout the war. News indicating a prolongation of the war consistently resulted in a downturn in the markets the following day and for the next 5 days. Enemy victories in battle or other advancements also tended to produce a drop in prices and increased market volatility. Positive news had the opposite effect and tended to create a rise in stock prices the following day and for the next 5 days (Choudhry, 2010, p. 1031). Though these changes in market value were generally not massive, they do demonstrate a certain level of market sensitivity to events on the ground as the war unfolded.

Ferguson attributes the hardihood of British equities during World War II to the US, and to itself in World War I, to the long run-up to the war. The run-up to the war was long and did not catch investors by surprise. They had time to diversify their portfolios into other commodities and equity markets, lessening their panic when war finally began (Ferguson, 2008, p. 462). World War I, in contrast, was relatively sudden for the UK and followed a century of peace under the balance of power system. Similarly, for a long time, the U.S. believed itself capable of remaining aloof from World War II until the attack on Pearl Harbor suddenly dragged it into a conflict it had struggled to avoid. Ferguson concludes that "when a crisis strikes complacent investors, it causes much more disruption than when it strikes battle-scarred ones" (Ferguson, 2008, p. 474).

The different reactions of London and US equity markets during the two world wars obscure trends and make any definitive lessons difficult to uncover. World War I demonstrated that the onset of war *can* be devastating to stock markets. But World War II showed that such is not inevitable and that markets can react differently to the same events and preparation can help generate resiliency in the market while surprise may lead to greater volatility and market loss.

Iraq wars

Viviana Fernandez took potential variability over time and location into account when she studied the impact of the 2003 Iraq War. Her study looked at major stock indices in North and South America, Africa and the Middle East, Europe and the Asia Pacific, along with two commodity indices. Her analyses revealed that the impact was greatest at the onset of the war and began to decline thereafter, eventually reaching levels of volatility even lower than before the war began. The major international stock markets were the most heavily affected during the period of greatest volatility (Fernandez, 2008, p. 3). Among her most important findings were that "volatility worldwide has primarily experienced transitory increments during 2000–June 2006, which can be primarily associated with volatility clustering. In addition, we do not observe in general more volatile financial markets than at the beginning of 2000" (Fernandez, 2008, p. 25).

Research by Wolfers and Zitzewitz found that for US markets specifically, volatility arose even prior to the initial onset of conflict and was affected by simply the increased probability of war. They found that a 10% increase in the probability of war was accompanied by a drop in the S&P 500 of 1.5% (Wolfers and Zitzewitz, 2009, p. 226). The S&P 500 lost a total of around 15% as the probabilities of war moved from 0% (no perceived chance of war) to 100% (the war was starting) (Wolfers and Zitzewitz, 2009, p. 234). The situation almost immediately began to reverse itself once the war began, and there was actually a rebound after the first 3 weeks of war of about 4% in the S&P 500, recouping about one-quarter of the prewar losses (Wolfers and Zitzewitz, 2009, p. 226). In comparison to other events of political instability, they found that "the S&P 500 fell by 7.6, 6.5 and 5.5% in the first two trading days after the Pearl Harbor bombing, the outbreak of the Korean War and September 11th, respectively" (Wolfers and Zitzewitz, 2009, p. 234).

In addition to US equity markets, Wolfers and Zitzewitz conducted statistical analysis on the impact of the 2003 Iraq War on 43 stock markets around the world using Morgan Stanley Capital International (MSCI) total return indices. The analysis concluded that stock market fell in 32 of the 43 countries as the probability of war increased. Markets in two countries, Austria and Indonesia, saw gains in their markets. The authors attribute the differences in how various markets were impacted by the probability of war to factors such as their proximity to Iraq and their dependency on oil imports. They also note that after the war commenced, the markets in these more initially vulnerable countries began to rebound (Wolfers and Zitzewitz, 2009, pp. 241–243).

Terrorism

Like war, terrorism can have a strong impact on equity markets, both locally and globally. Nguyen and Enomoto explain:

> *Acts of terrorism, such as the attack on the USS Cole in Yemen, the bombings in Madrid, Indonesia, and London, and the attacks on the World Trade Center and Pentagon in the United States, disrupt economic activity in the attacked nation and every nation that trades with the nation that was attacked. Profits of compa-nies in many nations are adversely affected. Furthermore, due to the interconnec-tedness of global financial markets, it is no wonder that the effects of terrorism are felt in every corner of the world. In terms of their effects on stock markets, terrorist activities create turbulence and uncertainty among investors, forcing them to get out of the market quickly, precipitating a drop in equity prices and returns.*
>
> **(Nguyen and Enomoto, 2009, p. 75)**

They argue that spillover effects of terrorist attacks can increase the economic costs of terrorism. Worried investors may avoid what they per-ceive to be higher-risk equities, being content instead with lower returns on more conservative investments. Investors may also avoid investing in markets located in countries perceived to be at higher risk being affected by terrorism. This can particularly undermine developing countries that have the most to gain from such investments, contributing to greater global inequality (Nguyen and Enomoto, 2009, p. 83).

Different markets are likely to be impacted differently by any given attack, based upon a variety of factors. Analyses of the effects of the attacks against the World Trade Center; bombings in London; and the attack on the USS *Cole* on stock markets in Tehran, Iran, and Karachi, Pakistan, led Nguyen and Enomoto to conclude that.

> *investors have different expectations concerning the effects of terrorist attacks on company profits. An act of terrorism occurring in a nation may lead investors to expect that company profits in Pakistan will be adversely affected while company profits in Iran will be largely unaffected. There are many reasons for this. Pakistan's exports to the attacked nation or trading partners of the attacked nation may be greater than Iran's exports to those same nations. There may be a greater likeli-hood of sanctions being imposed on Pakistan than on Iran by the rest of the world due to the terrorist attack. Pakistan may have more financial assets at risk abroad than does Iran. The result of all this is that while terrorism affects many different stock exchanges, it affects them differently.*
>
> **(Nguyen and Enomoto, 2009, p. 83)**

Ferguson agrees that terrorism can cause steep drops in equity markets—he points out the Dow Jones Industrial Average plummeted by about 14% between September 10 and September 21, 2001—but also draws our attention to the fact that these losses are often short lived. Only 2 months after the 9/11 attacks, the Dow Jones recovered to preattack levels. Though the market was slow in the following year, it picked up thereafter and the value of the Dow had nearly doubled by late 2007. Other markets, including markets from majority-Muslim countries like Egypt, Turkey, and Indonesia, did even better (Ferguson, 2008, p. 432).

Overall trends

Evidence from analyses of individual wars indicates that the reactions of equity markets vary. Some conflicts have greater impacts on certain markets rather than others, and for some the effects are long lasting while for others they are short lived. Here we will examine the research on broader trends rather than specific events or conflicts.

Wolfers and Zitzewitz derive generally pessimistic expectations from their research. They found that a 10% increase in the probability of war correlated a contraction of the S&P 500 of 1.1% and that in general, "global equity markets reacted very negatively to increases in the probability of war" (Wolfers and Zitzewitz, 2009, p. 233). They contend that investor's expectations about the repercussions of war largely determine the severity of the drop in equity prices and that the possibility, even if improbable, of a terrible outcome may weight those expectations toward the pessimistic (Wolfers and Zitzewitz, 2009, p. 234).

These researchers estimate that movement from a 0% to 100% probability of war will have a 70% likelihood of reducing the S&P 500 by 0%–15%, a 20% chance of a reduction of 15%–30%, and a 10% of a decline of more than 30% in the near term. The mean expected outcome is a reduction of 15% of value in the S&P 500. They also expect the market to rally by an average of 5% as the uncertainty of the war decreases, and especially as the probability of a disastrous outcome diminishes (Wolfers and Zitzewitz, 2009, p. 237). In general, they found that those stocks hit hardest at the onset of war, rallied most quickly as war progressed (although gold and IT were exceptions) (Wolfers and Zitzewitz, 2009, p. 240).

Research by Schneider and Troeger finds that investors flee equity markets when they expect a conflict to be prolonged. Pessimistic prognostications may result in market losses, while more optimistic predictions may actually see markets gain value. They confirm that negative trends can be reversed in rallies when things seem to be going well, pointing to a recovery of at least some market losses that occurred at the onset of the Gulf War in

1991 as the US military quickly demonstrated dominance and it became apparent that the war would be relatively short. They conclude that "the stock market reactions to international crises thus largely depend on the severity of an anticipated or real international event and the collective expectation that an event will materialize" (Schneider and Troeger, 2006, p. 643). Similarly, Choudhry finds that even escalations in conflict can lead to a rally as long as investors predict that such escalations are an indication that the war may be coming to an end (Choudhry, 2010, p. 1030).

Although the impact of conflict on equity markets has shown variability, how the markets reacted to World War I and World War II for example, and though there is no homogenous pattern that can be known with certainty, there are lessons to be learned. First, there is a strong probability that conflict will have at least a mild to moderate depressive effect on most equity markets. Second, these effects are likely to differ among different markets. Markets most directly impacted by the conflict—markets in the region in which the conflict is occurring, markets of the belligerents themselves, and markets that are most economically interdependent with the combatant countries—are likely to be those most strongly impacted. A third lesson is that such negative repercussions are likely to be temporary. If the worst outcomes of the war are initially avoided, it is likely that a rally will occur, recouping at least some of the loss. Markets generally rebound fairly quickly from these downturns.

Given the lessons learned from this historical analysis, the next section will outline some research-based strategies for investors faced with the potentiality of the onset of conflict.

Strategies to prepare for conflict

The lessons of history can be used by investors to protect their assets at the onset of conflict, and perhaps even to enhance their wealth based upon wise investing that take those lessons into proper account (Guidolon and La Ferrara, 2010, p. 682). It is also possible for governments to take into account the lessons of history to reduce the impact of conflict and terrorist attacks on their equity markets. This section will look at some of the ways that investors may be able to protect themselves—and to profit—from volatility in the markets and how government can act to reduce volatility in an effort to protect both the markets and their investors.

First, investors should remain aware of international events. Staying ahead and apprised of events is critical to being able to insulate oneself from them. Acting before conflicts unfold is likely to give one an advantage over those who merely react to them. Ferguson notes that "the stakes for investors had…been very high in the summer of 1914, although few of them seem to have known it before the storm broke" (Ferguson, 2008, p. 452). The lack of preparation brought on by the relative suddenness of the war, even though people knew a war was certainly possible, resulted in unmitigated losses for many investors who were in the dark.

The research indicates that the onset of conflict is likely to have a depressive effect on equity markets, particularly those that are most directly involved, in the region of, or economically interdependent with, the combatants. An investor aware of an international climate likely to result in conflict can take steps to protect her investments. Diversifying one's stocks into markets less likely to be impacted by the conflict is one potential strategy. Research conducted by Elie Bouri found that equity markets in the MENA region (Middle East and North Africa) may offer opportunities for remunerative diversification. This is because the markets in MENA countries are not as highly integrated as in other regions and may therefore be less affected by overall market trends (Bouri, 2014, p. 15). "While many researchers support the view that the globalization of capital markets reduces diversification on average, regional and international investors may still have an advantage from diversifying into some of the MENA stock markets" (Bouri, 2014, p. 4). Of course, if the conflict in question is located in this region, it would likely be wise to avoid investment in these markets.

Another strategy would be to move money out of stocks altogether into more conservative bonds. Research by Thomas Chadefeaux found that "the onset of war in a given week has a positive and strongly significant effect on that country's [bond] yields" (Chadefeaux, 2017, p. 319). He analyzed 2516 conflicts and government bond yields 3 months before and 3 months after those conflicts began, finding a clear increase in value immediately before and after the conflict (Chadefaux, 2017, p. 319).

The key benefit in moving from stocks to bonds is doing it soon enough—before one's equity values have been reduced and the value of bonds has risen. Chadefaux notes that "investors have historically underestimated the probability of war prior to its outbreak and the onset typically led a large correction. Market participants, in particular, could often have obtained better returns had they correctly estimated the risk of war" (Chadefaux, 2017, p. 313). Moving one's money out of potentially volatile markets and into safer bonds, which are likely to experience an increase in value if a conflict does arise, is one strategy for investors faced with the possibility of war.

Once war has begun, investors should also watch for indicators of positive changes in the direction of the war. Rallies are likely to occur with indications that the conflict may be resolved quickly. Buying when the markets are low after the onset of war and before a rebound occurs offers the potential for large rewards. Of course, a reversal of fortunes in the conflict may have a similar effect on the investor's fortunes, so sound analysis of the conflict and its likely trajectory is critical.

Making changes to investment strategy in advance of a crisis is harder to do when it comes to terrorist attacks, as there is often no warning to such events. But here, awareness of the international situation can help investors more quickly than the rest of the market and offer a buffer to make investment adjustments. Nguyen and Enomoto point out that "given the characteristics of each stock exchange, investors can make predictions about the reaction of the market after a terrorist attack and anticipate the magnitude of the effects. Those estimates can help investors evaluate investment decisions and select hedging strategies to neutralize the risk after such events" (Nguyen and Enomoto, 2009, p. 83). As their research demonstrated, different markets are likely to be impacted in different ways in different degrees by terrorist attacks. Predicting how that is most likely to play out, based upon geopolitics, international relationships, and other relevant factors, will help investors make wiser decisions in the wake of terrorist incidents.

Whereas individuals can alter their investment behavior through diversification, reinvesting in different markets, switching from stocks to bonds, and purchasing when the market is low and prior to an expected rebound, governments should also take swift actions to protect markets. In the immediate wake of terrorist attacks, monetary policies such as reducing interest rates and loosening credit, along with government spending and other forms of stimulus, may insulate the economy more generally, thereby buttressing equity markets more indirectly by bolstering confidence in economic fundamentals. There are also more long-term financial tools that governments can leverage to reduce the economic damage caused by potential future terrorist attacks. "Financial tools such as volatility options, bonds associated with terrorism events or insurance programs that protect investors after terrorist attacks can help reduce the likelihood of a market crash" (Nguyen and Enomoto, 2009, p. 84).

A drastic measure, but one that may be necessary under conditions of massive sell-offs, is for the government to close the markets altogether. Ferguson believes this was an important step at the beginning of World War I, "The closure of the stock market and the intervention of the authorities to supply liquidity almost certainly averted a catastrophic fire sale of assets. The London stock market was already down 7 percent on the year when trading was suspended—and that was before the fighting had even begun" (Ferguson, 2008, p. 449). The New York Stock Exchange and the Nasdaq also closed for 6 days after the 9/11 attacks. This was likely responsible for the avoidance of a massive panic sell-off that could have severely affected market value. Closing the markets in the aftermath of a major terrorist attack provides time for the situation to stabilize and the initial panic to dissipate, thereby potentially avoiding major sell-offs and loss of market value.

Conclusion

This chapter has outlined recent research on how conflict—primarily war and terrorism—impacts equity markets. Through looking at the historical research on how stock markets were affected by specific conflicts, as well as statistical research on how conflict impacts equity markets more generally, we were able to identify strategies that both individual investors and governments can take to protect themselves from conflict-induced market volatility. Though conflict often has a negative impact on markets, losses for the individual investor are not inevitable. In fact, conflict may present the wise investor with opportunities as well as dangers.

Ill-preparedness and panic are the two biggest threats to investors. A prepared investor, one who knows the geopolitical situation and can make knowledgeable decisions based on the situation, can adjust her investment strategy to insulate herself from the worst impacts of conflict—either through diversification, switching to bonds, or strategic timing in buying and selling. Doing well in the equities trade is reliant upon making sound decisions based upon research-based knowledge. This applies even more during times of conflict.

References

Baker, H.K., Filbeck, G., Kiymaz, H., 2020. Equity markets, valuation, and analysis: an overview. In: Equity Markets, Valuation, and Analysis.

Bouri, E.I., 2014. Israeli-Hezbollah war and global financial crisis in the Middle East and north African equity markets. J. Econ. Integr. 29 (1).

Chadefaux, T., 2017. Market anticipations of conflict onsets. J. Peace Res. 54(2).

Choudhry, T., 2010. World war II events and the Dow Jones industrial index. J. Bank. Financ. 34, 1022–1031.

Ferguson, N., 2008. Earning from history? Financial markets and the approach of world wars. Brook. Pap. Econ. Act.

Fernandez, V., 2008. The war on terror and its impact on the long-term volatility of financial markets. Int. Rev. Financ. Anal. 17, 1–26.

Guidolon, M., La Ferrara, E., 2010. The economic effect of violent conflict: evidence from asset market reactions. J. Peace Res. 47 (6).

Nguyen, A.P., Enomoto, C.E., 2009. On stock index returns and volatility: the cases of the Karachi and Tehran stock exchanges. Int. J. Econ. Bus. Res. 8 (12).

Schneider, G., Troeger, V.E., 2006. War and the world economy: stock market reactions to international conflicts. J. Confl. Resolut. 50 (5), 623–645.

Wolfers, J., Zitzewitz, E., 2009. Using markets to inform policy: the case of the Iraq war. Economica 76, 225–250.

CHAPTER 3

Energy markets

Introduction

Energy commodities are unique. Energy markets sit at the root of nearly all modern economic activity. Oil, and to a lesser but still important extent natural gas, fuels the world's economy. Oil is the most important economic commodity in the world and is by far the most heavily traded. This is only expected to increase as, according to the International Energy Agency, world oil demand is set to grow by 5.4 million barrels per day (mb/d) in 2021 to reach a total output of 96.4 mb/d (International Energy Agency (IEA), 2021). Oil far exceeds the value of any other commodity traded on international markets, including other important natural resource commodities such as natural gas, lumber, or diamonds. The oil market generates revenues in the range of ten to one hundred times that of the next most profitable natural resource (Colgan, 2013, Introduction).

In this chapter we delve into energy markets, particularly the global oil market, though also touching upon the more regional markets for natural. We first explain the basics of the oil and gas markets and describe the special importance placed on oil/gas production and distribution logistics strategies as a core part of international relations, including the dynamics of the Organization of Petroleum Exporting Countries (OPEC, 2018). Also discussed is how energy consumers have sought energy independence through new methods of extraction or technological developments such as solar and how that has impacted the oil and gas markets.

Next we move into the meat of the chapter, how oil relates to armed conflict. A section is devoted to describing how oil is variously theorized to cause conflict (or not) both within and between states. Also included here is a discussion of how oil relates to terrorism as well as the trend of extremist organizations and other nonstate actors capturing oil extraction facilities in oil-producing nations to fund operations. After having described the interrelation between oil and conflict, we move on to discussing the economic repercussions. We also give special attention to economies that are heavily reliant on oil resources and the sociopolitical problems that can result from such lopsided overreliance.

Markets and Conflict
https://doi.org/10.1016/B978-0-323-85525-9.00003-9

Basics of the oil and gas markets

As noted, oil is traded in a global market, generally meaning that disruptions will affect the price of oil relatively equally across the world, regardless of any particular country's domestic supply. Scholar Steve Yetiv notes, "Globalization and modern oil markets mean that a severe interruption in oil supplies will have a similar price effect across regions" (Yetiv, 2011, p. 167). Even being "energy independent" cannot completely protect one from the vagaries of global oil prices. Because industrialization is reliant upon oil, any disruption in supply will result in upheavals in production across the economic spectrum, not just in oil itself. This will result in a rise in the cost of nonoil imports, thereby affecting even those countries which are self-sufficient in oil itself (Yetiv, 2011, p. 167). No country is immune from the economic consequences of large-scale disruptions of the oil supply. Natural gas, on the other hand, is traded in more regional markets, making it more susceptible to regional disruptions—but offering some protection from price dislocations in other regions (Goldthau, 2012, p. 67).

Oil is generally categorized into very light, light, medium, and heavy, all of which are traded via future's contracts. Alqahtani and Taillard explain that

> these contracts are an agreement to purchase a standardized volume of a particular type of oil (the prices of which tend to be treated as a singular market) to be bought or sold (depending on your perspective) with a predetermined maturity date with a predetermined price, but the contract can be sold and resold on the secondary market between the time of purchase and the time of maturity. Since the price of oil changes during the sale date and the maturity date, the market price of these contracts change over time accounting for the differentiation between contract prices paid and the total value of the oil contractually obligated to be bought/sold at the predetermined price.
>
> **(Alqahtani and Taillard, 2019, p. 7)**

The market for oil is unusual in that there are relatively few suppliers catering to a massive number of consumers (Chevillon and Rifflart, 2009, p. 539). The early years of mass oil production, the first half of the twentieth century, was almost completely in the hands of just seven companies, colloquially referred to as the Seven Sisters. These were Texaco, Exxon, Royal Dutch/Shell, Mobil, Gulf, British Petroleum, and Standard Oil of California (Chevron). At the beginning, prices were largely determined by these producer companies based on considerations other than mere supply and demand. Instead, "the price was based on the need to accommodate the interests of both oil-consuming and oil-producing countries. Historically, all international oil contracts were conducted at a fixed price between the so-called upstream producers and the downstream refiners and retailers" (Yetiv, 2011, p. 28).

By the second half of the century, and especially by the 1960s and 1970s, pricing power was shifting decisively toward oil-rich states, with consumers having little power over the price they were forced to pay. In line with the principles enunciated in the Melian Dialogue, oil producers charged what they could, and consumers paid what they must. Much of this was the result of decolonization and the stronger insistence upon control of their own natural resources by states that had previously been politically dominated by the Western powers. Rather than allow foreign companies to control and profit from their oil resources, many oil exporting countries in the developing world nationalized the industry and set up state-owned enterprises to extract and market their oil (Ross, 2013, p. 7). In 1960 a group of exporting states formed the Organization of the Petroleum Exporting Countries (OPEC). Originally comprised of Saudi Arabia, Kuwait, Iran, Iraq, and Venezuela, its composition has expanded and altered over time. Its current members are Algeria, Angola, Equatorial Guinea, Gabon, Iran, Iraq, Kuwait, Libya, Nigeria, Republic of the Congo, Saudi Arabia, United Arab Emirates, and Venezuela. Nearly half of all countries have no oil whatsoever while only 10 of the most oil-rich countries possess 80% of the world's total supply (Kelanic, 2012, p. 44).

The relatively small number of oil producers means that the entire world is largely dependent on the output of only a few large producers, often located in troubled areas of the world. This concentration of supply in the hands of a few relatively unstable countries makes disruption more likely. Andreas Goldthau points out that there are a variety of potential causes of oil price volatility:

> Events triggering sudden price increases include domestic turmoil (for example, Nigeria's ongoing domestic conflict); political quarrels (for example, Venezuela's oil workers' strike of December 2002–February 2003); or regime change (for example, the Iranian Islamic Revolution of 1979), which—despite being limited to a single nation—all affected oil prices on a global scale. As a corollary, a sudden drop in demand in some parts of the world certainly has a revenue impact on all producer nations, not only on the ones supplying the economically depressed region.
>
> **(Goldthau, 2012, p. 69)**

Oil prices can also be impacted by overall economic activity. Economic recession can reduce the demand for oil, thereby depressing its price. Pascual and Zambetakis note the effects of both conflict and economic recession in oil prices during the 2000s. They point to an increase from $21 a barrel in 2002 before the Iraq War to $29 a barrel when hostilities began in March 2003 and an eventual rise to $48 by the beginning of President Bush's second term in 2005. The price of oil increased by more than 400% from its 2002 level to peak at $145 in July 2008. Prices dropped to a relatively moderate price of $50 a barrel by 2009 due to the global economic recession brought on by a crash in the U.S. housing market, though even this much reduced price was still twice as high as the 2002 price 6 years earlier. By Spring 2021, the price of oil had risen to around $65 per barrel, despite economic uncertainty generated over the previous year by the coronavirus pandemic (Pascual and Zambetakis, 2010, Chapter 1).

Production and distribution logistics and international relations

According to Yetiv, "oil has created an entire infrastructure, a way of life built around its discovery, production, and use" (Yetiv, 2011, p. 210). Natural gas also has its own unique infrastructure which differs from that of oil. Two key aspects of both are production and transportation. The United States is both the largest producer (18.6 mbd) and consumer of oil (20.5 mbd), accounting for about 20% of the global total for each. Saudi Arabia (11.01 mbd, 12%) and Russia (10.5 mbd, 11%) are the next two largest producers. The 13 OPEC countries are responsible for about 40% of total global production and 60% of all petroleum traded internationally (OPEC, 2018).

OPEC uses their combined position to manipulate supply through the setting of production targets for its members in order to maximize profitability. OPEC countries also control nearly 80% of the world's oil reserves, slightly less than 65% of which is in the Middle East. Oil reserves are the estimated amount of oil extant in a particular area but not currently being extracted. The U.S. Energy Information Administration notes that "because of this market share, OPEC's actions can, and do, influence international oil prices. In particular, indications of changes in crude oil production from Saudi Arabia, OPEC's largest producer, frequently affect oil prices" (EIA, 2021).

Once produced, oil must be transported from its point of origin to its consumers all around the world. Most of this transportation is via sea lanes, some of which are narrow and susceptible to potential interference, such as piracy, forced closure, or terrorist attack. Prominent sea lanes include the

Strait of Hormuz (which Iran occasionally threatens to restrict), the Bosporus Strait, the Strait of Malacca, and the Suez Canal (Gupta, 2008, p. 1195). These chokepoints generate vulnerability for the global oil supply and have been the focus of considerable protective measures, particularly by the U.S. Navy.

Natural gas, on the other hand, is more rarely delivered by sea (although oceanic transportation is increasing) and instead remains primarily regional in nature and dependent upon pipelines. With proper engineering these pipeline systems can be quite extensive. Pipelines bringing natural gas from Siberia in Russia to Western Europe traverse more than 5000 km. China's major West-East pipeline extends more than 4800 km and exceeds 9000 km when its various branches are included (Smil, 2015, p. 5). The United States, Canada, and Mexico also have an extensive network of pipelines that forms a regional market.

Natural gas can also be liquified and transported by tanker across land and sea, but this is more expensive than transportation via pipeline. Despite the additional cost, liquification is on the rise as it allows for cross-oceanic transport and has the potential to transform natural gas from a regionally traded commodity into a globally traded one. Most natural gas transport is still dependent on pipelines, however, and will likely remain so for the immediate future (Goldthau, 2012, p. 68). Because of the regional nature of the natural gas trade, there is no single global price and prices vary significantly across regions. In 2013, for example, prices in Europe were more than 2.5 times higher than in the United States and prices in Japan were more than 4.6 times higher (Smil, 2015, pp. 73–74).

Because both oil and gas are traded internationally (as opposed to most renewables, which are generally consumed by the producing nation), various geopolitical vulnerabilities arise. With natural gas, the fact that pipelines often cross the borders of numerous states creates the potential for instability. A prime example is that of Russia and Ukraine. Russia piped natural gas to numerous countries in Europe, much of which transits through Ukrainian territory. A pricing dispute between the two countries in 2009 led to several countries (Bulgaria, Romania, Serbia, Moldova, and Bosnia-Herzegovina) losing access to their Russian-provided gas supplies for 2 weeks, inflicting damage on their economies as well as Russia's (Goldthau, 2012, p. 71). This heightened overall geopolitical tensions between Russia and Ukraine. It also increased Europe's dependency on Russia for energy and may have slowed their initial response to increased Russian aggression against Ukraine, which eventually resulted in an invasion and still (as of this writing) ongoing war.

The vulnerabilities of oil, as already mentioned, primarily revolve around transit through strategic oceanic chokepoints and disruptive conflict in producer countries. Protecting sea lanes is an expensive and resource-intensive proposition, requiring substantial naval power. The United States bears most of the burden of protecting transit through the Straits of Malacca and the Strait of Hormuz, through which most of the world's oil flows on the way to international markets. Estimates of the cost to the U.S. taxpayer for the military protection of these sea lanes vary widely, from $13 billion on the low end to more than $140 billion on the high end, but is by all measures a significant expenditure—and one from which other oil producers and consumers benefit as it protects their supply and global pricing as well (Goldthau, 2012, p. 73).

The U.S. has also been uniquely responsible for the costs associated with the protection of suppliers, particularly in the Middle East. Yetiv points out that the Middle East is so crucial not only because of its annual production but also because of its spare capacity. Spare capacity is how much additional oil can be immediately brought to market (this differs from oil reserves as not all reserves may be readily exploitable). Approximately 80% of the world's spare capacity is in the Middle East and most of that is in Saudi Arabia (Yetiv, 2011, pp. 165–166). Since the early 1970s, when the UK pulled back from the Middle East, and increasingly in the 1990s and beyond due to the threat from Saddam Hussein, the U.S. put a massive amount of resources into protecting Saudi Arabia, Kuwait, and the Middle East generally. Since 1990, and not even including the cost of the 2003 Iraq War and occupation, estimated U.S. annual expenditures tied to defense of the Persian Gulf have exceeded the entire military budgets of all other states, with the exceptions of China and the UK (Yetiv, 2011, p. 167).

Criminal violence, terrorism, and civil wars

Oil is an important source of prosperity and wealth. Without, the world economy would come to an immediate and grinding halt. Our modern way of life and civilization floats atop oil. But, in addition to wealth and happiness, it also generates and supports criminal violence and terrorism. Oil and international relations expert Steve Yetiv referred to the connection between oil, globalization, and terrorism as the petroleum triangle. "The links between globalization, oil, and terrorism are many and varied," he wrote. "But they can be captured roughly in one general theme: while Middle Eastern oil has fueled terrorism, globalization has provided terrorists with global highways and side roads to traverse" (Yetiv, 2011, p. 3). Oil has enabled terrorism by acting as a source of funding, providing terrorist with political issues on which to recruit and motivate adherents, and has served as a source of anti-Americanism. It has also allowed states to fund the dissemination of extremist ideology, such as Saudi Arabia's funding of Wahhabi schools and other forms of indoctrination throughout the Middle East and beyond.

During Afghanistan's struggle against the Soviets in the 1980s, Saudi Arabia poured oil-generated money into the country, likely between four and five billion dollars, that supported not only military resistance but extremist ideological commitment. Monetary support continued to the Taliban even after the Soviets abandoned their occupation. This support to the Taliban in turn allowed them to host al-Qaeda and provide it a base of operations from which it was ultimately able to launch such attacks as those against the United States on 11 September 2001 (Yetiv, 2011, p. 169).

This is consistent with Collier and Hoeffler's contention that primary commodities—such as oil, but also including diamonds and other valuable raw materials—are a primary target for rebel groups seeking to increase their revenues (Collier and Hoeffler, 2004, p. 6). They argue that this can quickly create a vicious cycle that can escalate from minor isolated incidents to full-scale civil war. Rebel raids against commodity production sites, such as oil wells or other petroleum production or refining facilities, will lead to the imposition of defensive measures. Because of the geographic size of these resource extraction facilities, this will often require the services of an army. Armies are expensive, so this has the potential to increase the government's reliance on oil revenues even more. It may also result in higher taxation, which has the potential to drive more citizens into the ranks of the rebels. Faced with a defensive army, the rebels themselves will require additional firepower and more personnel, thereby incentivizing them to expand their efforts at recruitment and the scale of their attacks (Collier and Hoeffler, 2004, p. 7).

As with other crime, the returns on extortion can be decreased by defensive measures. However, whereas the most efficient defenders of commerce are law enforcement entities, protecting primary commodities usually entails defending a large physical space best suited to an army. The revenues associated with oil production not only attract rebel extortion but also incentivize governments to impose taxation. Revenues generated by oil give governments both an incentive and the ability to provide military defense. Faced with potent defensive measures, the rebel extortionists will also require considerable military power in order to challenge that force (Collier and Hoeffler, 2004, p. 7).

This can spiral out of control into full-out civil war as the government and its challengers form increasingly powerful armies in order to maintain or seize power over lucrative oil resources. This is one possible reason that, according to the research of Michael Ross, states with considerable oil reserves, particularly low- and middle-income countries, have been more than twice as likely to find themselves embroiled in civil wars than are states with no or little oil resources (Ross, 2013, p. 1). Cogan, citing a substantial body of research, points to at least three other reasons oil-rich states are more prone to civil war: "by providing finances for warring parties, especially rebels; by increasing the financial value of victory in a civil war, and thus the motivation to fight; and by encouraging corruption and weakening the institutions of the exporting states" (Colgan, 2013, Introduction).

Oil profits can motivate minority groups who feel disenfranchised or discriminated against to fight for control of it (Ross, 2013, p. 12). It is common for local groups to feel unfairly compensated for oil extracted by the central government, which then uses the revenues for itself or for the benefit of the majority ethnic group, who may live elsewhere in the state. This can result in preexistent rebel groups targeting oil to finance their ongoing rebellion or the fostering of entirely new groups which engage in violence in order to seize those oil resources.

Patricia Vasquez finds this second case to hold true in some Latin American countries. Her research found that

> very often, oil conflicts occur as a result of governance imperfections at the local level that affect the redistribution of oil revenues and the choice and subsequent implementation of local investment projects to benefit local communities. Poor procurement procedures, for example, ultimately jeopardize the use of oil revenues that should be available for sustainable community-development projects. This, in turn, results in conflict and discontent when the local population fails to enjoy the benefits of the oil projects being developed in their territories.
>
> **(Vasquez, 2014, p. 55)**

There are a number of examples of rebel and terrorist groups targeting oil facilities for extortion and other criminal purposes. Rebels have targeted oil facilities, primarily in Africa but also in Latin America, either for direct theft or for extortion. Oil production facilities in Nigeria have frequently been attacked by terrorist and extremist actors. Nigeria is the largest oil producer in Africa and oil is a critical element of the country's overall economy, thereby making it vulnerable to extortion. Much of its oil revenues come from transnational oil companies through either rents, taxes, or royalties

(Omeje, 2005, p. 321). Despite the economic gains attendant with oil production, those benefits have not always been shared with the local populace. In fact, Augustine Ikelegbe argues that

> *decades of oil exploitation, environmental degradation and state neglect has created an impoverished, marginalized and exploited citizenry which after more than two decades produced a resistance of which the youth has been a vanguard. A regime of state repression and corporate violence has further generated popular and criminal violence, lawlessness, illegal appropriations and insecurity. The Niger Delta is today a region of intense hostilities, violent confrontations and criminal violence.*
>
> **(Ikelegbe, 2005, pp. 208–209)**

A host of gangsters, robbers, thieves, and militias have metastasized in the area. These actors have engaged in theft, piracy, kidnapping of workers for ransom and extortion, and other violent attacks. This violence takes a heavy toll. Approximately 1000 people are killed each year in violence associated with oil production, and the struggle to control it, in the Niger Delta.

Oil has also funded violence in certain parts of Latin America. Vasquez points to Colombia as one example in which rebel groups have seized upon oil as a source of revenue for their violent movements. She notes that "following the discovery of oil in the 1980s, Colombian rebel groups strengthened and started to expand again, by using illegal practices—such as the economic extortion of foreign oil companies, and clientelistic arrangements—for capturing government oil revenues" (Vasquez, 2014, p. 132). Rebel groups such as the Ejército de Liberación Nacional (ELN) and the Fuerzas Armadas Revolucionarias de Colombia (FARC) resorted to kidnapping and extortion, much like similar groups in Nigeria. Though oil did not cause the long-term civil war in Colombia, it certainly helped prolong it.

International conflict and oil

"No blood for oil!" was a common refrain among protestors of the 2003 American war with Iraq. In addition to fueling violence among criminal and terrorist groups, and sometimes even rebellions and civil war, many politicians, activists, and some scholars believe that oil also contributes substantially to armed conflicts between states (international war). This remains controversial, however, and some scholars deny that oil causes such conflict at all, or if it does, very rarely.

Scholars such as Meierding (2020) argue that there are too many downsides to fighting over oil to make it worthwhile for most states, at least when it comes to international conflict. Invading and occupying foreign countries, for example, is very expensive in both lives and treasure. While states may frequently become embroiled in what she calls oil spats—minor conflicts over disputed oil rights, for example, that do not devolve into full-scale war—or attack oil facilities while already in the midst of wars, states very rarely start wars solely over oil (although they may sometimes claim to be doing so in order to obscure their true motives, which generally involve other political motivations). The reward for such drastic action, she argues, is rarely, if ever, worth the tremendous cost.

Rosemary Kelanic disagrees, arguing that despite the potential costs of fighting for oil, the costs of not doing so may be greater. She points out that the greatest motivator for states in an anarchic system is survival. A state's ability to survive is affected by oil because modern militaries (particularly those of great states) are uniquely dependent on it. Without oil military vehicles and equipment are inoperable. Modern armies run on oil and without it they are incapacitated. Kelanic argues that great states will therefore go to great lengths to protect their access to it, including preemptive war when threatened with loss of access. If they did not take such action, other states with the power of reducing, or even eliminating their power to defend themselves by blocking their access to oil, could coerce and blackmail them through the mere threat of doing so. She argues that "those nations most vulnerable to oil cutoffs do not sit idly by waiting for enemies to coerce them" (Kelanic, 2012, p. 173).

Instead of allowing themselves to be held hostage by oil producers, Kelanic claims that states in the twentieth century have frequently taken military action to secure access to this vital military product.

History is rife with examples of strategic anticipation. Japan attacked Pearl Harbor and seized the petroleum-rich Dutch East Indies to secure oil after a U.S. petroleum embargo cut off 80 percent of its imports. Determined to protect its stockpile and believing war with the United States was inevitable, Japan conquered its own supply and preemptively destroyed the lone naval threat to fuel shipments from the Indies—the U.S. Pacific Fleet. Fear of oil coercion spurred the British and French into the 1956 Suez War. Upon news of President Gamal Abdel Nasser's nationalization of the waterway, Prime Minister Anthony Eden lamented, "The Egyptian has his thumb on our windpipe," and the British cabinet resolved to keep the Suez Canal open by force if necessary. Oil disruption was the foremost concern; two-thirds of British petroleum imports transited through the canal, compared with just

one-quarter of the country's total imports. Indicative of this, oil was the only dis-
placed material that received attention by the British cabinet in their emergency
meeting following Nasser's nationalization of the canal in July.

(Kelanic, 2012, p. 2)

Due to the existential threat posed by catastrophic loss of access to oil, Kelanic argues that great powers formulate 'anticipatory strategies' to protect that access. These strategies can take a variety of forms, from more fully developing internal resources to full-out invasions of other states. Kelanic categorizes the three primary strategies as self-sufficiency, indirect control, and direct control. Self-sufficiency can include stockpiling of resources, more aggressive resource exploration and extraction, the provision of subsidies, and other measures to bolster domestic production. Indirect control generally involves forming treaty agreements and alliances with oil-producing states. This aids the state in securing its oil supply by formalizing and stabilizing agreements and often by deterring other states from interfering with the source of production through explicit security guarantees or even through military basing. The final strategy, direct control, is the most risky and potentially costly as it involves "conquest to capture oil-producing territory and transit routes" (Kelanic, 2012, p. 3).

Even if Meierding and other scholars who are skeptical of the idea that wars are started solely because of oil are right, it certainly has an impact on international conflict in other ways. Jeff Colgan demonstrates that, at least under certain conditions, oil revenues enable leaders and regimes with preexistent aggressive tendencies to engage in warfare more readily than they otherwise would. They can afford it. He points out that states which obtain 10% or more of their gross domestic product (GDP) from oil exports engage in conflicts at a rate more than 50% higher than other states and are among the most violent in the world. He notes that such states, which are a relatively small fraction of all states, have accounted for nearly one-fourth of all international conflicts since 1970. Colgan refers to this phenomenon as petro-aggression.

O'Sullivan also notes that even when oil doesn't cause war, it often is a major consideration for strategic decisions during war. "The history of grand strategy during that era [the twentieth century] was often the history of efforts to gain or deny access to energy. For instance, many pivotal moments in World War II—from Hitler's drive to the Caucasus to Japan's quest for Borneo to the failed drive of Germany's Afrika Korps across North Africa—were shaped decisively by oil" (O'Sullivan, 2017, Preface). Because oil is so crucial to the successful prosecution of war, it often becomes a primary objective during war.

Conflict, the price of oil, and the search for energy independence

Whether oil may or may not cause or impact conflict, conflict certainly has an effect on oil. Alqahtani and Taillard point out that a broad array of occurrences can heighten geopolitical risk and thereby alter market perceptions (and therefore behavior), including "foreign policy decisions, public rhetoric, cross-border terrorist and criminal activity, and a variety of other activities which increase the degree of uncertainty people have about the state of the world" (Alqahtani and Taillard, 2019, pp. 6–7). Geopolitical risk is especially heightened during widely reported violent events, such as the 2003 Gulf War; the terrorist attacks in New York and Washington, DC, in 2001 and in Paris in 2014; and the Russian-Ukrainian conflict in 2014.

A rather stable oil market between 1995 and 2004 was disrupted by the uncertainty generated by the war in Iraq and subsequently by negative outcomes associated with that conflict. This was exacerbated by other geopolitical events in other oil-producing countries elsewhere in the Middle East, Nigeria, Venezuela, Ecuador, and Russia (Chevillon and Rifflart, 2009, p. 547). Such changes are not easily predictable, however, and do not necessarily occur immediately or in sequence with the onset of international crisis. Statistical analysis conducted by Alqahtani and Taillard discovered that there is potentially a 1- to 2-month lag between the occurrence of a destabilizing event and the subsequent impact on the oil market (Alqahtani and Taillard, 2019, pp. 20–21).

Although there are a variety of ways in which volatility can affect oil prices, research by Zavadsk, Morales, and Coughlan found that shocks related to conflict generated greater levels of volatility than shocks driven by financial crises. Both the Gulf War of 1991 and the 2001 terrorist attacks in the U.S. generated higher levels of volatility and uncertainty than the Asian financial crisis of 1997–98 or the Global Financial Crisis of 2008. On the other hand, however, the effects of the financial crises were longer lasting. In other words, both types of crisis led to price increases and greater price volatility. The changes wrought by international violence, however, were greater in magnitude than those brought about by financial woes while financially induced volatility was more persistent. The authors conclude that

> the nature of the crisis plays a significant role in determining the behaviour of oil spot and futures prices and their lasting effects in terms of prolonged levels of uncertainty. As such, relevant market players should be aware that the crisis trigger

can denote significant differences in the magnitude of the reaction of oil prices to the market shock. Supply and demand related shocks are associated with higher levels of uncertainty, while economic and financial crises exhibit longer levels of persistence.

(Zavadsk, et al., 2020, p. 7)

Another major factor in oil price variability—and one that is likely to be more long lasting—is a change in supply. New technologies can increase the likelihood of finding new underground reservoirs and also offer novel ways to extract those new finds, or old finds that were previously too difficult or expensive to exploit. When new finds, or a new capability to extract long-known but previously unreachable deposits, are large enough, they can permanently alter the price structure and accessibility of oil. Similarly, a transition to other forms of energy, such as natural gas or renewables, also has the potential to permanently affect prices if the demand for oil is thereby reduced.

The United States offers a recent example of how the oil market can rapidly change. Beginning in about 2010, new technological developments began to allow for the extraction of oil and gas resources previously too expensive to commercially excavate. Whether accessible as a new type of oil or because of new extraction techniques, these new supplies are typically referred to as "unconventional oil." Meghan O'Sullivan explains:

Think of 'unconventional oil' as an umbrella term with many different unconventional oils grouped under it, including kerogen oil, gas converted to liquids, and tight oil (also known as shale oil). Likewise, the term 'unconventional gas' is also an umbrella term that encompasses several different types of natural gas, one of which is shale gas. There is also more than one unconventional extraction technique. The most well-known process is 'fracking,' which is used for extracting resources such as shale gas and tight oil. But oil sands, also considered an unconventional oil, is generally extracted by very different means: the intense heating of the resource while it is underground before extracting it.

(O'Sullivan, 2017, Chapter 1)

The availability of unconventional oil created a surge in U.S. oil supply, sometimes surpassing forecasted output by in excessive of one million barrels of oil per year. In this case, increased U.S. production offset diminishing supply coming from the Middle East and therefore kept market prices relatively stable. More important than price, which actually began to decline as more U.S. supply became available, was the shift in geopolitical considerations that it generated. Russia, whose economy was highly dependent on the production of petroleum, was weakened by this change, as were other traditional suppliers who now had less leverage over the market.

Because of oil's fundamental importance to every developed country's economy, large suppliers could potentially derive political benefit through threats of reduction in supply, even the mere perception of which could affect markets and therefore entire economies. As Goldthau notes, "An oil-importing nation, affected by a price hike, would probably experience an economic slump due to sharply rising costs of a key economic input factor; it would suffer from rising inflation, or experience an increase in unemployment" (Goldthau, 2012, p. 69). Meanwhile, supplier countries would likely benefit from windfall profits (though they may also suffer from currency appreciation). This places supplier nations not only in a position of economic but also of political advantage. By so vastly increasing its production capacity, the U.S. fundamentally altered both the economic and political structures of the global energy market.

Despite increased U.S. supply, Middle Eastern suppliers will still likely remain dominant in the near term. As Yetiv points out, "The conflict-prone Middle East will serve as the principal source of supply to meet rising demand over the next two decades. This will make the Gulf increasingly important to global oil pricing, oil supply, and the global economy" (Yetiv, 2011, p. 4). Reliance on Middle East oil will therefore continue to have geopolitical and economic repercussions for the foreseeable future, especially considering the global nature of the oil market, which lessens the impact of source diversification. In the long term, however, greater diversification by consumers—including with other forms of energy—to reduce their dependence on foreign producers as well as economic diversification on the part of suppliers in order to reduce *their* economic dependence on consumers will be necessary to break the cycle of energy market volatility and subsequent political disruptions (Pascual and Zambetakis, 2010).

A final factor with the potential to substantially and permanently alter oil prices is demand. Though the demand for energy is not likely to diminish, the sources of energy may. Primarily driven by the threat of global climate change, but also by the desire to reduce oil dependency, the developed world has made a massive push toward the development of renewable energy supplies, primarily wind and solar. According to the International Energy Agency (IEA, 2020), more than a quarter (27%) of global energy supply as of 2019 was derived from renewable energy sources. There is no reason to believe that this number will do anything other than increase over future decades.

Petrostates

Petrostates are those which generate a substantial portion of their GDP from the extraction, refinement, or export of oil. The reliance on this one product often results in various sociopolitical problems. Examples include Venezuela, Russia, Iran, Saudi Arabia, and many of the Gulf States. As discussed in earlier sections, excessive oil resources can result in increased bellicosity. It can also strengthen autocracies and stifle the development of an independent middle class and democracy.

Christopher Davidson points to the five Gulf monarchies, the United Arab Emirates (UAE), Kuwait, Qatar, Oman, and Bahrain, as examples of states that have maintained autocratic political systems in large part due to oil wealth. The rulers of these states have so far been able to essentially buy the acquiescence of their populations through the provision of direct payments, subsidies, public services, or highly compensated public sector employment. Made complacent by this largely effortless wealth (and what effort did go into it has largely been on the backs of low-wage imported labor from places in South and Southeast Asia), these societies never developed truly capitalist economic systems and did not develop the necessary motivations to challenge the political authorities. According to Davidson:

> Although at first glance seeming to have adopted capitalist modes of production, the Gulf economies never really spawned a proletariat—or at least not one that was interested in overthrowing the classes above it. Equally, though an urban, educated, and mass communications-literate population was undoubtedly emerging in the Persian Gulf...it hardly compared with the middle classes of more developed democratic states and nor did it seem keen to press for the kind of greater political participation...This ongoing apathy, or political demobilization, and the concomitant endurance of traditional monarchies on the Arabian Peninsula, can largely be explained by the region's unusual political economy, specifically the rent-based nature of the economic and political systems that emerged in all six monarchies...following their first significant oil exports.
>
> **(Davidson, 2013, pp. 5–6)**

Colgan comes to the same conclusion. Arguing that because income from oil can be easily controlled by a centralized government, it provides autocratic leaders with the ability to establish a patronage system which effectively forecloses political opposition and reduces the likelihood of political accountability for unpopular decisions. This has applied not only in the Gulf monarchies, but also bolstered Venezuela's socialist system and has propped up the Russian and Iranian regimes. Oil wealth not only imbued these petrostates with domestic political strength but also with regional and international influence. Dependence on energy imports fosters political deference, which petrostates have used to their advantage. Pascual and Zambetakis argue that oil has allowed petrostates like Russia, Venezuela, and Iran to "punch above their weight in regional and international politics" (Pascual and Zambetakis, 2010, Chapter 1).

These domestic and international advantages are prone to quickly unravel, however, with changes in the oil market or with internal dynamics. Though able to maintain political control for decades, these regimes may face increasingly threatening political instability if their domestic oil supplies dwindle, global prices become too low, or demographic changes (particularly a large increase in youth populations) strain their ability to continue providing the same level of economic incentives that have engendered political passivity.

> With the current slowdown in global demand from at least the traditional demand centers in Europe and the United States, lower oil prices have rattled the economies and politics of producer states that have come to depend on large export revenues to maintain stability at home and support muscular foreign policies abroad. That is especially poignant in countries like Iran and Venezuela, which highly subsidize social programs and fuel at the expense of economic growth and diversification.
> **(Pascual and Zambetakis, 2010, Chapter 1)**

Without the financial windfalls provided by vast oil revenues, these states will lose their ability to maintain the social spending programs that buy a quiescent population or the geopolitical leverage to maintain the same level of international influence, thereby simultaneously threatening the stability of their regimes and undermining their geopolitical positions.

O'Sullivan points to Venezuela as a country that has been devastated by a reduction in oil prices. It has eroded the government's credibility and legitimacy with its own people and greatly reduced its geopolitical influence in the region. Similarly, Russia has taken a major financial hit from lower energy prices. This has impacted its domestic economic situation and threatens to reduce its geopolitical power in the Caucasus and other areas within its traditional sphere of influence, not to mention its main market—Europe. The same situation is occurring in Saudi Arabia and various countries in Africa, such as Mozambique and Sierra Leone.

Oil revenues both empower petrostates and threaten that power. When the oil and gas markets are booming, it can allow such states to quell domestic opposition and lend them power in international negotiations. When those booms subside, however, populations accustomed to state beneficence may become unruly and the states once dependent on their energy supplies may become less deferential.

Conclusions

As demonstrated throughout this chapter, oil can be both a gift and a curse. Oil generates prosperity and drives economic growth. Without it, our modern civilization would come to a halt, at least until viable alternatives become more readily accessible. Oil is also critical to the effectiveness of modern militaries. Military vehicles and machinery are dependent on oil. Dependency creates vulnerability. Without oil, militaries cannot move. This has led Rosemary Kelanic to conclude that states, particularly great states, will go to extreme lengths to ensure ready access to the oil needed to ensure their survival. The very fact that oil is so critical to economic well-being and military capability makes it worth fighting over.

Additionally, the riches gained from oil can also fund tyrannical states, rebellions, and terrorist attacks. When oil revenues are not shared evenly, especially when it is distributed unevenly among different ethnic groups or geographical areas, it can cause splits in society. Sometimes those splits end in violence. Examples abound, particularly in developing countries in Africa and South America, of oil being the source of, and target of, violence. Oil has fueled not only machinery but also theft, extortion, and terrorism.

Oil, in short, can be a driver of conflict and violence.

On the other hand, while oil can drive conflict, conflict can also drive oil markets. Research has shown that disruptions in oil markets driven by conflict are generally more significant in magnitude than financially or economically generated shocks. Other research has demonstrated that this effect is usually not immediate and can take about a month to develop. These spikes in price, though significant, generally smooth over relatively quickly, at least in comparison to more financially driven increases.

Sudden increases in oil prices driven by conflict can have wide-ranging effects. Producers and investors are likely to experience large, though potentially short-term, profits while consumers will likely be subjected to significant economic pain, not only in oil prices but also through the effects of broader inflation since oil impacts the production and transportation of large segments of the economy. This knowledge may be valuable to governments and investors. The onset of violent conflict, especially in oil-producing countries, is likely to cause an increase in oil prices, though the effect generally takes some time to unfold. Investors could use this as an opportunity to purchase oil before prices go up with the intention of selling at a premium later. Governments can also use this time as an opportunity to take measures to blunt or minimize higher prices through official action, such as releasing reserves, boosting their own production, or securing other sources.

References

Alqahtani, A., Taillard, M., 2019. Global energy and geopolitical risk: behavior of oil markets. Int. J. Energy Sect. Manag.

Chevillon, G., Rifflart, C., 2009. Physical market determinants of the price of crude oil and the market premium. Energy Econ. 31 (4), 537–549.

Colgan, J.D., 2013. Petro-Aggression: When Oil Causes War. Cambridge University Press.

Collier, P., Hoeffler, A., 2004. Greed and grievance in civil war. Oxf. Econ. Pap. 56 (4), 563–595.

Davidson, C., 2013. After the Sheikhs: The Coming Collapse of the Gulf Monarchies. Hurst.

Goldthau, A., 2012. A public policy perspective on global energy security. Int. Stud. Perspect. 13 (1), 65–84.

Gupta, E., 2008. Oil vulnerability index of oil-importing countries. Energy Policy 36 (3), 1195–1211.

Ikelegbe, A., 2005. The economy of conflict in the oil rich Niger Delta region of Nigeria. Nord. J. Afr. Stud. 14 (2), 208–234.

International Energy Agency (IEA), 2020. World Energy Outlook. IAE, Paris. (2020). Downloaded from https://www.iea.org/reports/world-energy-outlook-2020. on 02/27/21.

International Energy Agency (IEA), 2021. Oil Market Report. IAE, Paris. (2021). Downloaded on https://www.iea.org/reports/oil-market-report-february-2021. on 02/27/21.

Kelanic, R.A., 2012. Black Gold and Blackmail: The Politics of International Oil Coercion. The University of Chicago.

Meierding, E., 2020. The Oil Wars Myth: Petroleum and the Causes of International Conflict, Kindle edition. Cornell University Press.

Omeje, K., 2005. Oil conflict in Nigeria: contending issues and perspectives of the local Niger Delta people. New Political Econ. 10 (3), 321–334.

Organization of Petroleum Exporting Countries (OPEC), 2018. OPEC Share of World Crude Oil Reserves. Downloaded from: https://www.opec.org/opec_web/en/data_graphs/330.htm. on 29 May 2021.

O'Sullivan, M.L., 2017. Windfall: How the New Energy Abundance Upends Global Politics and Strengthens America's Power, Kindle edition. Simon and Schuster.

Pascual, C., Zambetakis, E., 2010. The geopolitics of energy: from security to survival. In: Pascual, C., Elkind, J. (Eds.), Energy Security: Economics, Politics, Strategies, and Implications. Brookins Institution Press.

Ross, M.L., 2013. The Oil Curse: How Petroleum Wealth Shapes the Development of Nations, Kindle edition. Princeton University Press.

Smil, V., 2015. Natural Gas: Fuel for the 21st Century, Kindle edition. John Wiley & Sons.

U.S. Energy Information Administration (EIA), 2021. What Drives Crude Oil Prices? Downloaded from: https://www.eia.gov/finance/markets/crudeoil/supply-opec.php#:~:text=OPEC%20member%20countries%20produce%20about,the%20total%20petroleum%20traded%20internationally. on 29 May 2021.

Vasquez, P.I., 2014. Oil Sparks in the Amazon: Local Conflicts, Indigenous Populations, and Natural Resources. University of Georgia Press.

Yetiv, S.A., 2011. The Petroleum Triangle: Oil, Globalization, and Terror. Cornell University Press.

Zavadsk, M., Morales, L., Coughlan, J., 2020. Brent crude oil prices volatility during major crises. Financ. Res. Lett. 32, 101078.

CHAPTER 4

Agricultural markets

Introduction

On February 24, 2022, Russia launched an unprovoked attack against Ukraine, a smaller neighbor on its western border. As one of the primary exporters of grains and vegetable oils in the world, the European Union's (EU) second largest source of grains, and a critical source of food crops for a variety of countries in Asia and Africa, the conflict set off alarm bells for agricultural markets throughout the world (Maciejewska and Skrzypek, 2022). Most immediately, the invasion represented a threat to Ukraine's own food security. Such a massive disruption to its farms and agricultural markets threatened malnutrition and even starvation for its population without external support. But the repercussions were much broader than to Ukraine itself. As such a major supplier of agricultural food products, the invasion of Ukraine threatened to affect markets not only with its largest trading partners, such as the EU, but to the entire world.

Historically, agriculture has been targeted during conflicts as fields were burned or salted to destroy national food supplies. Throughout the entirety of human history food has been the single most important sector of production, so it comes as no surprise that it has been a primary target in times of war. Agriculture is unique in that a nation cannot allow its own food production to end, so how do farms survive when they are under attack and when their trade routes have been disrupted? What opportunities can they pursue when a conflict begins compared to when one ends? Everything depends on agriculture first, making this market particularly unique in how it behaves in times of conflict. And as noted with Ukraine, the implications of agricultural disruption may go far beyond those felt by the few countries directly impacted, especially in our modern globalized world.

This chapter will provide an overview of the fundamentals of agricultural markets. It will then detail the research on how agriculture can cause conflict and the deleterious, and sometimes disastrous, effects that conflict can have on agricultural production. In addition to general findings, brief examples from individual conflicts and historical periods will highlight some of the lessons that seem to be broadly applicable along with some trends that

Markets and Conflict
https://doi.org/10.1016/B978-0-323-85525-9.00001-5

may be more idiosyncratic or have changed over time. The chapter will also briefly touch on the importance of agriculture in postconflict redevelopment. Finally, the chapter will offer conclusions and lessons gleaned from the research.

Agricultural markets

Though agriculture as a profession has changed markedly over history, it is still small-scale farmers who account for the majority of agricultural production worldwide (Kneafsey, 2016, p. 12). Agriculture also remains the primary occupation of the majority of human beings, though the proportion of a country's population engaged in agriculture is roughly relational to its level of economic development, with more developed countries having a lower percentage of its citizens engaged in agricultural work (Capstick, 2019, p. 13). A country's level of economic development also impacts its mode of agricultural production. The United States and most European countries, for example, tend to have a smaller overall number of farms but they are large and highly mechanized, while many countries in Latin America, Africa, and Asia have a larger number of small farms that remain more reliant on human and animal power (Magdoff, 2012, p. 17). The most important crops for global food security are corn, soybeans, wheat, and rice which together comprise three-quarters of global food production as measured by caloric intake (Roberts and Schlenker, 2009, p. 1235).

No matter where in the world agriculture is being produced there are three primary factors of its production: the land on which it is grown and harvested; the labor which does the planting, reaping, and other agricultural work; and capital in the form of seeds, equipment, barns, and other material expenses involved (Capstick, 2019, p. 18). With the exception of subsistence farming, however, production is only the first step. Equally important is getting the produce to market, whether that be local or global in nature. Advances in transportation revolutionized this aspect of agricultural markets in the 19th century. When steam began to power ships and trains, perishable agricultural goods could suddenly be transported previously impossible distances and the importance of a farm's proximity to its ultimate customers became less vital. Refrigeration was another key technological development in the expansion of agricultural markets and the development of a global interdependence in agricultural goods (Capstick, 2019, p. 24).

These technological changes also increased the importance of comparative advantage. As farmers became less dependent on local markets and sold their produce further afield, they could increasingly focus on what they themselves could produce best and cheapest and import from other farmers what they in turn produced most efficiently. America, with its vast open prairies, became the world's primary exporter of grain, for example, while Australia and Argentina cashed in on meat (Capstick, 2019, p. 126). Similarly, tropical countries were able to market their fruits all over the world.

While land, labor, and capital are the three primary elements of production, cost, price, yield, and acreage are the four primary elements of agricultural profit (Williams, 2014, p. 10). Farmers want to obtain the highest prices for large yields of agricultural products harvested at the lowest cost possible. The capital involved in agricultural production—such as land, machinery, wage labor, infrastructure—is only part of the cost. Transportation, which is often dependent on extraneous factors such as the price of oil, also impacts the farmer's bottom line, and ultimately the consumers' wallets. The major role that transportation costs play in international agricultural markets is one of the primary reasons that there is growing correlation between energy and agricultural commodity markets, especially evident since 2008 (Szenderák, 2018, p. 288). For poor countries dependent on food imports, increased costs resulting from rising fuel prices or other factors can severely impact their food security (Williams, 2014, p. 12).

Fortunately, the overall trend has been a continual reduction in transportation costs which has increased trade. Free trade policies and the reduction and sometimes elimination of tariffs and other trade barriers have also spurred international agricultural trade (Zimmerman, et al., 2020, p. 23). According to the Food and Agriculture Organization of the United Nations (UN), "Trade in food and agriculture has more than doubled in real terms since 1995. Emerging and developing countries have become active participants in global markets, and they now account for about one-third of global trade…one-third of global agricultural and food exports are traded within a global value chain [GVC]" (Zimmermann et al., 2020, p. 11).

GVCs have become a critical element of international agricultural markets. GVCs entail a chain of steps between the farmer and the ultimate consumer that can include the famer selling to a local buyer, who in turn resells the product to a wholesaler after processing and packaging, who then send it to a retailer, who finally sells it to the customer who brings it home to their table (Magdoff, 2012, pp. 16–17). This process may occur within the borders of a single country, but it has become more and more typical for GVCs to cross borders at least once but often multiple times (Zimmerman, et al., 2020, p. 26). Transnational corporations (TNCs) have become dominant players in GVCs, exporting most major commodities. A small number of these corporations have come to have disproportionate market share in global agribusiness due to the efficiencies generated by private sector consolidation and economies of scale (Kneafsey, 2016, pp. 10–11).

GVCs have developed over time to increase efficiencies on the supply side of agricultural markets, but just like with any other economic interaction, agricultural prices depend on both supply and demand. Demand can rise or fall based on a variety of factors. Population growth, or decline, is an obvious variable. More mouths to feed will result in greater demand for agricultural products while fewer mouths will result in a reduction in demand. Income growth also plays a major role. People with larger incomes will tend to buy more food of better quality and of greater variety. Lower incomes will tend to reduce consumers' ability to purchase more expensive foods, such as meats, and cause a reversion to greater reliance on cheaper staple foods (Kerckhoffs et al., 2010, pp. 1–2). We will see later in the chapter that both sides of the supply and demand equation are impacted by conflict and that it therefore plays a major role in prices.

In addition to matters of supply and demand, uncertainty also effects price in agricultural markets as it increases risk. The normal uncertainties of any market commodity are compounded for agricultural products by the additional uncertainties and vulnerabilities attendant with their biological nature (Williams, 2014, p. 1). Crop yields may be diminished by disease, poor weather conditions, and other extraneous factors. Uncertainty also means that investors will seek to gamble in the hopes of making outsized profits, which can have major consequences on price. As Fred Magdoff notes, "speculation drives prices up and down further and faster, and as a result contributes to hunger for many—sometimes millions—when prices peak, and to the ruin of small producers when prices crash" (Magdoff, 2012, p. 22).

One of the primary ways of stabilizing agricultural (and other) markets is through hedging with futures. Futures trading allows both the seller and buyer to agree to a fixed price for a given amount of product at a particular date in the future. By doing so, the seller risks losing out on discounts if the actual future price is lower and the seller risks losing out on additional profit if it is higher, but both are also protected from losing out by either having to pay more if prices increase for the buyer or receiving less profit if prices fall for the seller. Futures trading reduces uncertainty and risk and can be particularly effective during unsettled times, such as during conflict (Sarris et al., 2011, p. 15).

Having laid out the basics of agricultural markets, the next section will delve into the impacts that armed conflict can have on those markets using several historical case studies.

Agriculture and conflict

Armed conflict often has substantial and long-lasting repercussions on agricultural markets and the cost of food and other agricultural products, such as cotton for fabrics. Agriculture can be damaged unintentionally and incidentally during conflict, through bombing, fires, troop movements, and other elements of fighting. But it is often targeted intentionally, with the hopes of ruining the enemy's livelihoods and of destroying the enemy's capacity to sustain their combat forces. Crops themselves can be targeted through burning, slashing, or chemicals, such as the United States' use of Agent Orange during the Vietnam War to reduce foliage (Özerdem and Roberts, 2016, p. 19). Livestock, which is both a product of agriculture but also remains a crucial element of agricultural labor on many small farms, can be slaughtered or confiscated. And agricultural infrastructure, such as barns, wells, mills, and other agricultural structures, along with fences and tools, can be deliberately destroyed, interrupting agricultural production and storage capacity.

When extensive, Emmanuel Kreike calls this activity environcide. "Environcide consists of intentionally or unintentionally damaging, destroying, or rendering inaccessible environmental infrastructure through violence" (Kreike, 2021, pp. 2–3). Throughout history combatants have often resorted to such tactics both to feed their own troops in the field and to deny sustenance to their foes (Kreike, 2021, p. 30). Though modern forces, at least those of highly developed countries, are not generally reliant upon the seizure of their opponents' crops for their own sustainment, the incentive to deny the benefits of agriculture to their enemies remains the same (Kreike, 2021, p. 14).

In addition to the direct and indirect destruction of crops and agricultural infrastructure itself, military conflict also deeply impedes agricultural markets by distorting normal trade routes. Blockades, on both land and sea, hamper trade directly. "The destruction of roads and bridges prevents access to local, national and international markets for small and large-scale agricultural producers" (Özerdem and Roberts, 2016, p. 22). Even if roads and bridges remain intact, the diversion of transportation vehicles, such as ships, trucks, and trains, typically used for distributing agricultural products to consumers, toward instead moving troops and war equipment can prevent producers from getting their product to consumers. A diminution of available agricultural labor as farmers go off to fight can also substantially reduce agricultural yields.

The repercussions of these various factors can be immense in terms of agricultural pricing and overall food security. As food becomes scarce, in other words, as the supply goes down, prices will rise. If less food is being produced and less food can make it to market, it will become more and more expensive. This is exacerbated by the fact that demand for food by soldiers will increase, as fighting burns calories. "A moderately active young man needs somewhere in the region of 2,800 to 3,000 calories a day, but a soldier in training needs about 3,429 calories a day; on active service in cold conditions, he needs 4,238 calories; and fighting in tropical conditions, 4,738 calories" (Collingham, 2012, p. 8). Increased demand and reduced supply sends prices soaring. This can severely harm consumers but be a boon to those agricultural producers whose fields avoid destruction and who can get their crop to market.

These factors make conflict one of the most common causes of food insecurity (Özerdem and Roberts, 2016, p. 19), and when extreme, it can result in famines and contribute to the outbreak of lethal diseases, as Kreike points out happened in Warsaw, Leningrad, the Netherlands, and Bengal during World War II (Kreike, 2021, p. 7). For consumers dependent on functioning agricultural markets, the disruption to those markets caused by war can mean malnutrition, disease, and death. Though some producers may profit due to increased prices, overall production is likely to be depressed. Messer and Cohen point out that "according to the Food and Agriculture Organization of the United Nations, conflict cost Africa over $120 billion worth of agricultural production during the last third of the 20th century. Given the importance of agricultural livelihoods to overall economic well-being, especially in conflict-prone countries in Africa, these losses were devastating" (Messer and Cohen, 2008, p. 3). Developed countries are not immune to these negative consequences. Research by De Winne and Peersman demonstrates that disruptions to international food markets affect the economy overall. "An unfavorable shock to the global food production index of 1 standard deviation," they find, "raises real food commodity prices by approximately 1.7 percent, which in turn leads to a 0.16 percent rise in consumer prices and a persistent decline in real GDP and personal consumption of almost 0.3 percent" (De Winne and Peersman, 2016, p. 188).

Other research has found a strong correlation between agricultural commodity prices and crude oil prices (Mokni and Youssef, 2020, p. 2), both of which are likely to be affected by conflict (discussed further in the chapter on energy markets). This can be doubly damaging to consumers who find both the cost of food and the cost of transportation to rise substantially and simultaneously. Further, even if agricultural production itself escapes the direct impacts of conflict, if crude oil prices rise due to that conflict the subsequently increased transportation costs will likely result in higher prices. Mokni and Youssef found in an analysis of oil shocks from 2003 to 2017 that immediate price effects are stronger than delayed effects, but that nonetheless delayed effects are frequently of long duration and may exceed 120 days. They warn policymakers and investors that oil shocks can result in long-lasting effects on the price of agricultural commodities (Mokni and Youssef, 2020, pp. 1 and 18). So even when agricultural markets are not directly impacted by armed conflict, they can still be indirectly affected by extraneous factors, such as increased crude oil prices.

Recent research has demonstrated that not only is agriculture affected by conflict, but that the reverse is also true. Agricultural markets can cause, or at least contribute to, the onset of armed conflict in the form of rebellions or civil wars. Hanne Fjelde's research links reduced profitability in agriculture in Africa with a greater likelihood of local armed conflict. She concludes that "negative changes to the local agricultural price index significantly and substantially increase the risk of violent events" (Fjelde, 2015, p. 525). On the other side of the ledger, Fjelde finds that "positive changes to the local agricultural price index—associated with increased employment opportunities and higher returns—are associated with a lower risk of violence at the location" (Fjelde, 2015, p. 529). Potential explanations for these findings are that lower economic returns increase unemployment and general poverty, which enhances incentives to join rebel movements and empowers rebel leaders to recruit adherents with monetary inducements (Fjelde, 2015, p. 525).

Other research demonstrates that since the Cold War those regions of the world most reliant on agricultural production in their economies—South Asia, Central, Africa, and areas of Latin America—have the highest concentrations of both domestic and international armed conflict. On the other hand, those countries with the lowest dependence on agriculture experienced much fewer conflicts. "Indeed, only five out of 63 states who exhibit a low dependence on agriculture have suffered armed conflict after the Cold War. Of these five, none have exceeded 1,000 battle deaths per year, and only the conflict in Northern Ireland has a cumulative death toll exceeding 1,000" (De Soysa et al., 1999, p. 17). The authors of this study again explain the connection between agriculture and conflict with the intervening variable of poverty. Agricultural societies are more vulnerable to economic deprivation, especially when experiencing downturns in agricultural markets, and are therefore more prone to violence (De Soysa et al., 1999, p. 18).

An example of this phenomenon occurred in coffee-producing areas in the late 1990s and early 2000s. Coffee prices plummeted precipitously during those years and armed conflict was a direct result. Research by Dube and Vargas determined that in coffee-producing regions the lower prices resulted in "4 percent more guerilla attacks, 7 percent more paramilitary attacks, 8 percent more clashes and 6 percent more casualties in the average coffee municipality, relative to a non-coffee area" (Dube and Vargas, 2013, p. 3). They attribute this to lower wages and a subsequent increase in the ability of rebel groups to recruit (Dube and Vargas, 2013, p. 1).

From this general examination of the interrelationship between agricultural and armed conflict we will move onto examine several more specific examples. First, we will look at the ancient world, then the American Civil War and World War II, and finally several other more contemporary conflicts. These examples will show how agriculture and conflict have been intertwined for centuries and what in that relationship has remained consistent and what has changed.

The ancient world

Agricultural production was a primary target of ancient armies. In ancient Greece, for example, the historian Victor David Hanson tells us that war "was inaugurated and often defined by a struggle to destroy, or protect, grain, vines, and olive trees" (Hanson, 1998, p. 5). This was true for at least three reasons: (1) to sustain one's own army, (2) to damage the enemy's ability to sustain themselves, and (3) to lure the enemy out from behind their walls of fortification and into open battle.

The first of these reasons was critical. As Hanson succinctly put it, "Armies need food. Any society that mobilizes troops must plan both to feed its own men and to seek to deny supplies to the enemy" (Hanson, 1998, p. 1). In the ancient world, armies had either to carry with them what they needed to sustain themselves or they had to forage for it wherever they went. These needs could be enormous. Historian Patrick Hunt has noted that "a consular army of several legions plus allies (around 20,000 men and 3,500 horses and pack animals) would consume around 35 tons of wheat and 25 tons of barley daily along with an optimum amount of 10,000 liters of wine and 2,000 liters of olive oil. Daily grazing of animals during the right seasons was an absolute given, but winter added a huge strain on food supply" (Hunt, 2017, p. 126). Food was a huge logistical challenge for ancient armies and necessitated living off the land as it was traversed and occupied. This in itself caused massive devastation on the agricultural lands armies encountered, even if the invading armies were not actively seeking to harm them.

But in fact, armies most often did actively seek to harm the agricultural infrastructure and products of their enemies. "Ravaging of cropland was central to warfare of most societies of the past" (Hanson, 1998, p. 4). Another obvious reason for this was to starve out the enemy. While the marauding armies needed food, so did those they were attacking. By reducing or eliminating their enemy's access to food, they could reduce or eliminate the effectiveness of enemy resistance.

Though Hanson demonstrates that the complete destruction of agricultural fields, harvests, and infrastructure was difficult, time consuming, and rarely wholly effective, agricultural catastrophe was often the result of ancient warfare due to "displaced populations, labor power losses, sieges, the unsettled conditions caused by brigandry and robber gangs, plagues, the desertion of slaves and hired hands, the loss of livestock and equipment, and the more enervating property and income taxes levied to pay for near permanent periods of hostility" (Hanson, 1998, p. xiii). Needless to say, this could be devastating for local populations.

According to James Thorne, cereals, such as wheat and barley, were primary targets. They were the staple crops of the ancient diet and would be highly vulnerable in the summer, when most military campaigns unfolded (Thorne, 2001, pp. 252–253). In order to avoid the worst depredations, under most circumstances defenders would have to decide either to capitulate to their invaders or come out and fight to protect their crops and lands. "To save their farms, the agrarian defenders felt they were obliged either to capitulate and thereby submit to terms or to engage in pitched battle to drive the invader away" (Hanson, 1998, p. 6). Remaining behind fortified walls may eventually result in the invaders departing in frustration, but the price was usually the destruction or carrying away of everything outside those walls, which included almost all agricultural lands. Invaders knew that it would be difficult for their enemies to helplessly watch their lands and economic futures being destroyed. Burning crops, slaughtering livestock, razing farmhouses and barns, and general devastation of farmlands was therefore a tactic to force a besieged target to come out and fight.

The degree of economic impact that seasonal marauding caused to agricultural economic production is disputed by classical historians. Hanson, for example, argues that farms would usually rebound within two or three seasons, so repercussions would not be long lasting and certainly not permanent. But even Hanson admits that the damage could be severe in the short term. And that's when people eat.

Thorne demonstrates that the invasions of Attica, which occurred between 431 and 425 BCE during the Peloponnesian War, contrary to Hanson's claims, caused major economic damage to Athens. The invading Peloponnesians used Attic crops to sustain themselves and destroyed what they could not use. He estimates that "the net effect was that Athens subsidised the rationing of the Spartan and allied armies on the order of 37 1/2 talents in 431, over 40 talents annually in the years 429–7, and 9 1/2 talents in 425, for a total of 177 talents throughout the course of the Archidamian War" (Thorne, 2001, p. 250). Though harder to quantify, the amount of crop destroyed was also likely to have been large. Together, these invasions had a significant impact on the Athenian economy, though they were able to weather the damage for some time due to their extraordinary wealth and access to imports. Most smaller populations would not have been able to sustain such losses. For any ancient society, "the substantial destruction of even one cereal harvest was a severe (by any definition) blow to the rural economy" (Thorne, 2001, p. 251).

Though our sources are not sufficient to give us a detailed understanding of the full economic consequences of agricultural destruction during ancient warfare, we do know that it was a major target of such warfare. It was used by invading armies to sustain themselves and to draw out their opponents from behind protective walls. When not prevented, agricultural devastation could have large, and sometimes existential, consequences for its victims. Agriculture was a central field of battle in ancient conflicts. It would remain so all the way up to the American Civil War.

American civil war

Agriculture was one of the primary differences between the Northern and Southern states in the American Civil War. The war itself was essentially fought over the South's "peculiar institution" of unpaid agricultural labor. The forced agricultural labor of enslaved people was the backbone of the

South's economy. The cash crops of tobacco and cotton, along with food products such as rice, corn, and wheat, reached a level of profitability for white enslavers that would have been impossible if they had had to pay the full cost of that labor. Maintaining this system was valuable enough to Southern states that they were willing to break apart from their country in order to safeguard it.

As the war began, Southerners were confident that their agricultural advantages would ensure that they outlasted their Northern brothers, now turned enemies. They believed that their vast output of agricultural production was a form of power that could not be matched by their opponents. According to R. Douglas Hurt, who has written a definitive book on the subject and on whose research this subsection relies upon, "The South possessed agricultural power, and it intended to use it to gain independence" (Hurt, 2015, p. 2). Unfortunately for the Confederates, they had failed to accurately measure the elements of agricultural power and would learn over the next four long, painful years that they were more vulnerable agriculturally than they had anticipated.

There were several reasons for this vulnerability. One was that due to the very fact that their economy was so reliant upon agriculture, any disruption of agricultural markets would ripple through the entire economic landscape. Another was that because the war was primarily fought on Confederate turf, their farmland was destroyed and ravaged by Union soldiers traversing and conquering it. Over time, even Confederate soldiers began to confiscate agricultural food products for their own survival, hurting their own farmers and undermining the South's primary economic engine. A third important factor that undermined Confederate agricultural power was a lack of transportation infrastructure to support agricultural markets. Finally, as soldiers died and needed replacing, young men were increasingly unavailable to work on the farms. At the same time, enslaved people were fleeing or being freed in ever larger numbers. The lack of available labor significantly dampened agricultural yield as the war dragged on.

The fact that the American Civil War was primarily fought on Confederate territory quickly took a toll on Southern agriculture. As Union forces captured more and more land, they were able to use those agricultural resources to feed themselves, while food became proportionately more scarce for Confederate soldiers and civilians alike. After Union victories in Middle Tennessee, it "had become not the breadbasket of the Confederacy but the food basket of the Union army" (Hurt, 2015, p. 172). The same applied wherever the Union army prevailed, and even in some places where they didn't, if they were able to damage crops during the fighting or while they were traveling through. Famous civil war battles and skirmishes are frequently named after the corn fields or apple orchards in which they were fought. Generals Philip Sheridan and William Tecumsah Sherman dealt a death blow to Confederate agriculture when they ransacked and pillaged the Shenandoah Valley of Virginia and the plantations of Georgia and North and South Carolina, respectively (Hurt, 2015, p. 10).

Another problem for the South was that agricultural product from relatively unscathed areas could not be transported in sufficient quantity to those areas that most needed it. The Union strategy included controlling vital waterways, such as the Mississippi River, enacting naval blockades around critical market ports, and destroying or commandeering train tracks. Even those trains that the South maintained control of were increasingly needed for the movement of troops and military equipment and could not also support the transport of sufficient amounts of agricultural product. "The South's railroads were too few in number to meet the wartime needs of the army and farmers" (Hurt, 2015, p. 10).

All of these factors decreased supply while demand was increasing. Soldiers on the march and engaged in combat require more calories, and as the supply dwindled, civilians found themselves in competition with soldiers for what remained available. Supply was negatively affected by the destruction of farms and crops, reduced labor, and the inability to get product to market. Supply for civilians was further curtailed due to impressment by Confederate soldiers who often confiscated food directly from farms, while it was in transit, or from markets.

Increased demand and decreased supply is a sure recipe for skyrocketing prices. Escalated prices benefitted farmers—at least those physically distant from the fighting—but undermined consumers and led to inflation throughout the entire Confederate economy. As Hurt put it, "Farmers, of course, enjoyed high prices. War is good for them unless an enemy army marches through or fights in their fields or kills them or their sons" (Hurt, 2015, p. 10). But even those farmers getting higher prices for their product began to resent the government as Confederate impressments at below-market prices increased, as higher agricultural prices led to general inflation, as their farms became unmanageable without sufficient labor, and as monetary depreciation began to eat away at their profits. Many farmers took the opportunity of 'trading with the enemy' when they could cross the lines and sell their goods to Union soldiers willing to pay with federal money.

Nonfarmer civilians were worse off by far. Riots broke out in cities throughout the Confederacy, but especially in Richmond and other eastern cities, as food became unaffordable and famine lurked. Not only was food lacking, but increased agricultural prices undermined the rest of the economy through inflation. In many ways, this set farmer against merchant, rural people against urbanites, and further divided a part of the country already divorced from its other half.

In the end, though farmers prospered for a time, "a host of war-driven causes" drove Confederate agriculture to near collapse and doomed the Confederate cause (Hurt, 2015, p. 5). What the South perceived to be its trump card at the beginning of the war turned out to be its Achilles' heel.

World War II

The role of agriculture, and food more generally, is an often-overlooked aspect of World War II. As Lizzie Collingham thoroughly demonstrates in her exhaustive examination of the role of food in World War II, agriculture played a major part in nearly all aspects of the war. The most tragic element being the toll in death and suffering that agricultural disruption caused. According to Collingham, more people perished during the war from lack of food than from violence. "During the Second World War at least 20 million people died…a terrible death from starvation, malnutrition and its associated diseases: a number to equal the 19.5 military deaths. The impact of the war on food supplies was thus as deadly in its effect on the world population as military action" (Collingham, 2012, p. 1).

The first way in which agriculture impacted the war was as one of its many causes. Both Germany and Japan "feared that their agricultural sectors could not produce enough food to feed the cities," and this fear was among the motivations that fueled their aggression (Collingham, 2012, pp. 1–2). Though Japan's reliance on foreign oil is often pointed to as driving its aggression, the additional element of food is less commonly recognized. Japan saw control of vast Chinese farmlands, particularly in Manchuria which Japan would take over and call Manchukuo, as offering a variety of valuable resources, "not the least of which was food" (Collingham, 2012, p. 2). During the 1930s and the lead up to World War II, Japan's invasion of China led to the eviction of thousands of Chinese farmers and the diversion of agricultural products away from China and into Japan. Japanese food diversion policies in the region created food insecurity and malnutrition in China but also to a famine in Vietnam that claimed an estimated two million lives (Collingham, 2012, p. 7).

Similarly, the desire for expanded crop lands was a major element of the Nazi idea of *lebensraum*, living space, which motivated its advances into Eastern Europe and to eventually turn on the Soviet Union, with whom it had signed a nonaggression pact. Collingham notes:

> It was the agronomist Herbert Backe who hatched the most radical plan to secure Germany's food supply. He argued that the Wehrmacht (the German armed services) could be fed by diverting Ukrainian grain from Soviet cities. This would solve the problem of feeding a vast army while conveniently eliminating the Soviet urban population, who would starve to death. Once the east was conquered and its former inhabitants had been forcibly eradicated, German agronomists intended to create an agricultural empire on the land. Altogether the regime's agragrian vision for the east generated plans to murder up to 100 million people.
> **(Collingham, 2012, p. 5).**

Though that plan was never materialized, Backe's arguments weighed heavily on Hitler's decision to go to war with the Soviet Union. Estimates of the number of Soviet civilians who died from starvation and malnutrition-induced disease stand between two and three million. Hitler's Nazi regime used food as a weapon throughout the war, leading to at least half a million famine-related deaths in Greece and widespread malnutrition in Czechoslovakia, Poland, France, Belgium, and Holland. Near the end of the war, a German blockade of parts of Holland that had not yet been liberated resulted in the death by starvation of 22,000 people. Lack of food also took its toll in Asia. Over half of the 1.74 million Japanese military deaths were the result of starvation rather than fighting. And in India, 3 million people died from lack of food (Collingham, 2012, pp. 7–11).

The Allied countries generally managed to maintain at least the bare minimum of daily calories, though prewar food production and distribution networks were severely disrupted. The United States, Australia, Canada, and New Zealand altered their agricultural economies to reduce variety and focus on basic foodstuffs. The war increased demand for food at the same time that it diverted farmers from their crop fields to the battlefields, the production of farm equipment and machinery was reduced as the need for war machines monopolized industrial production capacity, and key transportation routes were disrupted by blockades and fighting.

Because America was not at risk of invasion, its farmland remained unscathed by violence. And although considerable resources—both human and capital—were diverted from agriculture into war-making, America had such vast production potential that adjustments to agricultural practices were sufficient to keep itself and its allies fed.

> *America possessed sufficient resources to rise to the challenge and devised and implemented new agricultural techniques, the impact of which are still felt long after the war. But for most combatant countries total war placed an immense strain on the food system. Luxury foods fell by the wayside, and farmers switched to cultivating bread grains and potatoes rather than raising livestock for meat and milk.*

> **(Collingham, 2012, p. 9).**

Women increasingly replaced their husbands, brothers, and fathers in the fields, and farms became more efficient as they reduced in number but greatly expanded in size. Much as the automobile factories industrialized the production of war machinery, the American agricultural sector became industrialized. By the end of the war, agricultural production had actually increased over its prewar levels and farm incomes had grown by 156% (Collingham, 2012, p. 78). Though many small farmers went out of business and were absorbed into larger farms, overall the war was a boon to the American agriculture industry.

British farmers also did well. The demand for food led the government to pass generous compensation packages for its farmers. Even as Britain became more dependent on Western imports, it put great effort into propping up its own agricultural output, and between 1939 and 1945, farmers saw their incomes increase by a factor of four. As in America, war was good business for British farmers. At the same time, the British government protected consumers by keeping the cost of food artificially low by subsidizing it (Collingham, 2012, p. 89).

While Britain came to rely more and more heavily on the United States, Canada, and its other allies for food, despite its efforts to enhance its own self-sufficiency, it simultaneously sought to strangle food imports to Germany, primarily through the enforcement of naval blockades. Germany's lack of food production capacity—one of the motives for attacking the Soviet Union and seeking *lebensraum*—left it vulnerable to such disruptions to external food supply as it was heavily reliant upon imports. A powerful blockade instituted by Britain in 1940 essentially cut continental Europe off from the global food market. It was so effective that only 12 ships managed to circumvent it from 1941 to 1942 (Collingham, 2012, p. 35).

This, of course, had reverberations beyond Europe to the suppliers of those agricultural goods as well. Latin American coffee producers lost nearly half of their market. Cocoa farmers in West Africa, Caribbean banana producers, and other developing countries economically dependent on agricultural markets were also severely affected. The disruption of agricultural markets effected farmers around the world, not merely among the belligerent countries. And while some agriculturalists, such as those in the United States and the United Kingdom, prospered, others, primarily in the colonized developing world, suffered due to lack of access to markets and inability to sell their products (Collingham, 2012, p. 67).

These already poor countries suddenly had what few market advantages were available to them dry up. Beyond this economic threat to the world's poorest people, the historian Jamie Martin points out that this presented serious political problems to the allies.

> *Huge quantities of unmarketable primary goods piled up around the world—cotton in Egypt; citrus fruit in Palestine and Cyprus; palm products, oilseeds, and groundnuts in West Africa; sisal in East Africa; coconuts in the Pacific Islands; and bananas in Jamaica. A collapse of prices for these goods risked major political and economic consequences: the outbreak of anti-colonial unrest across Europe's empires, the defection of neutral countries and the colonies of occupied Europe to the fascists, sovereign defaults, the weakening of the blockade, and the global spread of Nazi influence. In the British government, some thought it threatened the 'collapse of the economic life of our Empire.'*
>
> **(Martin, 2021, p. 1).**

Both America and the British worked to stave off the worst effects to the developing world through a variety of measures. The Americans supported Latin American coffee growers with guaranteed prices, and the British Colonial Office similarly used price guarantees as well as "the direct purchasing of goods for immediate consumption, strategic stockpiling, storage for postwar relief, and grants-in-aid for the destruction of various perishable goods" (Martin, 2021, pp. 4–5). Many of the measures developed for international agricultural cooperation during the war resulted in long-standing agreements and institutions that long outlasted it.

Agricultural production and distribution, the struggle over farmland in continental Europe and Asia, and the disruption of the enemy's ability to produce food through conquest, deliberate destruction, and the blockade of trade routes all played a significant role in World War II. Farmers directly in the line of fire, particularly Soviet and later German farmers, were often devastated. Famines killed millions in Europe and Asia. On the other hand, the agricultural sectors in America and Great Britain prospered, and they were even able to prop-up their trading partners in developing countries sufficiently to stave off agricultural collapse in the wake of disrupted markets. The war affected both consumers and producers everywhere in the world, but in various ways depending on a variety of circumstances.

Other conflicts

"Ukraine is the breadbasket of the world. They grow enough food to feed 400 million people. Well, that's gone." So warned David Beasley, executive director of the UN's World Food Programme (WFP), during an interview with CBS News shortly after Russia invaded Ukraine in early 2022. In the same report the WPF's chief economist, Arif Husein, noted:

> This is the time for farmers to be out there planting corn. Right now. This is their time. And they are not. Why? Because farmers are soldiers. Why? Because there is not enough diesel. Look at wheat. Right now, in the ground is what is the winter wheat. It needs pesticides. It needs fertilizer. Same issues. No labor, no fuel, no machinery. Our estimates are between 30 and 50% will actually be harvested. Would that have an impact on the world? Hell yes, it will have an impact on the world.
>
> **(CBS News, 2022).**

Veronica Nigh, writing for the American Farm Bureau Federation (AFBF), made similar observations, pointing out that in 2021 Ukraine's agricultural exports topped $27 billion. Primary importers included the European Union (EU), China, Egypt, and Turkey, among others. Two of Ukraine's top agricultural exports are key food products, wheat and barley. Nigh predicted that "as the assault on Ukraine stretches on, the impacts to Ukraine's ability to produce the volume of tradeable commodities the global market has grown to depend on will become more significant. A substantial part of Ukraine's most productive agricultural land is in its eastern regions, exactly those parts most vulnerable to Russian attacks." Ukraine's export markets will be disrupted as croplands are destroyed by fighting, farmers put down their hoes and pick up their guns, and crops will be needed to feed their soldiers rather than hit the international market for sale (Nigh, 2022).

A significant reduction in Ukrainian export will have ripple effects in agricultural markets around the world. Reduced supply will mean increased prices, affecting people everywhere, but most strongly in poor countries where price increases weaken food security and threaten malnutrition. Though exporters of the same agricultural products from countries not affected by the conflict will likely see enhanced profits as prices rise.

Ukraine offers the most recent example of how conflict affects agricultural markets, but examples abound. Another recent example is Syria. There was a measurable drop in irrigated agricultural production of between 15% and 30% in the Syrian portion of the Orontes Basin between 2000 and 2013 after civil war erupted in 2011 (Jaafar et al., 2015, p. 436). A third recent example is on the other side of the world, in Colombia. There, conflict led to the breakdown of the International Coffee Agreement and the decline of international coffee prices at the same time as fighting ravished croplands. Local poverty increased and pushed more people into the production of illicit crops and trafficking them out of the country (Rettberg, 2010, p. 101).

Case studies of agricultural disruptions brought on by armed conflict and war could be reproduced nearly indefinitely. But those presented here are sufficient to demonstrate the most common impacts of war on agricultural markets. In the next section, we will see that many of those effects outlast the ending of war. Because a war ends does not mean its consequences do.

Agriculture postconflict

The devastation of croplands and the distortions of markets are not righted simply because a war ends. Instead, they can take years, or even decades, to return to normal—if they ever do. Agricultural markets in Canada during and after World War I present an illustrative example. Because Canada's territory was not threatened, it became a major food source for its allies, particularly Britain, during the war. The demand for wheat was so strong that many Canadian farmers altered their crop production to grow only wheat. In Canada's three Prairie Provinces, Alberta, Saskatchewan, and Manitoba, wheat exports doubled during the duration of the war. By the time the war was nearing its end in 1917, the price of wheat was three times what it was before the war. Canada's farmers profited significantly from these elevated prices (Thompson, 1976, p. 193).

As historian John Thompson explains, this distortion to Canada's agricultural markets would have long-lasting effects that were not as positive. In order to cash in on the enormous profits, many farmers had taken on additional debt to pay for more land, capital, and labor. Canadian agriculture also lost diversity as wheat came to replace a variety of crops once grown, causing damage to the land and overreliance on a single crop. "Western agriculture became concentrated even more heavily on the production of one staple crop for export to an unstable world market. In 1919 Western farmers were further from self-sufficiency than they had been in 1914" (Thompson, 1976, p. 202).

World War I Canada is an example of conflict altering the market properties of an exporting nation, but importing nations also may experience long-term changes to their market structures. Some countries become permanently, or semipermanently, reliant upon agricultural imports as their own production capabilities remain shattered. Research by Alpaslan Özerdem and Rebecca Roberts finds that "countries…that were self-sufficient before conflict become reliant on food imports during and after conflict because of an inability to increase food production to meet the population's needs" (Özerdem and Roberts, 2016, p. 23).

Reasons for continued agricultural dependence are many. In some cases, the land itself has become damaged or rendered inaccessible by unexploded ordinance and landmines that continue to pose a danger to farmers and to deprive them of the use of their lands for many years (Özerdem and Roberts, 2016, pp. 19–20). In particularly violent wars, many of the young men needed for farm labor are dead or maimed. This results not only in lost labor, but lost skill and agricultural know-how. Capital critical to farming, such as barns, machinery, and equipment, may also have been destroyed and difficult to replace. Agricultural market infrastructure, such as bridges, transportation vehicles, and physical markets themselves, may also have been destroyed or damaged. "The environment, infrastructure, social structures and skills, economy, and governance systems necessary to maintain agricultural production are fragile and easily damaged during conflict" (Özerdem and Roberts, 2016, p. 1). They can also be difficult to reconstitute after conflict.

A return to sustainable agriculture is key to societies, especially developing societies reliant upon agricultural as the primary element of their economy, being able to regain their footing and avoid reversion to war. "Without sustainable agriculture, populations remain vulnerable, increasing the likelihood of a return to conflict. Therefore, sustainable agriculture is central to the effective post-conflict recovery that provides human security as well as stability and rule of law" (Özerdem and Roberts, 2016, p. 1). A failure to reconstitute agricultural production in the aftermath of war can have devastating economic consequences that doom that country to a return to conflict, especially internal civil wars. "Poor conditions for agriculture hold grave implications for socio-economic development and sustainable peace" (De et al., 1999, p. 15).

Unfortunately, restoring agricultural production to prewar levels after conflict can be time consuming and expensive. Conflict zones in sub-Saharan Africa from 1970 to 1990 revealed an average reduction in agricultural output of 12% for each year that the conflict took place. A conflict lasting a mere two years would therefore wipe out nearly a quarter of agricultural production. Such devastation takes much time and investment to recuperate from, an especially difficult task in an already poor and war-torn country.

Conclusions

From the case studies of agricultural disruptions brought on by conflict and war presented in this chapter, we can detect some general patterns in the examples we have already seen. First, agricultural lands have throughout time been a target of invaders, both to feed themselves and to starve their opponents. As classical historian Victor Davis Hanson put it, "agricultural devastation remains an integral part of fighting. As long as people need to eat, and wars extend beyond the battlefield itself, generals and military planners will worry over how to protect and attack cropland" (Hanson, 1998, p. 5). Agriculture has always been and still is a target of war.

Second, the impacts of conflict on agriculture differ depending on a variety of factors. Those worst affected are the farmers whose land is directly targeted for destruction or as the site of battle and the consumers who either see higher prices or are not able to buy food at all, leading to widespread malnutrition, disease, and outright starvation. Because agricultural markets are international, the negative repercussions to consumers may be widespread and go far beyond the directly involved belligerents. This is especially the case when a major agricultural producer, such as Ukraine, is directly involved in the fighting.

A third lesson is that war doesn't hurt everyone in the agricultural business. The higher prices that result from greater demand and reductions in supply can be an economic windfall for those farmers who live a safe distance from the conflict zone and are still able to get their crops to market. War can bring a handsome profit to farmers, but this can also have long-term negative consequences for individual farmers and for their larger societies if profit incentives distort markets to an extent that do not normalize after war (De Soysa et al., 1999, p. 15).

Just as in the war itself, conflict brings both winners and losers in agricultural markets. Investors may find profitable opportunities in farms that are outside the conflict zone, maintain reliable access to global markets, and are focused on key staple food products that will be in high demand throughout a conflict. Consumers, on the other hand, should prepare for continually rising prices as demand increases and supply dwindles.

Because of the distortions that conflict wreaks on markets, governments often have an important role to play in avoiding famine. Subsidizing the cost of food for consumers, keeping trade routes open, and providing direct food assistance to areas in which markets have become dysfunctional may do much to avert starvation and horrendous humanitarian consequences. Governments also have a role to play in postconflict situations in feeding people, repairing transportation infrastructure such as bridges, helping farmers whose fields have been damaged by the conflict get back on their feet, and other interventions designed to return markets to normalcy.

References

Capstick, M., 2019. The Economics of Agriculture. Routledge.

CBS News, 2022. Economist: Loss of Ukraine's Exports May Be Felt Worldwide For Years. Downloaded on 07 May 2022 from https://www.msn.com/en-us/news/us/economist-loss-of-ukraine-s-exports-may-be-felt-worldwide-for-years/ar-AAWOGgY?ocid=msedgntp&cvid=65f708810537464eafb7fb956624f8c0.

Collingham, L., 2012. Taste of War: World War II and the Battle for Food. Penguin.

De Winne, J., Peersman, G., 2016. Macroeconomic effects of disruptions in global food commodity markets: evidence for the United States. Brook. Pap. Econ. Act. 2016 (2), 183–286.

Dube, O., Vargas, J.F., 2013. Commodity price shocks and civil conflict: evidence from Colombia. Rev. Econ. Stud. 80 (4), 1384–1421.

Fjelde, H., 2015. Farming or fighting? Agricultural price shocks and civil war in Africa. World Dev. 67, 525–534.

Hanson, V.D., 1998. Warfare and Agriculture in Classical Greece. University of California Press.

Hunt, P., 2017. Hannibal. Simon and Schuster.

Hurt, R.D., 2015. Agriculture and the Confederacy: Policy, Productivity, and Power in the Civil War South. UNC Press Books.

Jaafar, H.H., Zurayk, R., King, C., Ahmad, F., Al-Outa, R., 2015. Impact of the Syrian conflict on irrigated agriculture in the Orontes Basin. Int. J. Water Resour. Dev. 31 (3), 436–449.

Kerckhoffs, T., van Os, R., Stichele, M.V., 2010. Financing Food: Financialisation and Financial Actors in Agriculture Commodity Markets. Somo, Amsterdam.

Kneafsey, M., 2016. Global agriculture and the challenge of sustainability. In: Özerdem, A., Roberts, R. (Eds.), Challenging Post-Conflict Environments: Sustainable Agriculture. Routledge.

Kreike, E., 2021. Scorched Earth: Environmental Warfare as a Crime Against Humanity and Nature. Vol. 30 Princeton University Press.

Maciejewska, A., Skrzypek, K., 2022. Ukraine Agriculture Exports – What Is At Stake in the Light of Invasion? HIS Markit. Downloaded on 04/03/2022 at https://ihsmarkit.com/research-analysis/ukraine-agriculture-exports-what-is-at-stake.html.

Magdoff, F., 2012. Food as a commodity. Mon. Rev. 63 (8), 15–22.

Martin, J., 2021. The global crisis of commodity glut during the second world war. Int. Hist. Rev. 43 (6), 1273–1290.

Messer, E., Cohen, M.J., 2008. Breaking the Links between Conflict and Hunger in Africa. No. 566-2016-38943.

Mokni, K., Youssef, M., 2020. Empirical analysis of the cross-interdependence between crude oil and agricultural commodity markets. Rev. Financ. Econ. 38 (4), 635–654.

Nigh, V., 2022. Ukraine, Russia, Volatile Ag Markets. American Farm Bureau Federation. Downloaded on 04/03/2022 from: https://www.fb.org/market-intel/ukraine-russia-volatile-ag-markets#:~:text=These%20top%20five%20markets%20accounted,sunflower%20meal%20(%241.2%20billion.

Özerdem, A., Roberts, R., 2016. Challenging Post-Conflict Environments: Sustainable Agriculture. Routledge.

Rettberg, A., 2010. Global markets, local conflict: violence in the Colombian coffee region after the breakdown of the international coffee agreement. Lat. Am. Perspect. 37 (2), 111–132.

Roberts, M.J., Schlenker, W., 2009. World supply and demand of food commodity calories. Am. J. Agric. Econ. 91 (5), 1235–1242.

Sarris, A., Conforti, P., Prakash, A., 2011. The use of organized commodity markets to manage food import price instability and risk. Agric. Econ. 42 (1), 47–64.

De Soysa, I., Gleditsch, N.P., Gibson, M., Sollenberg, M., 1999. To Cultivate Peace: Agriculture in a World of Conflict. International Peace Research Institute, Oslo.

Szenderák, J., 2018. Correlation clustering: Analysis of Major Agricultural Commodity Markets. Int. J. Manag. Sci. Eng. Manag. 3 (3), 288–302.

Thompson, J.H., 1976. "Permanently wasteful but immediately profitable": Prairie agriculture and the great war. Can. Hist. Ass. Hist. Papers, 193–206.

Thorne, J.A., 2001. Warfare and agriculture: the economic impact of devastation in classical Greece. Greek Roman Byz. Stud. 42 (3), 225–253.

Williams, J., 2014. Agricultural Supply Chains and the Challenge of Price Risk. Routledge.

Zimmermann, A., Baldin, C., Dervisholli, E., Koroleva, E., Attaallah, H., Rapsomanikis, G., Dellink, R., 2020. The state of agricultural commodity markets 2020: agricultural markets and sustainable development. In: The State of Agricultural Commodity Markets 2020. Food and Agriculture Organization of the United Nations.

CHAPTER 5

Industrial markets

Wars can disrupt, reorganize, and even create new markets in ways that people don't always consider. The traditional wisdom related to the impact of conflict on industrial markets is that industry is damaged in the country where fighting takes place, and it is boosted in other countries involved in the conflict. Wars involve a reallocation of labor and capital that creates nuanced impacts on economies in general and industrial markets in particular. Beyond immediate impacts that include capital destruction or increases in demand for production, which industries shift to meet, industrial markets face secondary effects from changes in trade relationships. We can see this impact profoundly in industrial markets. While wars are often thought of as creating heightened uncertainty, in some ways they create greater certainty in industrial markets, even if only in the short term and in a limited capacity. Specifically, wars guarantee government spending and therefore production of specific goods. This includes military vehicles of various types, artillery, firearms, and munitions of all sorts. Additionally, governments shift spending and seek to boost production of a wide range of products, including computers, uniforms, medical supplies, foodstuffs, and building supplies, that are specific to military purposes.

Wars and production

While wars tend to result in increased government spending, their aggregate impact on economic performance overall and industrial production more specifically tends to be negative. Despite arguments by some that wars act as a form of economic stimulus, these arguments do not sufficiently consider how wars destroy physical and human capital. While limited portions of war-related spending might boost infrastructure or capital investments that have benefits to the civilian economy, much defense spending employs people for nonproductive purposes, removing them from jobs that would otherwise yield more benefit to the economy, and building equipment that is used for nonproductive ends, to be used only once despite high costs (munitions and ordinance), or to actively destroy physical and human

Markets and Conflict
https://doi.org/10.1016/B978-0-323-85525-9.00007-6

infrastructure and yield doubly negative economic impacts. Thus wars tend to lead to negative economic impacts in the aggregate, especially in the long term (Thies and Baum, 2020). Additionally, when wars involve great increases in government spending, we can see tremendous increases in industrial production, but these are not long-run changes in most cases, and such market distortions created by large increases in government spending rarely last once the war ends. This is why wars often see postconflict economic slumps, even in victorious countries (Thies and Baum, 2020).

While infrastructure is vital to healthcare access and the administration of key government services, it is a vital component of modern economies. Actions related to investment, management, and destruction of infrastructure impact industrial markets, both directly and indirectly. Wars spur a range of actions and outcomes relative to infrastructure. Active and potential wars can drive governments to invest in roads, rail, ports, and airfields, as these are important in the transportation and mobilization of troops, weapons, and materials used for war. During peacetime, these investments can yield great economic dividends by allowing more effective and efficient materials and components to factories for industrial production and goods to markets. Beyond the added efficiencies, adequate utilities and immediate infrastructure are vital to factories being able to function. Furthermore, the quality of infrastructure factors heavily in decisions to invest in building and/or expanding production facilities. During wartime, governments are often encouraged to build, upgrade, and/or expand infrastructure when possible. In many circumstances, infrastructure, including utilities and transportation infrastructure, is badly damaged during wartime. This damage hurts the effective functioning of many industrial manufacturers who depend on the infrastructure for transport. Additionally, damaged or weak infrastructure can act as a limitation on capital investments in societies due to how it impacts perceived utility and prospective profits. Even after the war, ineffective or delayed infrastructure rehabilitation impedes economic recovery more broadly.

Large-scale wars can be especially beneficial to the economies of countries not involved in the conflicts. Such countries may increase defense spending as a precautionary measure in some cases, but they generally do not see the same increase in the percentage of government spending and societal production that shifts toward nonproductive purposes. Nonwarring parties, of course, also tend not to see much, if any, damage to their domestic infrastructure or industrial facilities, and they do not suffer losses of productive workers temporarily to military service or permanently through war-related deaths. Noncombatant countries both avoid the destruction from war and sometimes see a macroeconomic boost from increased demand by warring parties. These societies that aren't involved in the war produce a wide range of products that are shipped in increased quantities to warring parties, including military hardware, foodstuffs, textiles, machinery, and many other items. We can see this in the examples of countries that remained neutral throughout the duration of World War II (Golson, 2019). While wars can create logistical challenges and limit who goods can be sold to, countries that aren't involved in conflicts tend to see a boost to their industrial outputs, provided that disruptions to trade caused by wars don't offset these gains.

Increased demand for military and nonmilitary items

International armed conflicts of sufficient size stimulate demand from governments that are involved to equip their militaries. The demand includes a wide range of products that impact arms manufacturers obviously, but they also impact textile, automotive, civilian aircraft, food manufacture, and a wide range of consumer products. Many of these industries are disrupted because their outputs are diverted to military purposes; their facilities are repurposed to serve military needs; or raw materials needed for their production are rationed, restricted, or redirected to government needs.

In large-scale armed conflicts, governments spend large amounts of money quickly, and there is often a rush to fill the needs created by the wars, including the need for manufactured products. This can place sudden price pressure on such products as well as materials and labor used to produce them or related things. Additionally, increased demand for materials and components used in manufacturing war-related products impacts unrelated industries as they compete for limited supplies as markets and supply chains struggle to meet increased demands. Without intervention, this creates substantial inflationary pressures.

Increased war-related demand by combatant parties impacts areas beyond what one might expect. Especially in the case of wars of mass mobilization, materials shift toward war-related production, which affects consumer goods production in complex ways. Many products are manufactured in far lower amounts as materials and factories shift toward production to support the war. Societies repurpose both materials and machinery away from standard societal uses to military uses. This sort of transformation mostly happens on a large scale in only the largest wars, but such shifts can have tremendous impacts on consumer goods in society. For example, during World War II, many warring countries' societies saw industrial production facilities shift from manufacturing consumer products to making products for military purposes (Vergun, 2020). Even societies that do not see full wartime mobilization still experience this on a smaller scale as companies seek opportunities and governmental demand for certain goods increases.

While the governmental demand for equipment is driven by the war itself, civilians can drive demand in other sectors during wartime. If households think that wartime shifts in industrial production will create shortages, they can drive inflation through speculation. For example, in the United States during the Korean War, inflation bit hard from 1950 to 1951 as many households increased their purchases anticipating shortages of many industrial goods that they experienced during the rationing of World War II. This caused demand to surge, and the supply could not keep up, causing inflationary pressures for which the country was not initially prepared given the more comparatively sudden entry of the United States into the war. The government chose to reinstate price controls in key sectors, but it did not resort to rationing in the same way that it did during World War II (Rouse et al., 2021).

Shift in government spending priorities

Wars generate new demands from governments, and they reorient government spending priorities. The size of the change depends on the size of the war, but wars require additional spending, redirected spending, or, at a minimum, replacement of resources expended during the war. Whether through increased taxation, redirection of budgets, or deficit spending, wars and preparation for them increase government spending in multiple industries. While wars can do this in ways that we might consider, the general defense footing and preparation of governments can have similar types of impacts potentially.

Increases in defense spending during war create substantial opportunity costs, even if wars do not involve mass society mobilization. Much of the increased spending in wars is financed by governments borrowing money, increasing taxes, printing more money, cutting spending in nonmilitary areas, or some mixture of these (Labonte and Levit, 2008). Any one of these approaches holds the potential to impact industrial markets. Increased printing of money, all things being equal, tends to create inflationary pressures that may pressure industries from multiple angles. Higher tax levels reduce the amount of money that households or corporations have to spend in the economy, thus decreasing demand for manufactured goods. Increased borrowing by governments can create the potential for government debt crises in some countries, which can cause investors to hesitate to invest in a country. Nonmilitary government spending, such as in infrastructure, often helps industries to operate more effectively and plays a vital role in attracting capital investments.

Supply chain disruptions

Wars offer the potential to disrupt supply chains in industrial markets. The manufacture of products can be delayed in both military and civilian contexts due to delays in deliveries of key supplies. This impacts the prices and availability of materials used to manufacture key materials.

Russia's invasion of Ukraine and the resulting sanctions have had substantial impacts on supply chains. While the war's impact on global commodity prices has been far more limited than many expected, it, along with experiences of the COVID-19 pandemic, has many businesses reconsidering their supply chains. One aspect of this disruption involves transportation routes between China and Europe. Traditionally, the overland route from Russia to Belarus and into the European Union was important in many industries. This method of transportation, which is faster than seaborne routes, was especially valued by industries such as electronics and automotive (*EU sanctions against Russia explained*, 2022).

One of the most profound lessons of war and its political accompaniments for supply chains is that wars present distorted conditions. Supply chains are typically built for stable and normal situations. This trend has perhaps been exacerbated by the increased use of quantitative approaches to data analytics and pushes for optimization to normal circumstances. While such approaches to supply management yield great benefits in most cases, war conditions create exceptions and distort normal market operations in many direct and indirect ways. Businesses are probably best served by using quantitative approaches in more creative ways by integrating them within frameworks that involve systems thinking.

In cases where one warring party is effective in preventing the flow of goods into or out of its opponent's territory, governments often work with industries to respond. Such blockades prevent both imports and exports, which can cause great difficulty in export-dependent industries, and it can create shortages in goods that are primarily imported. During the

War of 1812 in which Great Britain was highly effective at times in its blockades but did not conquer much land in the United States, the US saw high
levels of unemployment in ports and port-related jobs. To overcome shortages of typically imported goods, such as textiles, domestic industries were
given a boost, some of which remained profitable after the war
(Schakenbach Regele, 2019).

Conflict and capital flight

Investment of capital is one of the fundamental inputs in industrial productivity or any type of economic venture. Violent conflict generally increases
the perceived riskiness of an economic environment, which reduces expected
returns, and thus can deter capital investments. Of course, not all conflicts are
equal, and conflicts that are relatively stable and/or low intensity can be more
easily priced into investment calculations. The effect of conflict on decisions
to invest or withdraw capital from ventures in a country is driven by various
factors that impact the level of risk associated with the conflict, including the
intensity, duration, scope, and nature of the conflict (Davies, 2010).

Conflict does not simply cause capital flight and avoidance due to the
direct risk to investments. It also impacts incentives for capital reallocation
indirectly through the impact of conflict on inflation, which can be quite
high during conflicts in the absence of effective government interventions
and/or a degree of domestic stability within a country. When people see that
inflation rates are high, they are more likely to move their money to other
currencies and countries where it will not rapidly lose value. If countries can
keep inflation relatively low during the conflict, they will be able to reduce
the risk and rate of capital flight comparatively speaking. In postconflict societies, sufficient and properly structured aid for reconstruction is positively
associated with lower capital flights, likely due to a reduction in the dependence on inflationary monetary policies by governments (Adams et al.,
2008). While the direct risks of war are likely to decrease capital availability
and thus negatively impact industrial markets, if governments can control
inflation effectively during and after wars, they can avoid a secondary pitfall
that can further hamper industrial development and recovery.

Capital input and economic development

Wars shift incentives for capital investments in industrial markets. In societies that contain active war zones, perceived risks increase and incentives

for long-term investments decline. Conversely, in large-scale wars, investments in industrial capacity can increase tremendously, but the long-term impacts of such industrial boosts are often overrated. Unless such industrial investments are tied to new technologies that will continue in peacetime and provide additional societal productivity that didn't exist before the war, in the absence of wartime demand, such industries will often either decline or shift back to prewar levels and distributions roughly speaking.

During the Cold War, the United States moved into a standard expectation of high levels of military spending and something akin to a war footing during peacetime. Even with the end of the Cold War, with efforts to play a hegemonic role and decisions to stay involved in military bases and alliances around the world, the United States has continued to place substantial demands on manufacturing to support the military. This has caused the government to act as a large and consistent player in creating industrial demand for a wide range of products, including textiles, office supplies, munitions, semiconductors, military vehicles, and many more items. For example, the US military budget for FY 2024 included over $170 billion in military procurement alone (*Department of Defense*, 2023).

Labor inputs

Along with shifts in investment, consumption, and government investment patterns, wars impact labor force allocation. Wars of substantial size involve many people moving from civilian employment to military service. This means that these people are not available to work in industry or other fields, thus removing workers directly from these jobs and shrinking the available pool of potential labor. The opportunity costs involve moving able-bodied people away from productive roles in the labor force in which they typically produce utility for society overall by providing one of the vital inputs for production. Instead, they are actively moved to nonproductive roles that serve a purpose that is typically not directly involved in production or services that would otherwise hold value in a peaceful society. The opportunity costs are fairly simple in principle. Furthermore, because of shifting productive workers to nonproductive purposes, wars can create pressure that drives wages upward in industrial production as in other markets. Largely due to this, wars can serve as a driver to decrease the levels of inequality in labor markets as many traditional laborers join the military and are unavailable to work in the industrial labor markets.

Given the shortages that wars create in labor markets, industry, and other areas of markets, belligerent parties have often resorted to forced labor during conflicts. While such practices were commonplace in antiquity, changes in norms and modern treaty frameworks have caused forced labor during conflicts to typically become more limited and less inhumane. Military prisoners of war can be forced to carry out labor if it does not involve hostile military actions against their own countries and does not involve humiliating, dangerous, or unhealthy conditions. Civilians can potentially be forced into labor, but only under very narrow conditions (*Rule 95. Forced Labor*, n. d.). These conditions under the Hague and Geneva Conventions have typically been followed in the 20th and 21st centuries. Notable exceptions of widespread violations include practices by Japan and Germany during World War II. Civil wars are far more variable as they often do not involve legally bound parties, and these treaties were designed primarily to deal with interstate wars.

Wars create danger and uncertainty for many civilians as they face occupation and displacement. Even in cases where industrial production continues, people flee war zones and potential wars both reactively and prospectively. In the case of reactive fleeing of war zones due to heightened actual danger, industrial production often shuts down anyway due to the danger or impracticality of continuing to operate. In cases of prospective fleeing from a peaceful part of a country either under the shadow of a potential war or during an actual war, factories often continue to operate, especially if they are related to some military purpose. While these facilities continue to operate, they might face labor shortages as civilians who would otherwise be part of the labor pool relocate as internally displaced people or as refugees. Additionally, markets for civilian goods might be disrupted by the displacement of people in some cases. Demand may also shift to become more strategic during such times of crisis, creating opportunities and upward price pressure in some industries and the opposite in others.

Innovation and war

Wars create strong incentives for innovations that can help militaries perform more effectively. While the goals are typically narrow in their focus, wartime innovations can substantially change industries. Many modern technologies, such as in the field of aviation, grew by substantial degrees due to innovations spurred by the world wars, but military technology impacting civilian markets is nothing new. Even in ancient times, military needs drove innovations that served broad civilian purposes. Innovations in infrastructure have often been driven by military needs. Roads from Ancient Rome to modern highways in Germany and the United States were motivated in large part by military use.

War has driven many new technologies and innovations in food that have impacted civilian populations substantially. Writings as early as those of Sun Tzu noted the challenge of feeding soldiers and that the reliance on foraging and plundering meant that armies would see starvation at times. The Roman military created hard biscuits to allow legionnaires to carry their rations for days at a time without resupply. In the late 18th century, the French government, amid the French Revolutionary Wars (which later expanded into the Napoleonic Wars), offered a large reward to the person who could invent a process to store food safely. While it took him many years to perfect it, Nicolas Appert eventually created a process in which heat was applied that killed bacteria and then created a seal through the cooling process (Eschner, 2017). This process is so widespread in industry and normal kitchens that we take it for granted, but it may have taken many more years to create without the incentives created by war. Appert's process was limited as it initially involved glass jars, but in building upon the work, British and French innovators, driven initially by military needs, developed processes that used the same technique but with tin-plated steel cans. This provided safe, durable food with a long shelf life which also retained a high amount of the food's taste and nutritional value (Forbes-Ewan et al., 2016).

Many wartime innovations that have substantial industrial impacts don't come from intentional government efforts but from individual initiatives. A woman working at an ammunition factory in the US during World War II, Vesta Stoudt, noticed problems in the opening mechanism of ammunition boxes. She invented duct tape by applying adhesive to water-resistant duck cloth to create a tape that would provide a durable, waterproof, easy-to-open tape for ammunition boxes. Her initial suggestion was rejected by her supervisors, so she eventually wrote a detailed letter to President Roosevelt detailing the idea. He forwarded it to the War Production Board, and within weeks, they were actively working to apply Stoudt's idea (Gurowitz, 2012). During the war, this cloth-based tape that she created was quickly applied to other purposes, including patching clothing, equipment, and vehicles in many cases. Its use was quickly realized more broadly, and the original product was adapted to serve a wide range of industrial and trade uses, as well as eventually spreading to serve as a basic piece of many household toolkits.

New vehicles that are developed for military use sometimes find their way to civilian markets as companies realize the broader potential for these innovations that were made during wartime. The Jeep brand (and the modern love of 4-wheel drive vehicles) grew out of a 4-wheel drive vehicle developed for military reconnaissance in response to a request by the US Army in 1940 as it was preparing for the war (Hemmings, 2019). American Bantam developed a design for the Bantam Reconnaissance Car (BRC) in response. Because the Department of Defense was unsure that Bantam had the production capacity it needed, it ordered Ford and Willys-Overland Motors to produce the vehicle, of which over 600,000 were produced by the end of the war (*Bantam Jeep Prototype*, n.d.). The car's design was adapted as the war and production continued, and the various manufacturers made slight changes to it in consultation with the Department of War. There is some debate as to the origin of the term jeep, but by the end of World War II, the term was so popularized that people rarely referred to the vehicles as anything else. The most widely accepted explanation is that the term jeep came from a shortening of GP, which stood for General Purpose (Birth of the Jeep Name, 2021). Willys-Overland Motors continued to produce the Jeep after the war, popularizing the vehicle first among outdoor enthusiasts and then the broader population. The brand continued to be popular, eventually being owned by Chrysler, and now Stellantis (Hemmings, 2019).

The development of plastics in the United States during World War II is perhaps the most influential wartime industrial innovation. At the start of the war, plastics were in their infancy. Government investment in wartime production led to dramatic increases in the efficiency and versatility of plastic products. Plastics were used in parachutes, body armor, rope, aircraft cockpits, and many other products (Beall, 2009). They provided a material source that was not as sensitive to supply chain disruption and was flexible in ways that would revolutionize industrial production. Plastics yielded great benefits in medical technologies, and through increasingly efficient creation and use of plastics, consumer products dropped in cost tremendously in the second half of the twentieth century. Plastics, however, also led to tremendous waste and environmental destruction, both through increased emissions associated with plastics as well as through increased waste generation and proliferation throughout the environment, especially through single-use plastics and microplastics, which are found in a wide variety of products that are commonly found in average households. The use of these materials today is such that microplastics are found in even the most remote corners of the world (Johnston, 2018).

Industry after war

While wars can prompt great shifts in industry and might appear to have a stimulative effect, peacetime tends to yield greater economic benefits in the long term. In the wake of wars, government spending often decreases in ways that can result in economic slumps. Postwar reconstruction drives increased demand for building materials and construction machinery. Peace tends to decrease the levels of economic uncertainty, which increases the likelihood of individuals and corporations making long-term economic investments in industrial projects, including capital investments and expansion of production. Postwar economies tend to see substantial growth as investors seek opportunities and see investments as more feasible.

With effective postwar economic reconstruction, societies can reemerge stronger than before the war, but with poor postwar reconstruction, the problems that stemmed from war can fester in society for many years to come, leading to war recurrence in some cases. This dynamic is especially seen in the context of civil wars, where effective, equitable, and broadly shared economic reconstruction is highly correlated with better and more lasting peacebuilding efforts (Calame, 2005); however, postwar industrial reconstruction efforts can also play a strong role in preventing war recurrence in the case of interstate wars in some cases. One of the most notable examples of this can be seen in the case of Western Europe following World War II. The Marshall Plan provided funds that aided in rebuilding industrial capacity in the societies where it was substantially destroyed, and perhaps more importantly, it had a substantial impact in rebuilding infrastructure and housing that was important in supporting industry and the people who worked in it. The currency stabilization and accompanying control of inflation that it helped to achieve played a vital role in encouraging investment and restoring local trust in the postwar administrations. It also encouraged economic liberalization, which yielded great increases in the efficiency of industries across the region as cross-border trade increased substantially (DeLong et al., 1993). The European Recovery Plan was highly successful overall, seeing participating countries return to prewar production levels by 1950. Perhaps more importantly, the plan played a major role in encouraging regional integration in Western Europe by requiring recipient countries to work together to plan the postwar reconstruction and by erasing many barriers to trade within the region (Milward, 1984). The European Recovery Plan is often cited as an important step in the regional integration that ultimately led to the European Union, which helped to make war within the bloc unthinkable to most today.

While postwar economies often see great opportunities for industrial revival, postconflict societies also often see substantial instability in wages and prices. Several factors contribute to these unstable tendencies. Many former combatants reenter the labor markets, creating increased wage pressures unless other workers exit the labor force in the same period. During large-scale wars, the production of civilian goods is limited, and governments sometimes intervene to stabilize prices. With the end of wars, pent-up demand for consumer goods and services drives prices upward. If governments remove price controls on products, prices revert to an equilibrium point, which can be drastic in some cases, such as in the United States following the end of World War II (Rouse et al., 2021). Various actors benefit if they prepare themselves for the effects as markets regain more normal equilibrium points, often under new realities. Efforts in anticipating postwar trajectories are generally worthwhile for all actors involved.

Civil wars and industrial markets

Similar to interstate wars, civil wars destroy infrastructure and decrease the ability of factories to receive, produce, and ship goods. This has a similar impact as with interstate wars, but the impacts and effects tend to be differently distributed. One useful caveat to consider is that the major economies of the world have not experienced civil wars under conditions approaching the modern global economy. Therefore civil war in a country such as a G7 country, China, or India could have disruptive impacts that existing studies do not effectively address. The impacts of civil wars are felt keenly not only by the country undergoing a civil war but also by other countries in the region.

The effects of civil wars on industrial markets discussed later primarily focus on the countries experiencing civil wars, but it is worth remembering that civil wars have substantial indirect effects regionally on economic growth and patterns of investment. According to Murdoch and Sandler (2004), the impacts of civil wars on economic growth are felt years later regionally due to a mixture of supply chain disruption, decreased exports to and consumption from countries in the region experiencing civil wars, and the impacts of civil wars in the region on the perceived risk of industrial investments. The presence of multiple civil wars in regions (especially three or more) can retard economic growth for decades to come (Murdoch and Sandler, 2004).

The US Civil War resulted in tremendous disruptions to the economy on both sides of the conflict. Traditional scholarship has argued that the war resulted in a second industrial revolution in the United States, driving it to become a global economic superpower. The war resulted in a reduction of industrial production in the South by more than half during the course of the war. During the Reconstruction period that followed the war, the industrial capacity of the former Confederate states regrew at a relatively slow rate. While the South regained its nominal level of antebellum industrial production by 1871, it did not regain its share of national industrial production until 1890 (Davis and Weidenmier, 2004).

State investment in and facilitation of industrial markets can work to decrease the odds of a civil war outbreak, which is more likely under conditions of high levels of unemployment, especially among young men. Strong industrial markets allow options for employment among people of many educational and socioeconomic levels. High state capacity and strong economies tend to yield conditions that rarely see the outbreak of domestic conflicts (Fearon and Laitin, 2003). State investments in economic development and social services can decrease the likelihood of rebellion. For example, in Algeria, the plunging price of oil in the late 1980s led to the ruling FLN making democratic concessions of more open elections. When the electoral contests yielded unfavorable results and the government did not cede power, the country saw the outbreak of a bloody civil war (Entelis, 2011).

Modern civil wars are more fragmented than those that took place during the Cold War. In many cases, countries with active civil wars have multiple armed conflicts going on at once. Without consistent and unifying ideologies to guide combatants, we often see the institutional motivations of rebel groups cause civil wars to continue as new clients have come to rely on the rebel structures and funds derived to support the rebellion. Given this, preventing civil wars is especially important. Economic development in general and industrial development in particular play important roles in affecting the likelihood of civil wars. Uneven economic growth correlates positively with the likelihood of civil war onset. Thus achieving steady economic growth can prevent wars, and positive outcomes in postconflict economic reconstruction can help to break the conflict trap (Scheiber, 2015). Beyond steady economic growth alone, if countries can achieve lower levels of economic inequality, they will be less likely to see the outbreak of civil wars. Balen and Mumme (2013), applying principles of relative deprivation theory, found that higher levels of economic inequality consistently and positively correlated with the likelihood of civil war onset.

While interstate wars tend to strengthen the state, provided that it is not defeated and/or destroyed (Herbst, 1990), civil wars tend to be far more destructive to societies and states because the destruction and damage are entirely within the state in question, and civil wars often undermine, weaken, and corrupt state institutions, including police, courts, and systems of protecting and guaranteeing property rights (Collier, 1999). When these institutions are undermined, large-scale industrial developments become riskier and thus less desirable. Due to the prolonged nature of many civil wars, they often act as long-term forces that dissuade industrial investments and development for a variety of reasons. Collier (1999) found that while the end of long civil wars tended to result in rapid economic recovery, the peace dividend with the end of civil wars is far from a certain thing. According to this study, short civil wars tend to see a continued economic decline afterward. This may be due to the notion that the issues that drove the war were not effectively resolved, and war fatigue has not substantially altered the incentives for peace as opposed to war.

Sorens and Ruger (2014) find that, while civil wars tend to diminish access to foreign capital, higher levels of foreign investment do not correlate with a higher likelihood of governments compromising with dissidents to avoid or end civil wars. Pinto and Boliang (2022) argue that foreign direct investment by multinational corporations in developing countries tends to concentrate markets and result in high rents. Control over these revenues related to MNC investments can serve as fuel for domestic conflict, especially in weak states.

World War II as a case study

World War II provides an example of an extensive war in which societies and their resources were heavily mobilized toward a war footing. During the war, all major combatants saw war industries take priority and make up a tremendous portion of their national economies. The war tended to centralize economies and place broader sectors of industrial production under government production or heavier government regulation. This applied to a wide variety of decisions, including investment, production, prices, and labor rules. Many of these measures were temporary, but others resulted in a broader reconsideration of the roles of government in society.

By the 1930s, many countries in the world had become heavily industrialized with large-scale industrial production of a wide range of industrial and consumer goods. With the war, these industries were transformed to serve the war in sweeping and deep ways. Before World War II, countries with market-based economies produced a wide range of household appliances, civilian vehicles, farming equipment, industrial equipment, toys, and many other things. Following the start of the war, this tremendous industrial capacity that had been built in the United States, United Kingdom, Germany, Japan, and many other industrialized countries was now shifted to build weapons, vehicles, aircraft, ships, and numerous large and small things to support the war effort. For example, the automotive industry in the United States built approximately three million automobiles in 1941. Over the following 3 years, fewer than 200 civilian cars were manufactured; rather, they built guns, trucks, jeeps, tanks, and aircraft engines (Vergun, 2020).

World War II greatly increased the bargaining power of industrial workers due to labor shortages mixed with high demand. The impact of the war was such that it caused a new norm in the relationship between workers, businesses, and government. The war led to an empowerment of workers that helped to drive the most substantial modern decline in income inequality in the United States, as well as growth in the welfare state and advancement of civil rights.

In the years leading up to World War II, the United States demonstrated that it learned vital lessons from production problems in World War I. With the start of the war in 1917, the US government ordered 50,000 pieces of artillery, but only 143 were completed prior to the armistice in November 1918. The War Department created and revised its Industrial Mobilization Plan multiple times in the 1930s. Suspecting that the United States would eventually join the war, President Roosevelt announced the Protective Mobilization Plan on September 8, 1939, just 1 week after Germany invaded Poland. This enabled the United States to not only increase the size of its military but also dramatically increase production. In 1941 the United States produced over 26,000 aircraft, up by over 20,000 from 1939 (Morgan, 1994).

World War II demonstrated the tension between the civilian economy during wartime and the need for military-industrial output. A strong economy overall provides the tax base and productive capacity that are vital to support military effort, war industry, and generally maintain order during wartime. While the chair of the War Production Board in the United States regularly stated that a strong civilian economy is essential to war production, he nonetheless regularly fought against civilian production demands taking precedence over military production. Due to the repurposing of civilian industries, by May 1942, the normal production of civilian goods had halted as these production lines were directed toward military purposes. A wide range of products, including refrigerators, home radios, vacuum cleaners, vending machines, jukeboxes, pianos, and many more products, simply ceased to be produced for civilian use. This was due to both the materials and the production facilities being redirected to serve the war effort. By the end of 1942, more than six billion dollars of consumer goods production had been converted entirely to war production (Foyle, 1943).

With the overwhelming demands of the war effort, including both conversion of consumer manufacturers and direct consumption of goods by the military, many goods came to be in short supply. Responding to public distress and perceived need, the federal government implemented price controls and a rationing system. To buy scarce products, such as coffee, meat, bikes, tires, cars, clothes, and sugar, consumers had to both pay money (at fixed, government-dictated prices) and present ration stamps. The intervention to allocate scarce resources in fundamentally different ways for the US was partly a response to the experience of World War I, which saw very high inflation. The federal government created the Office of Price Administration (OPA), which engaged hundreds of thousands of employees and volunteers within communities. The goal was to make sure that people could afford key goods and were allocated a reasonable allotment that they could buy (Rosalsky, 2022). Such efforts were generally effective at controlling prices, but they took away the benefits that market forces can bring in allocating scarce resources effectively and providing rational incentives for actors in the economy to respond to price signals to restore equilibrium in the supply and demand curves. Additionally, as black markets sprang up, selling products at higher than permitted prices, the OPA had to ramp up its efforts to combat such activities. An interesting market response was one which has become common today; notably that of shrinkflation and skimpflation in which a smaller amount or lesser quality product or service is offered for the same price. For example, meats and other food products came to have increased amounts of fillers, packages became smaller where possible, clothes were sometimes made at lower quality, and meats were sold with more bones as part of the weight. One of the side effects of these controls was that the fixed price point of many goods moved farther away from what the supply and demand would naturally dictate, and when price controls were removed, the United States experienced substantial inflation such that President Truman quickly reintroduced some price controls in 1946 after removing them (Rosalsky, 2022).

Following the US entry into World War II, President Roosevelt set up the War Production Board to coordinate the activities of various defense industries. The federal government also became far more involved in many aspects of industrial production, including controlling prices, weighing in on wages, antidiscrimination measures, and working conditions in ways that were previously highly unusual. President Roosevelt created the National Labor War Board by executive order as a body that had the authority to settle labor disputes and keep production from being stopped. The board was controversial at times for both management and labor unions. While some measures such as government control of production and prices went away with the end of the war, other aspects stuck around after the war, whether through legal changes or shifts in power and norms of government regulation created under the war (Hoover, 1985).

The war greatly expanded the size and power of labor unions in substantial ways. Labor union participation more than doubled during the war, with membership expanding from about 7 million in 1941 to over 14.5 million in 1945. During the war, 12 million people were taken out of the domestic labor force and served in the military. This increased the bargaining power of workers. The National Labor Relations Act of 1935 gave unions in the private sector the right to organize, bargain, and strike. This law, coupled with the increased clout of unions from war production, created the basis that allowed unions to emerge more powerful after the war (Cintino, 2021).

With the end of World War II, cuts in wages and jobs by industrial companies and others led to widespread strikes in 1945 and 1946, with over 5 million people participating. In these strikes, unions demanded better wages and safer working conditions. While they were successful in many cases, these widespread strikes provoked a conservative backlash in the form of the Taft–Hartley Act in 1947, which placed substantial limitations on the framework in which strikes could take place. The creeping fear of communist infiltration of labor unions helped to provide cover for politicians in promoting these laws (Cintino, 2021).

With large sums of money flowing into industrial production and other private sector activities from the government, it created opportunities for waste and corruption. In March 1941, the US Senate approved the creation of a committee to oversee national defense spending, which informally came to be called the Truman Committee. The committee found widespread problems, including the production of faulty materials, falsified quality control reports, defective products, intentionally slow development, inflated prices, and other wasteful and fraudulent practices. The committee's work is estimated to have saved over 10 billion dollars over the course of the war (*Portraits in Oversight,* n.d.).

The experience of the United States during World War II serves as an example that demonstrates how war can impact the industrial markets and economies in countries that undergo widespread economic mobilization but do not see significant fighting within their borders. This combination of general circumstances is unusual, and it has led many to overestimate the economic benefits of war. Due to the scale and scope of the war, nearly every other major economy in the world was badly damaged by the war. Germany and the United Kingdom, for example, took approximately 20–30 years to fully rebuild from the war. The United States, though, found itself in an unusual set of circumstances. It had years in which it sold manufactured and other goods to warring parties while not being directly involved in the conflict. Some of these sales continued even after the US entered the war. The government's roles during the war demonstrated the ability of the central government to have large-scale influences on the economy and to act as a major employer and regulator in many new ways. US industry experienced large gains in productivity and scope, much of which continued and even expanded after the war as the country's factories shipped goods to recovering economies around the world (Tassava, n.d.). The war restructured labor markets and urban settlement patterns of the United States, increasing the wages of workers and the power of organized labor. Wartime production also led to a large shift in the population as more people moved to cities to work in factories. Despite World War II largely taking place "over there," US society was transformed in many ways by the industrial effort to support the war.

The Soviet Union engaged in tremendous industrial adaptation to support the production of military vehicles, munitions, and supplies during the war. As Germany launched Operation Barbarossa in June 1941, it caught the Soviet Union by surprise, overwhelming its military in the early stages of the campaign. In the several months following the invasion, the USSR evacuated hundreds of industrial production facilities from states such as Belorussia and Ukraine and moved them east of the Ural Mountains (Lieberman, 1983). Altogether across the western parts of the Soviet Union, over 1500 factories were disassembled and relocated to places such as Central Asian states, the Urals, the Caucus, and various parts of Siberia (Liberman, 1983).

During the first 18 months of the war, the Soviet leadership structure shifted priorities effectively to prioritize the war industry as a vital piece of the war and governance in general. The industrial evacuation campaign played a crucial role in avoiding an economic and military collapse during the early part of the war for the USSR. Central leadership figures, including Beria, Malenkov, and Molotov, oversaw key war industry segments, including Beria's supervision of armament and munition procurement. The adaptation of the political leadership of the Politburo was carried out in a top-down manner and proved effective in centralizing and focusing efforts on the mobilization and conversion of the economy for the wartime effort in a small number of key areas. Soviet leadership allowed greater flexibility at the lower level in other areas as many of the rest of the actors within the economy were given room to meet goals using localized initiative. The pressures of wartime production led to greater structure and bureaucratic regularity to achieve higher levels of efficiency (Harrison, 1988).

Japanese industry expanded rapidly following the Meiji Restoration in the late 19th century, laying the groundwork for the country establishing itself as a major regional power with victories over China and Russia in wars in 1895 and 1905, respectively. It also conquered and colonized Korea, using its natural resources to build industry on the peninsula. Japan's industrial revolution was largely inspired by a perceived need to strengthen itself following its abrupt and involuntary opening to international trade in the 1850s (Bernhofen and Brown, 2017). During World War I, Japan used this industrial base and stronger military to seize German colonies in the Pacific. Following World War I, Japan substantially increased investment in heavy and chemical industries. The need for industrial resources played a major role in Japan's decisions for expansion during World War II, including coal deposits in Manchuria, and oil and rubber resources in Southeast Asia (Honda, 1997).

While Japan's industry grew substantially before and during the war, especially in its efforts to serve the war industry, it declined substantially later in the war. By the end of 1942, the tide of the war turned against the Empire of Japan. It faced substantial setbacks in the naval war against the United States, and it eventually faced setbacks in its land campaigns, such as in 1943, when Chinese forces started to turn the tide. As Japan lost more of its military personnel, it drafted more men to serve in its army and navy. This led to a tightening of the industrial labor force. In mid-1944, the United States began intensely bombing Japan's home islands. This included citywide bombings, including conventional bombs, firebombs, and atomic bombs. Due to the destruction and decrease in resource extraction and industrial capacity from war-related factors, by the time the war ended in September

1945, Japan's mining and industrial capacity was around 20%–30% of its pre-war level. Between effective planning and prioritization and US aid in reconstruction, mining and manufacturing outputs roughly tripled between 1946 and 1950 (Tetsuji, 2016).

Instances of forced labor are one of many horrors from World War II. Such practices were especially common in lands occupied by Germany and Japan during the war. Forced labor in occupied territories and of prisoners of war was quite common in a wide range of ancient and medieval societies. In the past two centuries though, as slavery faded as an institutional practice and international humanitarian law took shape, widespread forced labor of POWs and civilians faded. For example, in the Franco-German War of 1870 and the Spanish-American War, warring parties used forced labor of prisoners of war on a relatively limited scale. With the length and scale of World War I, many of the warring parties began a widespread practice of forced labor among POWs in industry, but these practices generally conformed to the boundaries and guidelines laid out in the Hague Convention of 1907. During World War II, most belligerents engaged in practices of large-scale forced labor, but most did so in ways that were compliant with the Hague and Geneva Conventions (Spoerer and Fleischhacker, 2002).

During World War II, Germany faced dire labor shortages due to the large number of men serving in the military, and later, high levels of casualties. Much of this labor shortage was filled through the use of forced labor of various types. Civilian forced laborers were brought into and used in Germany and other parts of German-controlled territory to work in various industrial and service capacities. Additionally, millions of POWs, mostly from Poland, France, and the Soviet Union, were used in forced labor capacities in German-controlled lands. By August 1944, over 7.5 million forced laborers who were either foreign civilians or prisoners of war worked within German territory. These laborers were used in a wide variety of industrial capacities in both large and small companies, and they were even used in domestic capacities as household servants (Herbert, 2000). Beyond these two categories, Germany used concentration camp inmates as forced workers within its own borders, and it also used forced labor broadly among Jews within Germany and its occupied territories starting in 1939 (Herbert, 2000). Across these four categories of forced labor, the Third Reich used the forced labor of over 10 million people across the years of World War II (Herbert, 2000).

The Japanese government's use of forced labor among POWs has been depicted in pop culture, such as in *Bridge on the River Kwai*. In occupied territories, the Japanese government initially recruited local laborers on a voluntary basis, but as the war went on, Japan found its labor reserves depleted, and occupied populations were not willing to work in sufficient numbers to meet the needs. Later in the war, Japan enforced widespread forced labor of populations in occupied territories. Conditions at these work sites were dangerous. The setup of the sites lacked prior planning for sanitation and basic care, resulting in widespread outbreaks of avoidable diseases. Workers were often malnourished, and military overseers were often cruel and abusive. Due to a combination of these and other factors, mortality rates among these forced laborers were around one-third (Kratoska, 2005).

Postwar reconstruction led to complicated sets of disruptions, some of which are noted before, but the postwar period did not result in a sufficient economic slump for a complicated set of reasons. One piece of this was that the economies of countries where substantial fighting took place had seen widespread destruction of cities and industry. The case of Germany demonstrates this most directly. In Germany, most of the largest cities suffered widespread destruction. Following the war, especially with aid from outside, there was a great demand for industries that were involved in housing, infrastructure, and many other sectors (Brakman et al., 2004). Western European countries suffered substantial casualties but not nearly as high as those in Poland and the Soviet Union. Population losses during the war were offset by natural population growth and large-scale migration from outside countries. Despite the widespread bombing, fixed industrial capital assets in Western European countries grew from 1936 to 1945, and while these and electricity generation capacity needed some repair, they provided the basis for an effective postwar recovery. Effective central planning, along with a substantial influx of recovery funds from the United States, provided the groundwork for a robust recovery (Vonyo, 2019).

Russian invasion of Ukraine as a case study

As opposed to many cases of industrial production in the major powers during World War II, Ukraine had little opportunity to adjust industrial production before the war came to its lands. As Russia invaded Ukraine on February 24, 2022, many industries suddenly shut down as they fell under occupation or closed due to safety concerns over Russian attacks. For the year 2022, Ukraine's industrial production fell by over a third compared to 2021. During the same time, steel production dropped dramatically, including the production of finished steel products, which fell by over

60% over the same period (Kolisnichenko, 2023). The steel industry in Ukraine was particularly hard-hit because it was heavily concentrated in the Donbas region. Perhaps the most notable instance was the bombardment of Azovstal as the last holdout in the Battle of Mariupol.

The Donbas region of Ukraine is one of the most heavily industrialized parts of the country, and it has been the focus of substantial fighting. When the invasion started in February 2022, approximately one-third of all companies stopped production completely. The fighting has made it difficult to continue production, and facilities have been damaged or destroyed in many places. As Ukrainian defenders fought desperately to hold onto Mariupol, two of the largest steel plants were destroyed. These two plants alone accounted for approximately 40% of Ukrainian steel output. With close to 30% of the country's population displaced by the war and infrastructure disrupted, destroyed, and made dangerous in many parts of the country, production slowed tremendously, and transport of both raw and finished products dropped dramatically. Beyond the troubles with the land routes, Russia's Black Sea Navy imposed a blockade of Ukrainian ports, denying a vital route for both imports and exports. While grain shipments have been allowed to a higher degree than initially expected, thanks to a Turkish-brokered deal, Russia still generally denies sea routes to Ukrainian ports (Filippino et al., 2023).

Sanctions aimed to hamper Russian industry, especially in the area of military manufacturing. The Commerce Department imposed restrictions to curb high-tech exports to Russia, such as semiconductors, including goods that other countries produced using US technology (Berman and Siripurapu, 2023). Within 4 months of the invasion, global exports of semiconductors to Russia had dropped by 90% (*Chip Exports*, 2022). These chip export restrictions, which included the United States, Japan, Taiwan, and the Netherlands among others, caused difficulty in parts of the Russian economy. While Russia has complained before the WTO about these and other sanctions violating international trade rules, it is unclear the exact extent to which semiconductor export restrictions have harmed the Russian economy. There have been successful efforts by Russian companies to skirt sanctions. For example, exports of advanced semiconductors from Kazakhstan increased from about $12,000 in 2021 to $3.7 million in 2022, clearly indicating an effective avoidance of sanctions (Baschuk, 2023). Crucial semiconductors and other high-technology products have reached Russia indirectly from European countries through third countries (Nardelli, 2023). That said, the sanctions have made it more difficult and more expensive for Russia to obtain these and other vital materials and components for industrial activity within the country.

Whereas the Russian government's narrative related to sanctions presents them as largely ineffective, effects have been mixed and complicated, in part due to a relatively effective response from the Russian Central Bank and other actors. Stability was restored in the ruble after the turbulent early months of the war in which its value sank by over 50%. The International Monetary Fund estimated that the Russian economy contracted by 2.2% in 2022, well short of estimates early in the war, and it is not projected to shrink substantially in 2023. Over 1000 Western companies have divested from the Russian market since the start of the war. These hasty withdrawals may have generated something of a short-term windfall for the Russian economy and government, but these companies are not likely to return, and it will likely be a long time before Russia will receive a substantial capital influx from Western countries again. While Chinese, Indian, and other firms may eventually provide new sources of capital investments in Russia in the future, they are largely hesitant to make substantial investments due to the uncertain environment, limitations imposed by sanctions, and concerns about hurting business with the West. It is unclear how the exit of over half a million largely high-skilled workers from Russia will impact the long-term development of its tech industry. Russia's budget has increasingly become consumed by the needs of the war. Military expenditures have grown from 24% of Russia's budget to approximately 33% (Racz, 2023). Given the limited ability of Russia to borrow money, this increase in military spending has come largely at the cost of other budget areas, including the development of long-term industrial projects. While the trajectory of the war is uncertain as of Summer 2023, if it continues at high intensity over a long period of time, Russia may see increased currency pressures and substantial opportunity costs generated in the area of missed investments, whether from government spending or foreign capital. If these circumstances materialize, industrial investment will be limited, production rates will slow, and the Russian economy may see effects in labor and currency markets and decreased tax revenues.

Accessing accurate data regarding Russia's industrial output was challenging prior to the war, and since the invasion of Ukraine, the Russian government has restricted journalists more heavily, thus making it more difficult to confirm or refute government statements. While the official statistics report that industrial output increased by 1.2% from March 2022 to March 2023, data gathered by satellites operated by the European Space Agency (ESA) suggest a different story. According to the Tropospheric Monitoring Instrument, changes in emissions of nitrogen dioxide, ozone, and methane decreased in industrial regions by approximately 6% from April 2022 to April 2023. According to the ESA, its data show decreased emissions in construction, automotive production, and the defense industry (Rosen, 2023). These data suggest that Russia's economy overall and industrial markets are being hit far harder by the war and sanctions that many have concluded. If we were simply seeing a more typical weirding of the Russian economy, defense production, at a minimum, would have increased pollution as it increased output for the war. Most likely, sanctions and other disruptions to Russia's trade and other efforts to obtain materials and components have hampered its industrial production. While some of this may be spillover effects from the COVID-19 pandemic, given the drop in industrial production levels over the one-year period referenced before, which is over 2 years into the pandemic, most of it is likely due to the war and subsequent sanctions.

The war has placed stress on industries in both the two combatant countries and outside parties that are supplying them. One area of immediate impact is in the arms industries, especially those of European countries and the United States. Supplies of artillery shells have been stretched such that sending higher amounts to Ukraine would actively diminish military force readiness. Defense industries in the US and Europe have worked to increase production to meet the demands of the Ukrainian military. Having sent 1.5 million 155 mm shells to Ukraine, the United States finds its stockpiles substantially diminished. While the Department of Defense has taken measures to dramatically increase the production of artillery shells and other ordinances, it will be years until these results are fully realized (Judson, 2023). While both US and European defense companies have ramped up production in cooperation with their governments, they are not on the war footing that would be required to replace shells at the rate they are being used, even in combination. Because retooling or building new production facilities is a large, long-term investment, private companies do not face sufficient incentives to chase profits given that they do not know how long the war will last or how long the demand will stay high. Most of the increases in production have been from contracts signed between governments and private companies rather than defense companies. While this is not a terribly different structure than some of the production during World War II or other wars, the war in Ukraine has a strange dynamic to the defense production demand because the need is fairly immediate and the battle does not directly involve the countries contemplating large increases in defense production (except Russia, of course). Even in the case of Russia, the level of munition expenditure is that of a major war, but the government has been hesitant to fully mobilize society.

The attempts by outside economic powers to tighten the grip of sanctions on Russia may hit industries in many different countries as indirect supply routes are cut off. The war thus far has created numerous innovations, including tactics using old weapons, such as antiaircraft measures against drones carrying surveillance equipment and bombs. Ukraine finds itself in the position of using a mixture of Soviet-era weapons and a hodgepodge of NATO weapons that were designed largely for a war against the Soviet Union that didn't come. The trials of these weapons in a war against a major military power will inform the next round of major weapon orders by many countries as well as the designs of future generations of military weaponry in many areas. Manufacturers are taking notes and will likely respond to these signals.

Even 15 months into the war, the conflict and related sanctions continue to create an environment of uncertainty in industrial markets in warring parties and beyond. The political dynamics that develop as a peace deal is eventually made will play a vital role in signaling the level of certainty that investors and consumers enjoy postwar. Following the war, there will be many opportunities for a wide variety of actors across industrial markets, including arms manufacturers as they replenish spent stockpiles of ordinance and equipment and respond to new military hardware orders. Additionally, industries involved in reconstruction will likely see a boost in equipment and materials used in rebuilding destroyed infrastructure, buildings, and various items to fill these buildings, ranging from wiring, pipes, and ductwork to stoves, heaters, and furniture. The more solid the foundation for peace is, the stronger the signals for investors will be, but most likely, private capital will follow publicly financed rebuilding commitments more than it leads. Political actions by outside actors will have a tremendous impact on industrial markets, including decisions by G7 and EU countries on how they adjust sanctions against Russia and decisions by the EU on the degree to which it begins to integrate Ukraine into the economic bloc, as such decisions hold tremendous potential to reshape industrial and other markets in Ukraine. The postwar picture will depend on many factors, and decisions made in this context will impact the future prosperity of the region and prospects for stability in peacetime, militarily, politically, and economically.

Conclusion

Wars generally impact industrial markets by increasing certainty in the public sector in the short term and increasing uncertainty in both public and private markets in the long term. The certainty in the short term is brought about by predictable demands for some sectors and hesitation by private markets to react to most normal private demands from industrial markets. Additionally, consumption tends to be slowed in nonessential goods, thus sending signals to industrial markets to decrease supply in these areas. These market shifts create both increased risks and opportunities for industries and investors.

Conflict offers the potential to disrupt production in several different ways. Wars can destroy fixed capital assets as well as infrastructure that supports industrial activity. This includes services that are important to the operation of manufacturing facilities, such as electric and water utilities. Conflicts also result in the destruction of infrastructure used in the transport of materials and components to factories or finished products from factories. Additionally, labor is diverted that might otherwise go toward the industrial markets as people are directly involved in the conflict or flee the conflict areas. Furthermore, wars create conditions in which some industrial production ceases, whether because of safety conditions or inability to operate under war or occupation conditions.

Postwar recovery periods, similarly, provide market opportunities as industries involved in reconstruction can see substantial opportunities. One of the larger points of hesitation for investment in postwar industrial markets involves the question of demand from the postconflict markets. Due to logistical challenges, potential capital shortages, and limited demand in many cases, it can take industrial sectors many years to recover from substantial wars. Especially if political stability can be achieved, the threat of war is not imminent, and the typical fundamental economic factors are sound or well supported, postwar periods offer substantial opportunities for industrial markets. Because investment tends to trail development after wars, companies that can accurately assess the conditions for successful postconflict recovery before capital starts to flow more freely can potentially see substantial advantages.

As with other markets, war creates a series of disruptions and distortions for industrial markets. With careful planning, governments, investors, and businesses can navigate these difficult waters effectively. Lengthening and diversifying supply chains helps companies hedge against resource and component shortages that they may face during wartime if supply chains are disrupted. Governments often shift away from funding for industrial development during wartime as budgets become tighter and more immediate needs of security are more highly prioritized.

Industrial markets are substantially disrupted by war in complex ways outlined before. While wars create challenges in such markets, they also create opportunities. Similarly, peace creates not only business opportunities but opportunities to rebuild and reorient industrial markets in such a way that they contribute to effective peacebuilding in the long run. If economies are rebuilt and reoriented such that they distribute their gains and lessen inequalities in societies, the grievances that contributed to the onset of wars can potentially be ameliorated. This tends to yield benefits that are broadly shared across society, including among manufacturers. Greater levels of international and cross-regional economic integration, planned properly, can lead formerly warring parties to see not only economic benefits but higher prospects of peace, especially if closer economic relations are seen as sustainable, equitable, and reliable for the future.

References

Adam, C., Collier, P., Davies, V.S.B., 2008. Post-conflict monetary reconstruction. World Bank Econ. Rev. 22 (1), 87–112.

Hemmings Admin, 2019. If You Thought the Jeep Legend Began with Willys, Think Again. Hemmings Magazine. https://www.hemmings.com/stories/article/the-jeep-story.

Balen, J., Mumme, C., 2013. Does inequality lead to civil wars? A global long-term study using anthropometric indicators (1816-1999). Eur. J. Polit. Econ. 32 (December), 56–79.

Bantam Jeep Prototype, 1940, n.d., National Museum of American History Behring Center. Smithsonian Institute. https://americanhistory.si.edu/collections/search/object/nmah_841492.

Baschuk, B., 2023. Russia Lashes Out at the WTI for 'Illegal' Trade Curbs. Bloomberg. https://www.bloomberg.com/news/newsletters/2023-03-08/supply-chain-latest-russia-blasts-the-west-for-illegal-trade-curbs.

Beall, G., 2009. By Design: World War II, plastics, and NPE. Plastics Today. https://www.plasticstoday.com/business/design-world-war-ii-plastics-and-npe.

Berman, N., Siripurapu, A., 2023. One Year of War in Ukraine: Are Sanctions Against Russia Making a Difference? Council on Foreign Relations. https://www.cfr.org/in-brief/one-year-war-ukraine-are-sanctions-against-russia-making-difference.

Bernhofen, D.M., Brown, J.C., 2017. Gains from Trade: Evidence from Nineteenth-Century Japan. Microeconomic Insights https://microeconomicinsights.org/gains-trade-evidence-nineteenth-century-japan/.

Birth of the Jeep Name, 2021. Jeep. https://www.jeep.ca/en/articles/the-birth-of-the-jeep-name.

Brakman, S., Garretsen, H., Schramm, M., 2004. The strategic bombing of German cities during world war II and its impact on city growth. J. Econ. Geogr. 4 (2), 201–218.

Calame, J., 2005. Post-War Reconstruction: Concerns, Models and Approaches. Macro Center Working Papers. Center for Macro Projects and Diplomacy, Roger Williams University. https://docs.rwu.edu/cgi/viewcontent.cgi?article=1018&context=cmpd_working_papers.

Chip Exports to Russia Plunged by 90% After Curbs-U.S. Official, 2022. Reuters. https://www.reuters.com/technology/chip-exports-russia-plunged-by-90-after-curbs-us-official-2022-06-29/.

Cintino, R., 2021. (Host, Strike Wave (Season 2, Episode 5) to the Best of My Ability Podcast Series. The National World War II Museum. https://www.nationalww2museum.org/war/podcasts/best-my-ability-podcast/season-2-archive/episode-5-strike-wave.

Collier, P., 1999. On the economic consequences of civil war. Oxf. Econ. Pap. 51, 168–183.

Davies, V.A.B., 2010. Capital Flight and Violent Conflict: A Review of the Literature. World Development Report. 2011: Background Note https://openknowledge.worldbank.org/server/api/core/bitstreams/49983372-ff18-5c73-a81b-2a52d5aa4a1f/content.

Davis, J.H., Weidenmier, M.D., 2004. The Macroeconomic Impact of the American Civil War. Atlanta Federal Reserve. https://www.atlantafed.org/blogs/-/media/CFBC939B67FA46169DA711319F15FDD2.ashx.

De Long, J., Eichengreen, B., Eichengreen, B., 1993. The Marshall plan: history's most successful structural adjustment program. In: Dornbusch, R., Nolling, W., Layard, R. (Eds.), Postwar Economic Reconstruction and its Lessons for the East Today. MIT Press, Cambridge, MA.

Department of Defense Releases the President's Fiscal Year 2024 Defense Budget. 2023. U.S. Department of Defense. https://www.defense.gov/News/Releases/Release/Article/3326875/department-of-defense-releases-the-presidents-fiscal-year-2024-defense-budget/.

Entelis, J.P., 2011. Algeria: democracy denied, and revived? J. North Afr. Stud. 16 (4), 653–678.

EU Sanctions Against Russia Explained. 2022. European Council. https://www.consilium.europa.eu/en/policies/sanctions/restrictive-measures-against-russia-over-ukraine/sanctions-against-russia-explained/.

Eschner, K., 2017. https://www.smithsonianmag.com/smart-news/father-canning-knew-his-process-worked-not-why-it-worked-180961960/. (Accessed 18 June 2023).

Fearon, J.D., Laitin, D.D., 2003. Ethnicity, insurgency, and war. Am. Polit. Sci. Rev. 97 (1), 75–90.

Filippino, M., Hall, B., Tindera, M., 2023. The Economics of Russia's War in Ukraine. Financial Times. https://www.ft.com/content/75d5c6dd-afa8-449e-9876-81b25196f0c6.

Forbes-Ewan, C., Moon, T., Stanley, R., 2016. Past, present and future of military food technology. J. Food Sci. Eng. 6, 308–315.

Foyle, T., 1943. Civilian Production in a War Economy. CQ Press. https://library.cqpress.com/cqresearcher/document.php?id=cqresrre1943072700.

Golson, E., 2019. The Economics of Neutrality in World War II. Center for Economic Policy Research. https://cepr.org/voxeu/columns/economics-neutrality-world-war-ii.

Gurowitz, M., 2012. The Woman Who Invented Duct Tape. Kilmer House. https://www.kilmerhouse.com/2012/06/the-woman-who-invented-duct-tape.

Harrison, M., 1988. Resource mobilization for World War II: the U.S. S., U.K., U.S.S.R., and Germany, 1938-1945. Econ. Hist. Rev. 41 (2), 171–192.

Herbert, U., 2000. Forced laborers in the third Reich: an overview. Int. Labor Work. Class Hist. 58 (3), 192–218.

Herbst, J., 1990. War and the state in Africa. Int. Secur. 14 (4), 117–139.

Honda, G., 1997. Differential structure, differential health: industrialization in Japan, 1968–1940. In: Steckel, R., Floud, R. (Eds.), Health and Welfare During Industrialization. University of Chicago Press, Chicago.

Hoover, C., 1985. The economy, liberty, and the state. In: Blicksilver, J. (Ed.), Views on U.S> Economic and Business History: Molding the Mixed Enterprise Economy. Georgia State Press, Atlanta.

Johnston, K., 2018. Legacies of War: How the Commercialization of Plastics in the United States Contribute to Violence. SIT Digital Collections. https://digitalcollections.sit.edu/cgi/viewcontent.cgi?article=4150&context=capstones.

Judson, J., 2023. US Army Eyes Sixfold Production Boost of 155mm Shells used in Ukraine. Defense News. https://www.defensenews.com/digital-show-dailies/2023/03/28/us-army-eyes-six-fold-production-boost-of-155mm-shells-used-in-ukraine/.

Koliscnichenko, V., 2023. Industrial Production in Ukraine for 2022 Decreased by 36.9%. GMK Center. https://gmk.center/en/news/industrial-production-in-ukraine-for-2022-decreased-by-36-9/.

Kratoska, P., 2005. Asian Labor in the Wartime Japanese Empire: Unknown Histories. East Gate Books, New York.

Labonte, M., Levit, M., 2008. Financing Issues and Economic Effects of American Wars. Congressional Research Service. https://www.everycrsreport.com/files/20080729_RL31176_d5070b8a2d624c1e81ca4783e76b8d4d4d913c8b.pdf.

Lieberman, S.R., 1983. The evacuation of industry in the Soviet Union during world war II. Sov. Stud. 35 (1), 90–102.

Milward, A.A., 1984. The Reconstruction of Western Europe, 1945–51. University of California Press, Berkley.

Morgan, T.D., 1994. The industrial mobilization of world war II: America goes to war. Army Hist. 30, 31–35.

Murdoch, J.C., Sandler, T., 2004. Civil wars and economic growth: spatial dispersion. Am. J. Polit. Sci. 48 (1), 138–151.

Nardelli, A., 2023. Russia Is Getting Around Sanctions to Secure Supply of Key Chips for War. Bloomberg. https://www.bloomberg.com/news/articles/2023-03-04/putin-gets-military-tech-chips-semiconductors-despite-eu-and-g-7-sanctions#xj4y7vzkg.

Pinto, P.M., Boliang, Z., 2022. Brewing violence: foreign investment and civil conflict. J. Confl. Resolut. 66 (6), 1010–1036.

Portraits in Oversight, Levin Center, n.d., https://www.levin-center.org/harry-truman-and-the-investigation-of-waste-fraud-abuse-in-world-war-ii/.

Racz, A., Spillner, O., Wolff, G., 2023. Russia's War Economy: How Sanctions Reduce Military Capacity. German Council on Foreign Relations Policy Brief https://dgap.org/en/research/publications/russias-war-economy.

Rosalsky, G., 2022. Price Controls, Black Markets, and Skimpflation: The WWII Battle against Inflation. Planet Money, National Public Radio. https://www.npr.org/sections/money/2022/02/08/1078035048/price-controls-black-markets-and-skimpflation-the-wwii-battle-against-inflation.

Rosen, P., 2023. Russia's economy is suffering from industrial decline as satellites detect less pollution in the air. Bus. Insid. https://markets.businessinsider.com/news/stocks/russian-economy-industrial-decline-air-pollution-satellite-data-ukraine-war-2023-5.

Rouse, C., Zhang, J., Tedeschi, E., 2021. Historical Parallels to Today's Inflationary Episode. The White House Council of Economic Advisors. https://www.whitehouse.gov/cea/written-materials/2021/07/06/historical-parallels-to-todays-inflationary-episode/.

Rule 95. Forced Labor, International Humanitarian Law Databases, n.d., https://ihl-databases.icrc.org/en/customary-ihl/v1/rule95.

Schakenbach Regele, L., 2019. Manufacturing Manufacturing Advantage: War, the State, and the Origins of American Industry, 1776–1848. JHU Press, Baltimore.

Scheiber, C.M., 2015. Two Steps Forward and One Step Back: An Assessment of how Uneven Economic Development Affects the Number of Civil Wars. The Cupola, Fall.

Sorens, J., Ruger, W., 2014. Globalisation and intrastate conflict: an empirical analysis. Civil Wars 16 (4), 381–401.

Spoerer, M., Fleischhacker, J., 2002. Forced laborers in Nazi Germany: categories, numbers, and survivors. J. Interdiscip. Hist. 32 (2), 169–204.

Tassava, C.J., n.d., The American Economy during World War II, Economic History Association, https://eh.net/encyclopedia/the-american-economy-during-world-war-ii/.

Tetsuji, O., 2016. Industrial Policy in Japan: 70-Year History since World War II. Research Institute of Economy, Trade and Industry. https://www.rieti.go.jp/en/papers/contribution/okazaki/06.html.

Thies, C.F., Baum, C.F., 2020. The effect of war on economic growth. Cato J. Winter 2020 https://www.cato.org/cato-journal/winter-2020/effect-war-economic-growth#references.

Vergun, D., 2020. During WWII, Industries Transitioned From Peacetime to Wartime Production. DOD News. https://www.defense.gov/News/Feature-Stories/story/Article/2128446/during-wwii-industries-transitioned-from-peacetime-to-wartime-production/.

Vonyó, T., 2019. Recovery and Reconstruction: Europe after WWII. Center for Economic Policy Research. https://cepr.org/voxeu/columns/recovery-and-reconstruction-europe-after-wwii.

CHAPTER 6

Trade and currency

Conflict often drives substantial shifts in trade relationships and currency values. We see this in both the case of violent conflict and trade and currency wars. Trade and currency values often suffer as a negative side effect of violent conflicts. More specifically, these types of markets are impacted as states impose sanctions in response to conflicts. Warring parties have their trade relations impacted by a sharp decrease, but the relationships are not necessarily always severed completely as one might expect. Sanctions can have substantial and surprising impacts on trade relationships, trade flows, and supply and demand relationships in ways that are not always easy to predict.

This chapter discusses several topics related to trade and currency, and how they intersect war and international nonviolent competitions known as currency and trade wars. This section starts with a general discussion of currency and trade, how governments view them and are affected by them, and how national governments use tools of currency and trade in an attempt to accomplish their broader goals. Next, the chapter discusses theories of the relationship between international trade and the likelihood of war. The following sections discuss the impact of war on international trade as well as the impacts of trade and currency wars.

After these general sections related to international interactions, we discuss the impacts of civil wars on international trade and currencies. The subsequent sections include two case studies. The first one pertains to the trade and currency wars of the 1930s. The second case study examines the impact of Russia's 2022 invasion of Ukraine and the effects of this war on trade and currency. We also address the questions of how sanctions and other trade measures have been used to punish actors in and related to this conflict. The chapter then concludes with a summary of lessons learned and their application for the future.

Currency value and modern markets

Modern currencies exist largely to facilitate economic transactions, and they effectively permit them to be carried out with ease. Currencies are typically

Markets and Conflict
https://doi.org/10.1016/B978-0-323-85525-9.00005-2

issued or selected by national governments and declared by legal authority to be valid financial instruments within the countries. Even though most economic transactions are facilitated electronically, the management of national currencies by governments is still important to modern economies. Cryptocurrencies offer a complement to national currencies, but at this point, they are fairly new and do not offer a serious prospect of replacing them altogether soon; therefore, this chapter will not discuss cryptocurrencies.

Government-issued currencies and their value in the modern era are determined by government action and market response. Currency value is typically expressed as the exchange rate relative to other currencies, or the amount of another currency for which one could hypothetically exchange a unit of a particular currency, such as the ratio of British pounds to Japanese yen. Typically, the general population and central bank within a country pay the most attention to the exchange rate relative to global reserve currencies, such as the US dollar.

Currency value can also be conceptualized in terms of what a unit of the currency can purchase, such as the Big Mac Index, created by *The Economist* in 1986, which compares the price of a Big Mac from McDonald's across countries as an estimate of the relative cost of living. Of course, this is far from the best measure, but it has served as a lighthearted way of comparing the cost of living and measuring inflation across at least some countries in the world (Economist, 2023). Similar measures that are more comprehensive and use standard items in society serve as the basis to calculate purchasing power parity (PPP) measures of GDP as they provide a notion of the relative utility of money in a society.

A more traditional comparison would be to the price of a currency relative to a precious metal. Gold once held a central role in currencies as the key global currencies were once backed by gold and centrally exchangeable for a set amount of gold. While no countries use the gold standard in such a way today, gold still maintains an important role in national reserves to create a sense of stability in national currencies, and it serves as a useful benchmark for currency values.

Currency exchange rates matter a good deal to countries because they have substantial impacts on prospects for macroeconomic stability and growth, government stability, and quality of life for people. While there is substantial debate about the exchange rates that are desirable for a given country, there is broad agreement that relative stability in currency value is highly desirable. Countries need to achieve a relative degree of currency stability to attract investment, both from internal and external sources.

The prospect of relative loss through currency value loss both deters invest-ment and encourages capital flight from a country. A relatively stronger currency can decrease the desirability of exports from a country as they become more expensive, and the prospect of a currency strengthening can decrease the desirability of establishing such export relationships and decrease the desirability of loans from a country's banks as the rising exchange rate would effectively raise the costs. Countries pursuing an export-led growth strategy or otherwise seeking to boost their exports may prefer a weaker currency to make the relative price of their exports lower.

National currency values are generally determined by a fixed (also called pegged) exchange rate, a floating exchange rate, or some variation of one or some mixture of both. In the case of a fixed exchange rate regime, a country will typically choose to peg its currency value, either precisely or approxi-mately, to the value of a major global currency, such as the US dollar or the euro, or a composite or basket of other currencies. By doing so, the thought is that governments can bring about a greater degree of macroeconomic stability and achieve greater benefits for the country, such as by controlling inflation more effectively, making exports more competitive, or achieving some other goal through the more stable, and possibly artificially manipu-lated, currency value.

A country may choose to use a fixed/pegged exchange rate or a floating peg, in which it maintains the value of its currency within a certain range relative to another currency. If countries are to achieve a valid peg relative to another currency's value, the central bank will most likely have to use its powers to tweak the underlying factors that impact the perceived value of a currency, such as by buying or selling foreign reserves (foreign currency instruments) or by altering national reserves of precious metals, such as gold. If a country maintains the peg artificially, this will increase the pressure on the currency as these societies will typically see large-scale capital flight and substantial black market activity in which people are not willing to sell goods at the formal exchange rate prices, which can also scare away investors as the real currency value becomes increasingly detached from the official exchange rate.

In a floating exchange rate regime, a country allows the price of its cur-rency to be set through market behavior, largely driven by the perceived value and desirability of a currency. Under such an exchange rate regime, countries nonetheless need to pay attention to the values of their currencies as they impact investment, capital exchanges, and many economic decisions made by actors both domestically and internationally. For example, irresponsible monetary policies by central banks and other governmental actors must be avoided as these will have ripple effects throughout the economy if the currency value crashes.

Many exchange rate regimes lie somewhere between a true fixed and a true floating exchange rate, and even those governments that have a floating exchange rate nonetheless keep the exchange rate in mind and typically factor it into fiscal and monetary policy decisions. Other countries opt out of these exchange rate policy questions partially or altogether by either adopting a shared currency under a currency union, such as the euro, east Caribbean dollar, or the CFA franc; or by adopting the currency of another country altogether, such as the euro or the US dollar. Over four dozen sovereign states use one of these two tactics by which they relinquish sovereignty over their currency management and thus sidestep the question of how they will manage their exchange rates altogether. While these policy choices often create greater currency stability for these countries, they also result in these societies being vulnerable to currency fluctuation due to the policy choices of other bodies.

A large part of currency value is based on perceptions, especially in the modern era where countries are decoupled from a gold standard. Essentially, the underlying value of a national currency is based on the demand for the currency relative to its supply. Even countries with fixed exchange rates must pay attention to these underlying forces if they don't want to suffer substantial hardships (Segal, 2021).

Aside from choices in exchange rate regimes, countries can impact the relative value of their currency through both fiscal and monetary tools. Fiscal policy involves taxing and spending behavior. When a country runs substantial deficits, especially if its ability to repay its debts comes into question, the result is often a weakening of the currency as such patterns tend to lead to a decreased demand for it. On the other hand, countries that are perceived as being on a sound footing fiscally tend to have, by and large, relatively stable currencies.

Monetary policies include central bank exchange rates as these can be used to manipulate the perceived desirability of a currency indirectly and money supply, which directly affects the supply/demand equation. Additionally, central banks hold reserves of major foreign currencies, often held in the form of government bonds, and other assets, such as gold. The supply of these assets can play multiple roles. It serves as a supplementary backing to the perception that the country can honor its financial commitments by providing an additional method of paying loans, and it can be used to cushion a country from economic shocks. Additionally, decisions to buy and sell these reserve assets are some of the main methods that a country can use to manipulate the value of its currency. If a country buys its national currency with a foreign currency, it increases demand, and if it buys a foreign currency with its national currency, it can artificially increase the relative value of the other currency, thus decreasing its own currency's value (Hargrave, 2022). Regardless of its exchange rate regime and policies, well-run countries pay attention to their exchange rates, aim for stability, and are mindful of how fiscal, monetary, and other policies impact their currencies' values.

Because the stability of exchange rates is important to the effective functioning of the global economy (and political stability indirectly in some cases), the International Monetary Fund (IMF) devotes substantial attention to monitoring and studying the global economy and individual national economies, especially among those countries receiving IMF loans. As part of the effort to advance global economic stability in the post-World War II era, the United States led the creation of the International Monetary Fund (IMF) at the famous Bretton Woods Conference in 1944. The structures developed under and by the IMF were especially beneficial to the capitalist-oriented economic and political bloc that would emerge after the war.

Two of the greatest concerns of the organization are to avoid currency wars and to prevent national financial crises from spreading and becoming global crises. The concern about currency wars was driven by the recent example of the series of competitive devaluations by many countries as they sought to boost exports and stimulate their economies during the 1930s. These measures, along with accompanying trade wars, deepened the Great Depression and brought about deeper economic suffering and political tensions internationally. To address this problem, under the IMF's Articles of Agreement, all member states agree to not artificially manipulate their currencies' value or aspects of the international monetary system. The goal is to avoid the creation of either a balance of payment problem or one country trying to gain an unfair advantage relative to other member states in export markets through a lower currency value. Whether it is due to the work of the IMF, the global economy has largely avoided currency wars since its creation (Bird and Willett, 2011).

Nearly every country in the world is a member state of the IMF, and of those, over 90% participate in one version or the other of the Data Dissemination System that the organization established to standardize and share economic and financial information. The organization engages in regular dialogue with governments to monitor exchange rate conditions and underlying governmental policies that might impact exchange rates (*Economic Surveillance, 2022*). The IMF can issue temporary loans to governments to help them correct balance of payment issues that affect currency stability. The goal of the institution is, through these loans, the provision of advice and expertise, and other measures, to assist governments in maintaining greater levels of exchange rate stability and macroeconomic stability.

Overall, international currency markets facilitate trillions of dollars in transactions each year using computer networks and foreign exchange brokers from countries around the world. Furthermore, currency markets enable international trade by allowing firms to purchase foreign currency to buy products from a firm in another country. They also support investments for businesses and easier exchanges by central banks. In addition to the practical role that foreign exchange markets play in facilitating transactions, they allow people to invest in currencies as they would in stocks and other securities. By having the currencies held, often virtually, in the market, people can exchange currencies without the need to physically hold such currencies (Kenton, 2022). This ability is especially beneficial to economic transactions in the digital age, and for better or worse, it facilitates additional profit-driven speculation in national currencies by investors seeking profit. While these actions of foreign exchange traders can exacerbate volatility in currency values, they also can help currencies reach new equilibrium points more quickly.

Modern trade

International trade is the exchange of goods and services across international borders, allowing consumers to access goods that they would not otherwise be able to reach and producers to enter markets that they would otherwise not be able to access. Through trade mechanisms, in situations where countries and markets are more open to international trade, we tend to see more competition within markets, placing higher competitive pressures on firms.

Liberal economic theory holds that all things being equal, unrestricted trade will lead to greater levels of aggregate productivity and prosperity as firms and societies will focus production on things where they have either a comparative or relative advantage. Because in an open trade regime, consumers in a given market can access goods from all over the world, they can purchase most goods from producers somewhere in the world even if they do not operate within the borders of their country. Additionally, free markets create opportunities for arbitrage in which merchants purchase goods in one market and sell them in another market at a higher price. This dynamic creates additional economic opportunities for both individuals and countries. Through trade, governments potentially gain additional tax revenue, whether by increased economic activity that is then taxed domestically or by taxing imports coming into the country through tariffs.

Trade is an old activity, tracing its roots to prehistoric times. Community trade goes back to Neolithic peoples when it largely consisted of trading primitive tools, hides, and food (Royal Geographical Society, n.d.). As humans developed agriculture, more sophisticated tools, higher degrees of specialization, and methods of long-range transportation, trade routes became common and regularized in many parts of the world. Long-distance and regular trade routes developed in many parts of the world, including Northeast Africa, over 5000 years ago (Amin, 1970). By the end of the first millennium B.C.E., long-distance regional trade routes and networks were well established in a wide range of places around the globe, including Central America, the Indus Valley, Africa, the Fertile Crescent, Europe, Ancient China, and across the Steppes. Over these centuries, these trade networks linked to one another increasingly, apart from the Americas, but these links were often indirect, and they were not part of a cohesive global framework of trade (Magie, 2023).

As European colonialism brought the Americas into contact with Africa, Asia, Oceania, Europe, and other parts of the world, the trade routes became interconnected and more global in nature. With 19th and 20th-century technologies, distance and time became figuratively shortened. The gradual development of engines for transportation, from steam engines to combustion engines to jet engines, increasingly reduced the time that it took to travel great distances. Furthermore, communication technologies that developed in the late 20th century allowed for the transmission of information and human connection across the world in a manner that came to be nearly instantaneous, and later very inexpensive as well.

While these once disparate parts of the world became increasingly and more deeply connected, the impacts of wars came to be felt more widely across the world as trade partners, trade routes, and material and component suppliers were disconnected and disrupted by those conflicts. The very manner of these disruptions became equally more complex over time.

Modern, global systems of trade are quite different in their breadth, depth, and speed from their earlier forms. Modern global value chains

(GVCs) have developed in such a way that the production processes for many goods have become truly global in complex manners that make trade deeply connected with production in a way that did not exist before. While raw materials were shipped to far-off lands for manufacturing processes for centuries, modern GVCs involve not only the movement of raw materials but also component parts in the production at multiple stages of extremely complicated finished products. Facilitated by trade liberalization efforts of the 20th century under the GATT and WTO framework, GVCs have made it difficult to discuss the manufacturing of a product as belonging to a single country. Through processes of natural learning, almost in an evolutionary sense, businesses developed practices of vertical specialization by businesses and entire market segments to serve not broad markets in exports but specific clients in global supply chains (Hummels et al., 2001).

The integration of supply chains to the extent that has developed by the 2020s means that the impact of trade wars has become highly complex, and the impacts are felt more broadly and deeply than they were in previous eras where supply chains were not as heavily integrated globally. This means that rather than markets simply losing out on the potential efficiency advantages encouraged through free markets, supply chains are now deeply impacted in ways that might not be fully anticipated when sanctions are imposed. Despite the number of studies that have been conducted on how wars impact the global economy, with the relatively recent development of these GVCs, the comprehensive effect of a major and prolonged conflict on the global economy is difficult to anticipate. The war between Russia and Ukraine is likely to give some evidence of how global supply chains and trade routes respond to such a conflict.

Barriers to trade

Barriers to trade, including both imports and exports, come in a wide variety of forms, and they have more subtlety than one might expect. Such restrictions can be broadly targeted at a country, or they can be far narrower and limited to a specific sector, resource, good, company, or person. Subsequently, economic tactics can have a wide variety of motivations, including the protection of domestic industries, bolstering government revenues, punishing target countries or individuals through sanctions, or the pursuit of other goals. Whatever the motivations, trade barriers can have impacts far broader than the product, service, or country they target. The secondary impacts and responses and effects are often far wider and deeper as firms, governments, and consumers respond to the new realities brought about by these measures. This applies to both trade restrictions and barriers to financial transactions.

Not only do trade barriers come in many shapes and forms, but they also have different potential impacts. Embargos are full exclusions on trade with another country, which typically apply to both imports from and exports to that country. Embargos can be unilateral or multilateral in their structure, but they are relatively uncommon except when countries are at war with one another. Tariffs, on the other hand, are far more common and are part of the regular trade regulations of most countries. They are typically structured as duties, or taxes, on imports coming into a country. These taxes increase the prices of the goods to which they apply, and they can create a comparative advantage to some degree for domestic goods or goods from certain countries.

Tariffs can be structured generally around a specific material or product, they can be targeted at specific countries, or some combination of the two. Nontariff barriers to trade beyond embargos are more complex and include a wide variety of measures, including subsidies or a complex set of technical, health requirements, or customs procedures that make the import of certain goods more cumbersome or altogether impractical. Some common nontariff barriers to trade include regulations on acceptable manufacturing practices, requirements on how a product is handled, or how it is advertised. Such rules on trade may require that imported goods must be accompanied by proof of their country of origin. Countries may also impose import quotas that limit the amount of a product that can be imported in general or from a specific country. Altogether, these nontariff barriers to trade typically limit trade far more heavily than tariffs today (Institute for Government, 2017).

Trade, economic interdependence, peace, and war

International relations (IR) scholars have long debated the relationship between economic interdependence and war. Liberal IR theorists have argued, in one form or another, that closer economic relationships make war less likely. Such theorists tend to argue that international economic liberalization tends to promote peace for one or more of the following reasons: (1) higher levels of trade increase opportunity associated with war due to a loss of trade during wartime; (2) higher levels of economic interdependence lead to a greater array of tools for communication and allow for states to send more credible signals to one another, helping to avert wars caused by failure of effective signaling; or (3) increased cross-national contacts across international boundaries by many different actors lead to increased trust (and trade is a piece of this).

Despite the potential pacific impacts of a more interconnected global economy, critics point to the record of colonialism and imperialism, partly driven by economic motivations, as driving substantial numbers of wars. In their desire to control trade routes, specific goods, and access to markets, countries (especially major European powers) entered a multitude of wars over the centuries of colonization. For example, the Opium Wars were largely driven by desires to protect commercial operations and open Chinese markets to British goods. The US did not fight such a war but used the explicit and physical threat of force to open Japanese markets to outside trade more fully in the 1850s. Gilpin (1987) argues that trade often serves as a tool through which more powerful states seek to dominate weaker ones. By using trade and other economic tools to pursue strategic advantage and relatively more beneficial economic gains, states can sew the conditions that lead to war (Gilpin, 1987). Mearsheimer (1994–1995) argues that, given the concern of states about their security in the international system, highly interdependent relationships lead to increased insecurity as concerns about losing out on gains relative to potential rivals become amplified and lead to an increased potential for conflict.

Neo-Marxist theories, such as developed by Wallerstein (1979), argue that firms in wealthy countries are rationally driven to seek profits, both domestically and in foreign countries. Borrowing from earlier Marxist ideas, such theories see the actions of the state in a capitalist society as largely an extension of wealthy class interests. As such, the interests of the capitalist class will project force abroad when it is beneficial to secure resources, supply routes, and investment opportunities. Wallerstein (1979) argues that the capitalist world system is inherently steeped in violence and that dominant states in the system use wars at times to build and maintain the system.

Theorists dating back to the 18th century, including Montesquieu and Kant, argued that these pressures meant that greater commerce could make war less likely. Kant saw greater economic interdependence as one of three legs in a tripod of peace, along with democracy and international law and organizations (Doyle, 1983). While Kant's formula for perpetual peace may seem utopian to some, there is evidence for a version of such a triangulation, as offered by the work of Oneal and Russett (2000), along with many other scholars. From a dyadic sense, countries that are both democratic, have closer trade relationships and mutual membership in high numbers of international organizations tend to triangulate toward a low probability of interstate war. Thus, while earlier versions of commercial peace theory that held higher levels of trade greatly discourage conflict may have been lacking, when paired with more robust and complex economic interdependence and other factors, closer economic relations, properly constructed, can greatly reduce the risk of war (Oneal and Russett, 2000).

According to other liberal theories that argue in favor of the pacifying effects of international trade, the higher the value of an economic relationship between states, the higher the opportunity costs of war. Higher levels of trade and economic interdependence generate benefits that are dispersed among multiple actors in society and for the state overall. Additionally, wars generate direct costs in terms of lost human and physical capital (Arad et al., 1983). Economic relationships between states in conflict are severed or suspended to a large degree, even if not entirely, in times of war; therefore, the opportunity costs of war are raised in the case of countries more economically interconnected with potential rivals and the world in general. Therefore, due to material self-interest, states will be less likely to go to war with states when they have closer economic relationships.

Many scholars argue that economic liberalization, coupled with closer international economic ties, tends to decrease incentives for war. Gartzke (2007) finds support for the hypothesis that countries with liberal economies and high volumes of international trade tend to engage in fewer wars, especially with one another. He offers economic liberalization as at least a partial explanation for the finding that countries with democratic regimes rarely, if ever, fight one another. He argues that the explanation is not simply economic liberalization strictly but about this coupled with a substantial decrease in the value of land as a factor of production, which reduces incentives to conquer lands. The norm of border fixity and mutual recognition of international boundaries in most cases has also provided a stable boundary in which states can compete within the capitalist global economy. Additionally, liberal states developed substantially overlapping policy goals in the post-World War II era. In this context, modern markets in a globalized market system allow an alternate avenue along which states can compete with one another; yet the system provides substantial incentives for states to work out their disputes nonviolently in most cases and avoid paying the opportunity costs incurred with the loss of trade during war (Gartzke, 2007).

One of the broader questions that are still being debated is how the globalization of trade and integration of supply chains change the calculations of how trade relates to prospects for peace. Martin et al. (2008), for example, argue that globalization decreases the opportunity costs of war as substitute trade partners are more readily available in the modern era. Sadeh and Feldman (2020) similarly argue that globalized trade allows for easier substitution of trade partners, increases the difficulty of imposing sanctions, and increases routes and resilience of credit and foreign investment. They argue that the peace benefits of trade have not disappeared but that they have lessened. The difficulty in fully and effectively assessing the impacts of globalization, aside from the obvious methodological challenges, includes the fact that interstate wars have been far less likely during the globalized era; therefore, studies often rely on studying militarized international disputes or other similar events.

Lee and Hyun (2009) find that increased integration into multilateral trade frameworks, such as the GATT/WTO, decreases the risk of war. They also find that higher levels of bilateral trade correlate with lower risks of war. This effect is especially pronounced in pairs of neighboring countries. When considering both reciprocities in trade relationships as a cumulative effect and geographic proximity, the effects of economic interdependence are far greater. After all, very few states are capable of waging wars over great distances; therefore, most wars take place between states that border one another. Hegre et al. (2010) find that when distances and sizes of country pairs are considered, there is a strong and positive correlation between economic interdependence and the likelihood of peace.

Other liberal theorists argue that closer connections across societies create a wider array of tools at the disposal of states and stronger common incentives to address shared problems. For example, in their theory of complex interdependence, Keohane and Nye (1977) argue that a wide variety of actors are involved in creating relationships among states and societies. In pairs of states where there is a wide range of deep connections across societies, issues in interstate relationships are less hierarchical, there are many routes of connection, and military force becomes far less important in such relationships (Keohane and Nye, 1977). For example, in the case of the US-Canada relationship, companies, civic groups, schools, local and regional governments, and millions of individuals have regular and collaborative relations across the international border. This allows many issues that might arise between the two states to be addressed by a wider range of actors. Additionally, the interests of states involved in a complex interdependent relationship become so intertwined that the needs of the other cannot be easily dismissed, and through the complex, broad, and deep relations across the countries, trust increases, fear decreases, and the likelihood for violent conflict becomes dramatically less likely and unthinkable in the eyes of most (Rana, 2015).

Copeland (2016) developed an explanation for the relationship between trade and the likelihood of war that is based on the future expectations of the trade relationship. This theory holds that the probability of conflict among major powers is largely driven by a combination of the level of economic interdependence between the states and the future expectations in the realm of trade and investment. In a large-n quantitative analysis, the study testing the theory found that a large portion of the variation in war outcomes was driven by trade and investment expectations (Copeland, 2016). Therefore policymakers need to consider how their actions create and frame expectations, rather than simply how these measures advance their immediate goals.

War and trade

Wars tend to lead to decreases in trade, especially for countries in which wars are being fought. This causality applies to international and domestic wars as both often see reductions in foreign and domestic trade, which is one of the major contributors to a reduction in aggregate GDP. The decrease in trade volumes is the result of a complex set of factors, including a decrease in aggregate consumption, lower investment in human and physical, and disruptions to both production and transportation (Thies and Baum, 2020). Of course, wars vary widely, and the scope and intensity of conflicts will impact whether these effects are felt and the degree to which they are felt.

While wars often lead to combatants on opposite sides severing trade relations altogether, they sometimes continue such relations in ways that initially appear surprising. For example, during the Crimean War, the United Kingdom thought carefully and strategically about how it should approach its trade relations with Russia while the two fought on the battlefield. Cabinet officials carefully weighed the strategic impact of trade choices, the immediate economic impact, and the country's long-term economic interests. Additionally complicating the matter was the question of how decisions made relative to Russia economically would impact the UK's relations with neutral parties, such as Austria and Prussia (Levy and Barbieri, 2004).

Furthermore, wars tend to dramatically, and sometimes entirely, sever trade relations between warring parties. These effects are severe, and they tend to last beyond the war itself as it takes time to rebuild after the war, given the loss of human capital, infrastructure, industrial facilities, and systems for facilitating stable financial flows in the private sector. Additionally, it takes a while to rebuild economic relations and trade and distribution networks. Beyond these physical concerns, there is sometimes a stigma that outlasts the war against the products of an opponent. In the cases of the two world wars, it took approximately a decade from the end of the war on average for pairs of formerly warring countries to regain their prewar levels of trade with one another (Glick and Taylor, 2005).

Beyond these negative consequences, the effects of wars spill over to neutral countries that do not participate in the conflict. Those spillovers include instances in which wars can provide an economic boost for neutral parties as one or more sides in a conflict might trade more with those states to substitute for suspended exports and imports with their enemies. However, these effects tend to be focused on a limited number of sectors. Overall, wars tend to decrease productivity and trade, thus generating a negative externality for the global economy that is felt by neutral parties through a reduction in trade with warring parties, lowered economic productivity in the warring countries, and heightened overall economic instability (Glick and Taylor, 2005).

In examining pairs of countries from 1885 to 2000, Feldman and Sadeh (2018) found that hostile third parties tended to reduce trade with warring states by about 30% on average, and these hostile third parties tended to see similar trade reductions with third parties friendly to their indirect enemies. Third parties tended to see no reduction in their overall levels of trade, on average (Feldman and Sadeh, 2018). Therefore the impacts of wars on third parties tend to depend on the size of the wars, their location relative to the third-party countries, and their preexisting relationships with the warring parties. The level of reduction in trade generally correlates with the breadth and depth of the war. Larger wars tend to generally result in greater trade reductions, and global wars result in the greatest losses in international trade (Glick and Taylor, 2005).

Sanctions and war

Attempts to inflict economic harm and prevent economic gains have long been a feature of warfare, including blockades and trade embargos.

For example, Athens banned Greek merchants from rival city-states during the Peloponnesian War. Additionally, blockades and sieges have been used as tactics in warfare across the world (Mulder, 2022). Until the past century or so, however, economic sanctions were primarily thought of as measures that were used when one was already at war with another country, rather than as tools to compete without war, punish another country without directly engaging in war, or even as measures meant to seek peace and prevent war.

In the world today, countries use sanctions as part of a tactic to smooth relative imbalances in power and to preserve the status quo in the balance of power internationally. In doing so, states use sanctions to deprive a rising power rival of potentially gaining capabilities that would disrupt the status quo and force the existing dominant power into a preventative war. In such instances, economic sanctions may offer a route for great power competition to play out that does not result in open warfare (McCormick and Pascoe, 2017).

Sanctions are often used by outside parties in a conflict to weigh in on the conduct or existence of the conflict without directly engaging in the war. Sanctions are used or threatened at times in attempts to deter a potential aggressor from carrying out a war. They are also implemented at times to punish a party that is seen as an aggressor in a war or that has engaged in behavior that violates norms or treaties under international law. For example, when Iraq invaded and annexed Kuwait in 1990, the UN Security Council authorized heavy sanctions against Iraq under United Nations Security Council Resolution 661 in an attempt to compel it to reverse course (*Resolution 661*, 1990). Sanctions are used at times to punish certain parties or try to limit the war-fighting ability of one party in a war, such as those imposed on Yugoslavia in response to its actions in wars in Croatia and Bosnia. At times, such as in the example of Yugoslavia or the case of Liberia, sanctions are used to punish those who commit human rights violations (Dimitrijevic and Pejic, 1995).

In the case of Russia's invasion of Ukraine, sanctions carried out by the EU, United States, Japan, and others allow these countries to weigh in on the conflict without becoming active belligerents. Actively entering the war would be a risky and politically dangerous move, especially for leaders in democratic regimes. Sanctions are far easier to justify and support politically, and they allow countries to signal strong disapproval of a war without directly entering it. We can see this in many conflicts throughout the years, including as a response to both interstate and intrastate wars.

Trade wars

Trade wars are nonviolent conflicts between or among countries that involve substantial increases in protectionist trade policies. They start when one country imposes tariffs or other import restrictions or barriers on imports from another country, and this country takes punitive trade measures in turn. This can lead to a cycle of escalation in which both countries suffer damage to their economies. The damage can impact domestic businesses and consumers relatively directly, as the price of materials, components, and goods increases for businesses and consumers, and as exports decrease for domestic firms. Perhaps more importantly, trade wars often hurt the diplomatic relationships between participating countries, and they can strain the relationships of these countries with their allies, as trade war participants may place pressure on allies to join in the trade war.

In general, scholars and practitioners in the field broadly agree that free trade brings certain benefits to consumers, namely, lower prices and an increased variety of goods. Raising tariffs might be tempting to some countries because the negative effects of increased costs can be offset by various mechanisms, including changes to the nominal exchange rate as the balance of trade shifts (what trade economists call a terms-of-trade externality). However, this result can only be enjoyed if there is no response to the increased tariff levels and the prospects of negative responses from other countries can serve as deterrents against substantial protectionist tendencies. In many cases, state responses result in feeling only the pinch of increased prices without the offset from a shift in exchange rates. Nonetheless, political incentives can align in certain circumstances such that politicians may see political benefits from choosing to initiate a trade war (Lechthaler and Mileva, 2018).

Realist theorists in international relations argue that trade wars could be rational for states to engage in, even in the modern, globalized world. They would argue that states are primarily concerned with relative gains, whether in military or economic balance. Therefore states might potentially engage in a harmful trade war, provided that they think the other side will suffer more or fail to gain as much in the long term. Therefore realists argue that utility calculations could potentially favor what might seem like a suboptimal outcome from a traditional economic perspective (Copeland, 2016).

Neoliberal institutionalists largely argue that trade wars are suboptimal outcomes that, like physical wars, can be prevented or made less likely by effective regimes to facilitate cooperation. Regimes developed among states can provide rules, norms, and procedures that provide a basis around which actors' expectations converge and their behaviors are coordinated for mutual benefit (Keohane, 1982). The GATT/WTO framework, and later, institution, was developed specifically to institutionalize stable and more open trade relationships in a multilateral framework on a global scale. In a supplementary manner, many countries developed strong, regional trade agreements or trade unions, such as NAFTA, the EU, MERCOSUR, CARICOM, ECOWAS, and ASEAN. These mechanisms have facilitated much more extensive and consistent levels of international trade, and they have provided effective mechanisms for states to work out trade disputes peacefully.

Given the incentives countries face, trade wars are often modeled as a Prisoner's Dilemma, wherein parties bring about harmful outcomes for the group through individually rational behavior. In this structure, the idea is that, even though countries gain from more open trade interactions, they face incentives to impose import duties unilaterally because this lets them benefit at the cost of the other countries. In this case, trade wars happen when multiple countries in trade relationships with one another decide to impose such restrictions, either simultaneously or by one country in response to the other (Ossa, 2019). Ossa estimates that, in a maximally escalated trade war, countries would impose tariffs of nearly 60% in attempts to shift prices and trade balances in favor of their domestic firms, which, in turn, would decrease economic gains from trade by about a quarter (Ossa, 2014).

Currency wars

Currency wars are international competitions in which states use currency policy to gain a competitive edge and stimulate national economies. The typical version involves competitive currency devaluation policies in which countries lower the relative value of their currency to make their exports more attractive to buyers in other markets. Countries devalue their currency either directly by artificially manipulating the value of the currency, such as through buying or selling their foreign reserves. If a country has some version of a fixed exchange rate regime, it will also adjust the official rates of exchange between its currency and foreign ones. Countries achieve devaluation effects in other ways, such as simply printing more money, but these measures run a far greater risk of immediate inflation for domestic consumers and could potentially result in far wider economic consequences. Devaluation policies are often driven by a desire to correct imbalances in international payments, to promote growth through one mechanism or another, to encourage consumption and investment, or to boost domestic production, especially in the industrial sector as currency devaluation not only makes one's exports more attractive abroad; it also makes domestic products cheaper relative to imported ones (Majaski, 2023).

The strategy of keeping a relatively low currency value is often a vital part of export-led growth strategies. When there is no response by other countries to such a strategic devaluation by one country, we do not see currency wars (Dadush and Eidelman, 2010). It is not always possible to tell whether currency devaluation is the result of an intentional strategy with a separate goal, an unintentional result of things outside the government's control, a side effect of another action, or the result of competitive devaluation policies.

Currency wars have side effects, both in domestic industry and international relationships. Currency devaluation can hurt domestic industries if they rely heavily on imports for raw materials, components, or equipment that they use in their operations. Furthermore, currency wars may result in spillover effects that lead to heightened political tensions between countries and potentially lead to trade wars, which tend to hurt multiple countries. For a variety of reasons, higher levels of policy coordination to reduce currency misalignment would likely lead to decreased tensions and would help to reduce global financial uncertainty and risks of instability (Bird and Willett, 2011).

Currency during war

Like other macroeconomic features of countries at war, we tend to see increased currency volatility in states involved in conflicts, especially those with substantial combat in their own territories. Armed conflicts drive volatility in currency prices due to a variety of factors. Especially in the case of sudden-onset large-scale wars, we tend to see a desperate attempt by investors and regular people to ensure the value of their money.

Wars often lead to increased strength in the traditional safe-haven currencies as people seek to ensure the value of their savings and/or investments. These safe-haven currencies include both traditionally strong currencies, such as the US Dollar, and other instruments that are often seen as having intrinsic financial value, such as gold. With war, we tend to see upward pressure on the values of these currencies. In parallel, we see currencies in the countries involved in armed conflicts weaken, especially when the conflicts take place in their territory. Additionally, we sometimes see secondary pressure on currencies from the impact of sanctions if these are imposed by third-party countries to a conflict.

The example of Iraq in the 1990s provides a powerful example of the impact that substantial international economic sanctions can have on a currency. Iraq in 1990 had already seen pressures on the Iraqi dinar. The official fixed exchange rate had been about 1 Iraqi dinar to 3 US dollars for years at that time. In part due to the pressures of spending to finance the war with Iraq in the 1980s, the dinar was already trading at a rate well below the official exchange rate. The dinar did not plummet initially from the pressure of sanctions but in a delay starting years later. With the UN-imposed sanctions on Iraq following its invasion of Kuwait in 1990, Iraq's oil was banned from global markets, and the country lost its main source of foreign reserve income; however, the Iraqi dinar did not face the anticipated price pressure because, during and following the Persian Gulf War, speculators from other countries in the region, such as Jordan and the UAE, bought Iraqi dinars, effectively making a bet that the UN sanctions would be lifted and that the dinar would recover as Iraqi oil reentered the global market fully and the value of the dinar would rebound (Hedges, 1993). As the sanctions became a more permanent fixture, nervous investors took their assets out of Iraq to the extent that they could, and foreign investment had not yet returned. As a result, the value of the Iraqi dinar plummeted from 1993 to the mid-1990s, and never truly recovered (Foot et al., 2004).

Wars generally decrease demand for local currency for a variety of reasons, leading to rapid or gradual devaluation of currency prices. In addition, conflicts tend to decrease physical and legal certainty in a territory, leading to decreases in investment (both domestic and foreign). Additionally, governments often invest in long-term projects, such as infrastructure, that decrease the likelihood of private investment. Speculation by currency traders and the uncoordinated behavior of many other actors can accelerate these processes. Currency traders seek to avoid losses from current investments, and they often see opportunities for profits in the anticipated currency volatility. At least in the early stages, they exchange currencies of countries directly engaged in war or short these currencies, especially if the war is taking place in these countries' territories.

While nonconvertible currencies are protected from this market vulnerability, they still can suffer from both direct and indirect currency pressures, largely through various forms of capital flight. Capital flight drives down currency values substantially, and it can take place rapidly, especially with modern electronic bank transfers. Even in cases where we do not see electronic transfers, people in times of uncertainty tend to prefer to have cash on hand instead of in bank accounts, especially if those bank accounts or banks might be frozen by law under emergency measures or seized by force. People also often convert funds into what they see as more secure instruments, whether this involves foreign currencies or other secure instruments, such as gold.

Beyond the direct pressures on currency through transfers noted before, wars create secondary, and sometimes long-term, devaluation of currencies. Conflicts also tend to lead to increased government spending, decreased revenues, and increased government debt. While the impacts might not be felt as strongly for some countries, such as the United States, those effects hit other states more acutely. Even the US dollar tended to depreciate relative to gold during wars that it found in the past, including extended military action in Korea and Vietnam, as well as during both wars with Iraq (Warburton, 2009).

One of the most notorious cases of currency depreciation as a result of war is that of Germany following World War I. During the war, Germany financed its efforts heavily through borrowing, confident that it could repay these debts after the war through reparations from the defeated countries. Additionally, the country suspended the gold standard for its currency. Following the war, not only did Germany fail to see the financial windfall of reparations, but it was saddled with a hefty price to pay to the victorious parties in the war. While the Weimar Republic reinstituted the gold standard and briefly recovered a semblance of currency stability, the tentative balance brought about in part through external loans fell apart. The underlying factors from the war and the reparations under the Treaty of Versailles made it difficult for Germany to establish long-term trade stability, but with the Great Depression, increased barriers to trade by outside countries, a dramatic decline in exports, and an eventual loss of loan availability, currency pressures built. As part of the response, the Weimar government printed more money, and Germany saw an episode of hyperinflation that is notorious to this day, which is credited as part of what enabled the rise of the Nazi Party in the 1930s (Balderston, 2002).

If a country takes on too high of a debt load, its bonds become devalued, and it can lose its ability to borrow, leading to further devaluing of its currency. In general, if a country's ability to pay its debts comes into question, it leads to lower currency value. Beyond the potential pitfall of borrowing to finance a war, if investment and exports decrease as a result of the war, this tends to lead to decreased demand for a country's currency. If post-conflict reconstruction is ineffective, these problems linger long after the conflict ends.

Civil wars and trade

As with international wars, civil wars have a substantial impact on international trade and are impacted by it as well. Civil wars, generally speaking, act to reduce levels of international trade in both imports and exports (Bayer and Rupert, 2004). They tend to reduce exports from countries in which the conflicts take place due to disruptions to investments, labor, production, and transportation through various mechanisms. Analysis of civil wars from 1989 to 2006 indicates that, in a bilateral trade relationship, civil war in either country in a pair reduces trade levels by 40% on average. The effects of trade reduction tend to be felt throughout the duration of the conflicts, and they are even more substantial for ethnically based civil wars (Bayer and Rupert, 2004).

The impacts of civil wars in countries are not limited to dyadic effects but tend to reduce levels of trade overall in the broader region (Assem, 2019). Because of this dynamic, Martin et al. (2008) argue that international trade can both exacerbate and limit the likelihood of a civil war's inception. They argue that international trade could potentially work to provide insurance in that it could potentially provide a replacement for domestic trade and therefore lower the opportunity costs for war. However, since international trade generates economic gains for both rebels and governments, the prospect of losing the ability to trade could act to deter the escalation of domestic conflicts in many cases, thus providing a deterrent effect. Martin et al. (2008) find in their analysis of civil war onset risk that high levels of trade openness tend to be associated with a higher likelihood of the onset of low-intensity conflicts but with a lower risk of high-intensity conflicts.

The civil war in Syria has devastated the country's trade relations through a mixture of mechanisms. From 2010, the last full year before Syria's civil war started, to 2016, Syria's total exports dropped from about $19 billion to $555 (Calder, 2019). The losses are partly due to sanctions imposed on Syria as the government fired on peaceful protestors and has been accused of carrying out other atrocities during the war. These sanctions have included bans on imports of key Syrian industries, freezing of the financial assets of the government and its officials, and embargos on investment in

Syria. These sanctions have been imposed by many countries and organizations, including Turkey, the United States, the Arab League, and the European Union. Beyond sanctions, explosive munitions have damaged and destroyed productive facilities, storage facilities, infrastructure, and other economically significant resources. Syrian people and businesses have often been deprived of goods that they need to be productive, transport goods, and survive. Not only have infrastructure and capital assets been damaged and destroyed, but over half of Syria's prewar population was displaced by the war at one point or another, including approximately one-fifth of the country's population fleeing the country altogether. The war has both produced a humanitarian catastrophe and a dramatic reduction in both potential laborers in export-oriented industries and consumers who might consume some imported goods. Additionally, the war has served to scare away investors who would not be deterred by other factors as the war creates greater uncertainty (Calder, 2019).

Civil wars and currency

Civil wars, like interstate wars, tend to create loss and uncertainty; therefore, we often see heavy inflationary pressures for largely the same reasons. These pressures include increases in government spending, often financed through increased debt and higher perceived risks by investors and regular people. Thus we tend to see a decreased demand for the currency. Especially if the civil war is large in scope, we tend to see substantial inflationary decisions. In addition, wartime inflation both causes and is exacerbated by capital flight. With capital flight, accompanied by decreased demand and decreased production, we tend to see inflationary pressures on currencies. Speculative pressures are common additions in the early stages of civil wars or during major changes in the progress of the wars. War termination often has unpredictable impacts on capital flight and currency pressures as well (Davies, 2010). If sufficient signals related to long-term stability are sent to markets, such as through improved and stabilized economic performance and sound fiscal and monetary policies, capital flight tends to decrease and sometimes reverse. In such circumstances, currencies are more likely to stabilize.

One of the most substantial impacts of civil wars on currency values is related to the degree of capital flight that takes place. Capital flight has a downward pressure on the exchange rate value of a currency as it increases the frequency with which people exchange a country's currency for more stable currencies and other more stable instruments, such as gold. A large portion of the decisions made by people to withdraw capital from a country are driven by perceptions of the expected intensity, scope, and duration of the conflict (Davies, 2010). In the early stages of a high-intensity conflict, or when a conflict intensifies, countries can see substantial capital flight if they do not impose strong capital controls and provide sufficient assurances to the public.

Syria's civil war provides a stark lesson in the potential impact of civil war on a currency. The Syrian pound has suffered significantly during the war, declining to less than 10% of its prewar value by 2017 as Syria saw a substantial economic decline and was effectively excluded from global financial systems through sanctions. Syria's lifeline to foreign exchange operated primarily through its neighbor, Lebanon. The war and subsequent sanctions made Syria much more dependent on Lebanon's financial system, and with the liquidity crisis in Lebanon, both the Syrian economy and the value of its currency plummeted (Al-Khalidi, 2019). The value of the Syrian pound tumbled further to less than 1% of its prewar value (*Syria Exchange Rate*, 2023). It is unclear how or when Syria, once a middle-income country with a relatively modern economy, will recover from the devastation of its civil war. The woes of the pound are exacerbated by sanctions that effectively exclude Syria from international financial institutions and structures through which it could potentially receive loans to stabilize its currency (Calder, 2019).

Case study: Trade and currency wars of the 1930s

As the Great Depression set in and spread across the world, policymakers took economic policy steps that caused greater destruction than they anticipated. In attempting to boost their domestic economies and gain a competitive edge, dozens of countries engaged in competitive devaluations of their currencies and increased barriers to imports. These policy moves led to trade and currency wars that likely deepened and prolonged the economic difficulties of the 1930s. While even the most liberal and coordinated trade and currency policies would not have avoided the international economic chaos of the 1930s, the Smoot-Hawley Tariff Act, enacted in June 1930 by the US government, likely exacerbated the economic calamity around the world more than perhaps any other policy decision enacted by Washington or any other state (Arndt, 2013).

By the turn of the 20th century, the United States had developed both an advanced industrial sector and a thriving banking, rendering its tariff policy out of step with its actual economic strength. The United States had used high tariff barriers to develop industrially, selling its surplus of raw materials and agricultural goods and using tariffs to protect its young industries. As World War I engulfed Europe and Africa, Washington's emergence as a leading lender to the embattled Europeans made its rising status as the world economic powerhouse abundantly clear. Nonetheless, the traditional role of tariffs as protection for industry and a major source of government revenue was well entrenched.

Prior to the notorious 1930 Smoot-Hawley tariffs, the United States likely laid some of the seeds for the Great Depression through its extreme economic protectionism in the early 1920s. In September 1922, Congress passed the Fordney-McCumber Tariff Act, which set a range of tariffs that led to an average statutory tariff rate of over one-third of the total value of imports. The goal of the act was to protect domestic manufacturers from foreign competition. These barriers to US export markets for European countries caused difficulties in rebuilding their economies in the postwar period. Many states responded with retaliatory tariffs against US goods overall or focused on specifics such as wheat or automobiles (Hayford and Pasurka, 1992). Even before the Great Depression, these barriers to trade, along with others, created more fragile conditions in the global trade system as the United States had not yet adapted to its role as the largest economy in the world, subsequently helping to lay the brittle ground for the Great Depression (Rothgeb, 2001).

In 1930 the United States found itself in the early stages of what came to be known as the Great Depression. In an attempt to protect domestic producers, Congress passed the Smoot-Hawley Tariff Act, which dramatically raised tariffs against imported goods (Irwin, 2012). These tremendous tariff hikes exacerbated the existing imbalance in current accounts as the United States found itself in a position of an established industrial power with protectionist trade policies and large export surpluses, while at the same time serving as a large international creditor (Arndt, 2013).

In response to Washington's dramatic tariff hikes, trade partners protested, and many imposed retaliatory trade measures, including actions specifically targeted against the United States, such as those aimed at its automotive industry. By the end of 1931, over two dozen countries had also raised tariffs (Arndt, 2013). Beyond strategically targeted import duties, countries used nontariff trade responses, including quotas, and many consumers and corporations boycotted or reduced consumption of US exports (Mitchener et al., 2022). Most-favored nation restrictions did not prevent either the imposition of the Smoot-Hawley tariffs or the retaliatory measures that were targeted toward the US.

The direct impacts of Washington's tariffs and subsequent retaliation measures taken by trade partners resulted in slight expansionary effects on the US economy due to the large size of the domestic market available to consumer goods that might otherwise have been exported (Eichengreen, 1986); however, this does not tell the full picture. The global economy, and the United States, suffered as the indirect effects of both the tariffs and their consequences were felt through a series of economic shocks. The overall volume of trade globally fell by nearly two-thirds in gold-to-dollar terms from 1929 to 1933, and even when accounting for changes in currency and gold values, we still see a decline of one-quarter in global trade over this period. Trade contracted in a spiral as countries responded to one another's policies and as economic effects of both policy changes and economic downturns were felt in ways that spread and caused increased economic pain across the globe (Irwin, 2012).

In countries that were harmed by and retaliated against the tariffs, Mitchener et al. (2022) estimate that welfare gains from trade fell by 8 to 16% compared to normal trade conditions. Even the United States, with its large domestic economy, did not gain in the aggregate (Mitchener et al., 2022). Furthermore, one of the more notable indirect impacts of these tariffs was felt in the disruptions that they dealt to international capital markets and the stability of the international monetary system (Eichengreen, 1986).

The increase in tariffs under Smoot-Hawley led to a dramatic decrease in imports to the United States, which placed pressure on many outside economies that relied on this market, especially those recovering from World War I in Europe. With the decrease in consumption of their products, countries struggling with war debt saw a slowdown in production. Coupled with a withdrawal of a decrease in capital availability from the United States due to the stock market crash and a reorientation toward domestic markets, debtor countries in Europe and South America faced a serious balance of payments problem. As their foreign currency and gold reserves declined, these countries faced the dilemma of devaluing their currencies or adopting foreign exchange controls. Additionally, the economic pressures amid the economic decline and balance of payments deficit led countries that held war debt to gradually default on sovereign bonds held in the United States in 1933, except for Finland, further deepening the economic difficulties and tightening capital availability (Arndt, 2013).

The current account deficits that many countries experienced also put pressure on their currencies that debt defaults alone could not solve. While the retaliatory trade measures were partly driven by an attempt to mitigate the economic effects of external tariffs, they were also part of a desperate attempt to even the balance of payments and relieve pressure on national currencies. In cases where the current account balance was not restored through successful trade balance adjustment, countries faced difficult monetary policy decisions. Even countries that did not engage in retaliatory trade measures found that they faced the current accounts deficit problem, and they often responded by devaluing their currencies. For example, the Netherlands and Belgium primarily relied upon increased trade barriers to maintain their currency. The Nordic countries, on the other hand, allowed their currencies to depreciate, and they were able to deal with the balance of payments problem through this mechanism.

While the term "currency war" was only created in the 21st century, episodes of the early Great Depression have been cited as prime examples of a currency war. Currency policy coordination among major economies of the United Kingdom, the United States, and France, which had brought about relative currency stability in the 1920s, ceased. Additionally, many countries abandoned or relaxed the gold standard to allow greater fiscal flexibility. Following the market crash of 1929, the United States and France began to build up their gold reserves as a hedge against expected instability in the pound sterling. This policy led to a self-fulfilling prophecy as it put downward pressure on the pound, especially when coupled with the actions of others who followed suit. Combined, these processes played a major role in precipitating the Sterling Crises of 1931. During the 1930s, a total of 20 countries engaged in currency devaluation, and some did so several times, including the United States, which was relatively late in suspending the gold standard in 1933 (Dadush and Eidelman, 2010).

During the 1930s, many countries relaxed or abandoned the gold standard and/or increased the printing of money to boost the domestic economy through two mechanisms. Increasing the prospects for inflation would incentivize investment and consumption over saving, introducing more money into the economy. The hope was that this policy would work against the instinct of many to be more conservative with funds in turbulent economic times. Additionally, devaluation offered a route for correcting the balance of payments problem, albeit an imperfect one. While it accomplished the second goal effectively in the short term, in some countries, such as Germany, the currency devaluation opened the country up to the notorious runaway inflation that serves as a cautionary tale today.

While the devaluations and abandonment of the gold standard created multiple shocks to both national economies and the global financial system, countries that ceased to use the gold standard tended to see better economic outcomes, all things being equal, compared to those that kept the gold standard during the 1930s. In times of economic downturn, countries on the gold standard often saw people redeem currency for gold, taking the currency out of circulation and reducing the supply of money relative to the level of economic activity. Adherence to the gold standard by major powers tended to permit periodic deflationary shocks, which could lead to banking panics, such as those we saw in Austria and Germany in 1930 and 1931 (Eichengreen and Sachs, 1985). The gold standard and the way international financial and trade transactions were tied through it allowed the transmission of these deflationary shocks from one country to another, including through impacts on debt (Bernanke and James, 1991).

The Tripartite Agreement of 1936 between the United Kingdom, France, and the United States ended the destructive currency wars that started in 1931. It was too late, however, to quickly undo the economic damage that the competitive devaluation dealt to international trade. More important, perhaps, was the political damage that the currency and trade wars had caused to many countries and the faith in the international financial system (Harris, 2021). These tensions helped to justify more aggressive economic measures taken by Germany and others and paved the way for more assertive foreign policies to be welcomed by weary publics.

The trade and currency wars of the 1930s yielded long-term lessons for both economists and policymakers, and they heavily informed postwar economic planning. One of the broad lessons was the need for more effective international coordination on currency and trade policy, which took the form of the Bretton Woods system and the General Agreement on Tariffs and Trade (GATT) framework. The goal of these two interrelated systems was to avoid the disastrous trade wars and competitive devaluations that were so harmful to the global economy and that many saw as fueling the conditions that led to World War II.

The Bretton Woods system set up a coordinated system of exchange rates for countries within the system in which their exchange rates would be fixed as a set exchange rate to the US dollar, which in turn would be exchangeable for a fixed amount of gold. Under the Bretton Woods agreement, two institutions were set up to promote global financial stability. The International Bank for Reconstruction and Development (IBRD), which would later become the World Bank, was created to provide development loans to help countries rebuild their economies after the war.

The International Monetary Fund (IMF) was created as a mechanism to monitor currency values and monetary policies and to provide stabilization loans where needed to allow countries to adjust their balance of payments using foreign currency.

The GATT framework was established through a series and, later, rounds of treaties starting in the late 1940s to systematically reduce tariffs in a mutually beneficial multilateral framework. Eventually, these agreements included more countries until they were subsumed within the framework of the World Trade Organization (WTO) which provides a forum for countries to agree on certain rules designed to liberalize trade. Furthermore, WTO provides mechanisms for monitoring, adjudicating, and enforcing rules of trade and allows members a route to redress trade grievances. WTO tribunals can authorize punitive trade measures for aggrieved parties through which states can seek retribution for what are deemed to be unfair trade practices within the rules in a way that runs a much lower risk of escalating into trade wars.

Economists today generally hold a consensus view that trade protectionism and competitive, uncoordinated currency policies played a substantial role in deepening if not causing the Great Depression. While mechanisms were developed to mitigate these problems in the forms of the World Bank, IMF, and WTO, some of these lessons are being questioned by some practitioners. While countries do occasionally engage in strategic devaluations of their currency, competitive devaluations are fortunately not practiced today. Even instances where countries are accused of engaging in currency wars are much milder and far more limited. Additionally, policymakers cannot take dramatic monetary policy measures in modern currency regimes as easily.

The current dynamic between Washington and Beijing serves as an example of such a challenge. In the past 5 years, the United States and China have engaged in policy competition that many see as risky for the global economy and, possibly, for peace. The rivalry between the status quo power and rising power offers the potential to escalate into greater trade competition and fragmentation. The lessons of trade competition from the 1930s can offer useful lessons to those seeking to avoid similar economic and political devastation in the modern era, but it is unclear how well they will be heeded. Policymakers in the US and China seeking an edge in what many have described as a trade war find themselves limited by the realities of modern global value chains. As the disruptions of both the competitive trade measures between the US and China and disruptions caused by the COVID-19 pandemic have shown, modern economies are intricately intertwined. Despite the bluster that trade wars are easy to win from the Trump administration, and similar policy measures from the Biden administration, the realization of these modern realities will add a note of caution to policymakers in both Washington and Beijing.

Case study: Russia's invasion of Ukraine

While the war following Russia's 2022 invasion of Ukraine involves only two countries on its face, many outside states and international organizations have become involved deeply, even if in noncombatant capacities only. Aside from large shipments of arms and substantial financial assistance to Ukraine, the US, EU, and other allied countries have conducted extensive operations on the financial and trade side of the equation against Russia to punish its government and hamper its war effort. In the months following Russia's invasion of Ukraine in February 2022, the G7, EU, and other allied countries imposed widespread sanctions on Russia that attempted to undermine political support for Vladimir Putin and hinder Russia's ability to wage war against Ukraine. These efforts included targeted sanctions against Russia's financial system and foreign reserves.

The war started quite suddenly from the perspective of Ukraine's government, but the National Bank of Ukraine made substantial changes rapidly to stabilize the hryvnia. The Ukrainian National Bank imposed capital controls and quickly deployed a fixed exchange rate currency regime (Skok and de Groot, 2022). In the decade before the open war with Russia, Ukraine's currency lost substantial value following the Russian invasion and annexation of Crimea in 2014 and with the Russian-backed separatist conflicts, especially the prolonged war in Donbas. Over the year following the February 2014 invasion of Crimea, the hryvnia dropped to about one-third of the value it held in January 2014; however, it held a relatively stable value over the next 7 years. Despite the move to a fixed exchange rate and the imposition of capital controls, Ukraine saw significant inflation in the first year of the war, and the National Bank of Ukraine devalued the hryvnia multiple times (Skok and de Groot, 2022). Fearing additional increases in inflation, the bank also took the unusual step of considerably raising interest rates. Despite these measures and extensive foreign aid, there are substantial worries about inflation, especially given the high borrowing rate by Ukraine's government given the increased war costs and decreased tax revenues (Harmasch, 2023).

The specific range of sanctions involved a sweeping set of trade and financial measures that were unprecedented in targeting an economy the size of Russia's so comprehensively. These sanctions included EU and G7 countries primarily banning the export of not only military goods previously banned but also a prohibition on many dual-use goods that could be used for either military or civilian purposes, such as computer chips and vehicle parts. These countries also banned the export of luxury goods to Russia.

Altogether, sanctioning countries froze Russian foreign reserve assets located under their authority swiftly in a way that caught the Russian government off-guard. In total, they froze well over $300 billion of Russia's foreign reserve assets, which amounted to over half of the country's holdings. This action was carried out in a coordinated manner so that the Russian government did not have time to withdraw its holdings from allied countries. Furthermore, Russian banks were mostly barred from using the SWIFT financial messaging system, making it difficult for Russian businesses to carry out international financial transactions. Beyond these measures, the UK froze the assets of Russian banks, and it barred Russian companies from borrowing money from British banks.

Russia has skirted trade and financial sanctions through a variety of methods. It has dedollarized much of its trade to deal with exclusion from the SWIFT system and other routes through which it would normally have accessed dollars used in international transactions. One interesting secondary impact of the war is that, with bans on Russian access to the US dollar for international transactions, Russia has carried out many transactions in the Chinese yuan (Tan, 2023). This has contributed to increased chatter about dedollarization in many international transactions. If the war contributes to this discussion, it could be a piece of the US dollar losing its special status as the predominant currency of global reserves and trade. While the US dollar has not lost its dominant status in international trade, transactions in CNY have more than doubled since the start of the war (Lockett and Leng, 2023). Nonetheless, the Chinese yuan has little prospect of becoming the dominant international currency without major policy changes due to a range of factors, including the fact that its value is managed related to the US dollar (De Mott, 2023). Russia has used a variety of ghost trades through second-party countries to sell its goods and to obtain dual-use components and goods that can be used for military equipment, sometimes indirectly from countries that have banned direct export of the same goods to Russia. It has assembled a fleet of tanker ships that carry its oil exports abroad, skirting the price cap on Russian oil above which Western insurance firms will not insure tankers carrying oil shipments (Tan, 2023).

Sanctions also targeted and restricted imports of goods from Russia. The US and UK banned all imports of oil and gas from Russia, and the EU banned the import of both refined oil products and coal. While the EU did not ban imports of gas or oil, the EU and G7 countries placed a $60 price cap on Russian crude oil, banning insurers from underwriting oil shipments at prices above the cap (*Sanctions on Russia*, 2023). Additionally, the EU created ambitious plans to end its dependence on Russian fossil fuels by 2030 (Roberts and Bowden, 2022). While the bloc has made tremendous efforts toward these goals in a relatively short time, the full impact of these measures will have a long-term negative impact on Russia's economy as European policymakers are unlikely to reverse course anytime soon. It may be that, when coupled with concerns about carbon dioxide emissions by EU countries, Russia may have accelerated the permanent loss of European energy markets.

Germany, long criticized for increasing its dependence on Russian gas through the construction of the Nord Stream 2 gas pipeline, canceled the opening of the pipeline from Russia and has permanently abandoned the project. The EU has worked to both accelerate its move to dramatically decrease carbon emissions and, in the shorter term, to replace Russian gas imports by looking to other markets, including Azerbaijan and Algeria. The organization has also increased LNG imports from places like the United States (Roberts and Bowden, 2022). While Russian oil and gas earnings gained on higher prices in 2022, the International Energy Agency estimates that Russia's earnings on gas and oil exports fell by over half from April 2022 to April 2023 (*Sanctions on Russia*, 2023).

Russia's invasion of Ukraine shows the tremendous difficulty of cutting a major economy out of the global economy. This is partly due to the sheer size of Russia's economy, but it is more substantially driven by Russia's position as a producer of key natural resources. European countries have continued to import billions of dollars in gas and oil each month from Russia. Russian natural gas continues to transit through Ukraine to EU countries via pipelines in the country. The United States continues to import a large portion of the enriched uranium that its nuclear power plants use from Russia, sending billions of dollars to Russia's nuclear emergency agency (Bearak, 2023). Even efforts in Congress to limit imports of uranium from Russia recognize that domestic uranium production and enrichment must increase substantially if the country is to cease enriching Russian producers (Rodgers, 2023).

Beyond the denial of goods and markets, one of the central goals of the sanctions' effort was to undermine the value of the Russian ruble. In the early days of the conflict, the price of the ruble plunged dramatically, dropping to less than half of its value at the start of the year. In response to the capital flight and fears of a currency collapse, the Central Bank of Russia and other parts of the government reacted quickly, imposing a set of extraordinary measures that are credited with stabilizing the currency. On February 28, the Central Bank of Russia increased its interest rates to 20%, offering a strong incentive to keep money in the bank in ruble form.

Additionally, Russian businesses were required to change a minimum of 80% of their foreign earnings into rubles. Russian brokers were barred from selling any securities owned by foreigners, including Russian government bonds and domestic securities of any type. Moreover, strict capital controls were put in place on regular Russians, including caps on foreign currency conversions. Moscow also demanded that foreign buyers of Russian gas pay for these transactions in rubles rather than the typical euros or dollars. Altogether, these measures limited capital flight and artificially stimulated demand for rubles, thus propping up the currency's value (Hirsch, 2022). With these extraordinary measures, by late March 2022, the value of the ruble had stabilized and partially recovered (Davidson, 2022), and by June, it was valued higher than at the start of 2022, at its highest value in over 7 years (Sivabalan, 2022).

Even with the ruble's decline in value in the first half of 2023, its value is approximately where it was before the war as of May 2023. Economic analysts at Commerzbank estimated that the ruble will weaken in the near- to medium-term future, predicting an exchange rate of 80 rubles to the dollar by the end of 2023 and 90 rubles to the dollar by the end of 2024 (*Ruble to Weaken Medium,* 2023). With the increased economic warning signs in Russia, the failure of the country to make more progress in its war, and the signals of uncertainty sent by the June 2023 Wagner Group insurrection, the ruble's decline has accelerated (Sullivan, 2023).

While this estimate indicates a weakening of the ruble, it is far from the collapse the G7 and EU countries sought with the sanctions they imposed in response to Russia's invasion of Ukraine. While the Russian Central Bank has proven itself quite adept at stabilizing the currency's value, it remains tentative at best, and it is unclear whether it can be maintained without substantial state intervention, leading some commentators to label the ruble a Potemkin currency (Bartholomeusz, 2022). These same measures that have rescued the ruble simultaneously limit the willingness of foreign firms to make long-term investments in the Russian market.

Beyond the impacts noted before, the war has had substantial direct and indirect impacts on many other currencies around the world. In the period following the start of the war, currencies within much of Europe saw inflationary pressure as nervous investors searched for more stable markets. The euro depreciated substantially, as did other currencies closely tied to it, such as the Polish złoty, Hungarian forint, and Czech koruna (Komuves, 2022). While these European currencies have generally recovered most of the value they lost in the early months of the war (Harper, 2023), as of June 2023, they were still trading at rates below their prewar levels. Along with the depreciation effects in many European currencies, the war led to the substantial appreciation of other currencies, most notably the US dollar and the Chinese yuan. Appreciation of the US dollar has contributed to inflationary pressures on many currencies far from the conflict, increasing the price of imports. In many countries, a majority of imports are priced in US dollars. Combined with US interest rate hikes aimed at fighting inflation, the war in Ukraine, and the accompanying decreased global risk appetites, the price of imports and the cost of dollar-denominated debt have increased for many African countries (Kemoe et al., 2023). While much of the inflationary pressure on these countries' currencies has been driven by interest rate hikes by the Federal Reserve of the United States, these interest rate hikes were driven in part by inflationary pressures unleashed by the war in Ukraine. This, combined with the draw of safe-haven currencies and financial instruments during wars, has inflationary effects on third-party countries, where it places increased pressure on consumers, firms, and governments.

Overall, the Russian Central Bank has proven itself adept at preventing large-scale capital flight and at stabilizing the ruble's value, but the long-term consequences of such measures may hamper investment long term not just from the G7 and EU countries but from firms in BRICS which might be nervous about investing heavily in the Russian economy if the Russian Central Bank's currency stabilization measures become more permanent. While Russia has largely prevented the currency and broader economic collapse sought by sanctioning countries, the war creates long-term opportunity costs that may outlive the war itself. In the best-case scenario, it will be years after the end of the war before foreign investment and economic engagement with Russia resume at prewar levels. Under these conditions, Russia's economy will likely be more dependent on the state and the energy sector, which will set the conditions for more difficult economic hardship if energy prices collapse in the coming decades.

While Russia has proven savvy at finding replacement markets for goods banned from other markets and at finding replacement routes for many of its key imports, the sanctions have damaged the Russian economy, though not to the extent the US and other sanctioning countries had hoped. The Kremlin holds tremendous economic weapons that it could use to strike back at participants in this trade war, but it is hamstrung in its ability to do so. Moscow's greatest weapon in a trade war comes from its oil and gas resources. Prior to the war, European countries, were the main importers of these goods from Russia, but since the start of the war in Ukraine, European countries have worked hard to lessen this vulnerability by decreasing their dependence on Russian energy.

One of the important lessons from the study of sanctions as a tool of coercive diplomacy is that the greater the cost of the change in policy behavior, the less likely that the sanctions' target will shift its behaviors. Therefore it is difficult to imagine the sanctions having the effect of causing Russia to end the war (Kulikov, 2023). If the goal is to prevent future wars, perhaps sanctions can have some future deterrent effect. Furthermore, it is possible that sanctions indirectly affect Moscow's incentives toward ending the war sooner, along with mounting Russian casualties. That said, given that only about half of the world's economy and fewer than a quarter of its countries are participating in meaningful sanctions, they are far less likely to be effective. Especially when combined with Putin's framing of the Ukrainian war as existentially important to Russian identity, economic sanctions are predicted to not be sufficiently compelling to push the Kremlin toward ceasing its hostilities toward Ukraine. The failed use of sanction threats as a deterrent will be studied extensively to determine whether the sanction threats were too vague, not signaled credibly enough, or insufficient in size to deter the invasion. If the sanctions cause long-term harm to Russia's economy, they may serve as a deterrent in other cases and/or weaken Russia in the long term.

Conclusion

Trade and currency are tightly intertwined with conflicts. They affect and are affected by wars, and they can, at times, serve as a forum in which competition among countries takes place. These peaceful forms of competition create tensions between states, but they also provide strong incentives for peace, especially if the countries involved see a positive benefit in the relationship's future. Therefore policymakers are well served to consider the long-term implications of interactions related to trade in the broader context of a country's foreign policy. When examining Russia's recent invasion of Ukraine, for example, scholars and policymakers will likely ask how the reduction in trade between the two, as well as the international sanctions, in the wake of Russia's annexation of Crimea, affected the calculations of the Russian government to invade Ukraine.

Both civil wars and interstate wars tend to lead to an overall reduction in economic activity and trade, all things being equal. That said, these effects are felt more acutely within the region where wars take place, even for countries that are not involved in the wars. Civil wars tend to decrease trade volumes, especially in the case of large-scale wars. Given the wide range of variation in the nature, structure, and intensity of civil wars, it is harder to generalize their impact. However, it is safe to say that they tend to negatively impact international trade, both for the country involved and for the broader region.

Firms that rely on complex supply chains can employ strategies to cushion themselves against war-related disruptions to trade. They can seek to diversify their supply chains and/or hold greater inventory where possible. Both strategies come with costs but limit risk. These strategies cushion against short-term disruptions that can be caused by war. Another strategy, which may be even more expensive, both in transaction costs and opportunity costs, involves onshoring or nearshoring as much production as possible. A broader approach would include pricing international conflict as part of the risks when building supply chains for production and operation. Importers and retailers can use similar strategies to manage risk and consider the impacts of wars on trade relationships and business operations. Investors, in navigating their decisions, can consider the exposure of companies to war-related risks. While this could be broadly applicable and is considered at the point of extraction and/or production, lessons drawn from the research on war and trade indicate that trade disruptions from large-scale, especially global, wars tend to be long term. Civil wars often have shorter-term implications for trade relationships, but they can have regional effects beyond what one might initially expect, both due to regional trade disruptions and how civil wars impact the perception of risk.

While warring parties typically cut off trade altogether, doing so is often complicated due to both long-term calculations and immediate needs. Therefore trade and other economic transactions sometimes continue to happen between embattled states, albeit in a more limited capacity. This dynamic includes direct trade, informal or illicit transactions, or indirect transactions through third parties.

Wars generally increase the volatility of currency values. National currencies tend to see downward pressure with the onset of wars, and they are impacted by productivity variations from the war, changes in the balance of trade, government borrowing, fluctuations in foreign investment, capital flight, speculative trading, or secondary measures, such as sanctions. The currencies of countries in which war engagement takes place are most likely to be hard hit, especially if fighting is widespread throughout the country. While capital controls can stem some of these problems, countries experiencing conflict must take active measures if they want their currencies to avoid substantial losses in currency value. Traditional safe-haven currencies, as well as gold, tend to increase in value as people and firms seek stability. A secondary effect of these activities tends to be inflationary pressure on many countries as inflation of the US dollar and other reserve currencies increases the cost of imports and foreign debt.

Through a mixture of changes in modern economic systems, collective learning, and improved policy coordination, currency wars are extremely rare in today's world, and trade wars are quite uncommon and limited in nature. Despite the dire predictions that are occasionally proposed, devastating currency wars are very unlikely. Any actions related to strategic currency choices are likely to be far more limited, such as those carried out by the United States under its quantitative easing policies or China's managed float of its currency. Modern currency regimes are more dynamic and complex and far more likely to absorb market changes. Additionally, currency markets tend to facilitate currency values finding equilibrium relatively quickly. Therefore investors can reasonably anticipate that most war-related disruptions to currency values will be short lived except in circumstances of widespread devastation in a country or unless state behavior in reaction to the conflict fundamentally undermines confidence in the stability of monetary policy, such as we saw in the case of Germany during World War I.

Future currency competition is unlikely to center around competitive devaluations, generally speaking; however, this does not mean that currencies will not be important in political and economic competition. Actions in 2022 and 2023 have indicated a decreasing appetite of many states and firms to continue to rely as heavily on the US dollar as a reserve currency and standard for international trade. This is driven by a mixture of factors, including the rise of non-Western economies and the desire of many actors to decrease the political clout of the United States and its allies. The recent experience of Russia, a major economic player, largely losing access to dollars, has served as a reminder of the leverage that a dollar-denominated trade system allows the United States. While the conversations about a potential BRICS currency are relatively early and may not bear fruit, they indicate the appetite for much of the world to become less dependent on the international monetary system built by the US and other G7 countries.

In the case of the ongoing trade war between the United States and China, both sides have shown substantial restraint to avoid escalating the consequences of the conflict. The shape of this great power rivalry in the coming decades will provide new information about how the modern globalized economy impacts competition among major powers in an era of global value chains. The manner in which the two countries manage their trade relationship impacts how they view each other, and if they reduce their level of economic interdependence, the prospects for violent conflict could increase. Therefore the potential trade war between the two powers, as well as the broader political relationship, carries the potential to reveal much about the relationship between economic interdependence and conflict in the modern era.

References

Al-Khalidi, S., 2019. Lebanon Crisis Wreaks Havoc on Syria's War-Torn Economy. Reuters. https://www.reuters.com/article/us-syria-economy-lebanon/lebanon-crisis-wreaks-havoc-on-syrias-war-torn-economy-idUSKBN1Y31I7.

Amin, M.A., 1970. Ancient trade and trade routes between Egypt and the Sudan, 4000 to 700 B.C. Sudan Notes Rec. 50, 23–30.

Arad, R., Hirsch, S., Tovias, A., 1983. Economics of Peacemaking. Palgrave Macmillan, London.

Arndt, H.W., 2013. The Economic Lessons of the Nineteen Thirties. Routledge, New York.

Assem, H., 2019. Trade and Civil Conflicts. Economic Research Forum. https://erf.org.eg/app/uploads/2019/02/11-150-Hoda-Assem.pdf.

Balderston, T., 2002. Economics and Politics in the Weimar Republic. Cambridge University Press, Cambridge.

Bartholomeusz, S., 2022. Nothing is Quite as it Seems: The Illusion of Russia's Potemkin Markets. Sydney Morning Herald. https://www.smh.com.au/business/markets/nothing-is-quite-as-it-seems-the-illusion-of-russia-s-potemkin-markets-20220329-p5a8sh.html.

Bayer, R., Rupert, M.C., 2004. Effects of civil wars on international trade, 1950-92. J. Peace Res. 42 (6), 699–713.

Bearak, M., 2023. The U.S. Is Paying Billions to Russia's Nuclear Agency. Here's Why. New York Times. https://www.nytimes.com/2023/06/14/climate/enriched-uranium-nuclear-russia-ohio.html.

Bernanke, B., James, H., 1991. The gold standard, deflation, and financial crisis in the great depression: An international comparison. In: Hubbard, R.G. (Ed.), Financial Markets and Financial Crises. University of Chicago Press, Chicago.

Bird, G., Willett, T.D., 2011. Currency wars: rhetoric and reality. World Econ. 12 (4), 121–136.

Calder, A., 2019. Civil War in Syria: How Conflict Erodes Trade. Hinrich Foundation. https://www.hinrichfoundation.com/research/tradevistas/sustainable/trade-during-war/.

Copeland, D.C., 2016. Economic Interdependence and War. Princeton University Press, Princeton.

Dadush, U., Eidelman, V., 2010. Currency Tensions: Four Lessons From History. Carnegie Endowment for International Peace. https://carnegieendowment.org/2010/12/09/currency-tensions-four-lessons-from-history-pub-42108.

Davidson, K., 2022. Biden Turned the Ruble into Rubble. Then it Quickly Came Back. Politico. https://www.politico.com/news/2022/03/31/ruble-recovery-russia-biden-sanctions-00021850.

Davies, V.A.B., 2010. Capital Flight and Violent Conflict: A Review of the Literature. World Development Report 2011: Background Note. https://openknowledge.worldbank.org/server/api/core/bitstreams/49983372-ff18-5c73-a81b-2a52d5aa4a1f/content.

De Mott, F., 2023. De-Dollarization Has Started, But the Odds that China's Yuan Will TAKE Over Are 'Profoundly Unlikely to Essentially Impossible. Markets Insider. https://markets.businessinsider.com/news/currencies/de-dollarization-renminbi-dollar-vs-yuan-takeover-china-russia-usd-2023-4?op=1&trk=public_post_comment-text.

Dimitrijevic, V., Pejic, J., 1995. UN sanctions against Yugoslavia: Two years later. In: Bourantonis, D., Wiener, J. (Eds.), The United Nations in the New World Order. Palgrave Macmillan, London.

Doyle, M.W., 1983. Kant, liberal legacies, and foreign affairs. Philos Public Aff 12 (3), 205–235.

Economic Surveillance, 2022. IMF Annual Report 2022. https://www.imf.org/external/pubs/ft/ar/2022/what-we-do/economic-surveillance/.

Economist, 2023. Our Big Mac Index Shows How Burger Prices are Changing. https://www.economist.com/big-mac-index.

Eichengreen, B., 1986. The Political Economy of the Smooth-Hawley Tariff Act. National Bureau of Economic Research. Working Paper 2001 https://www.nber.org/papers/w2001.

Eichengreen, B., Sachs, J., 1985. Exchange rates and economic recovery in the 1930s. J. Econ. Hist. 45 (4), 925–946.

Feldman, N., Sadeh, T., 2018. War and third-party trade. J. Confl. Resolut. 62 (1), 119–142.

Foot, C.W., Block, K.C., Gray, S., 2004. Economic policy and prospects in Iraq. J. Econ. Perspect. 18 (3), 47–70.

Gartzke, E., 2007. The capitalist peace. Am. J. Polit. Sci. 51 (1), 166–191.

Gilpin, R., 1987. The Political Economy of International Relations. Princeton University Press, Princeton.

Glick, R., Taylor, A.M., 2005. Collateral Damage: Trade Disruption and the Economic Impact of War. Federal Reserve Bank of San Francisco Working Paper Series https://www.frbsf.org/economic-research/wp-content/uploads/sites/4/wp05-11bk.pdf.

Hargrave, M., 2022. Foreign Exchange Reserves: What are They, Why Countries Hold Them. Investopedia. https://www.investopedia.com/terms/f/foreign-exchange-reserves.asp.

Harmasch, O., 2023. Ukraine's Inflation Hits 26.6%, But Lower Than Forecast. Reuters. https://www.reuters.com/world/europe/ukraines-2022-inflation-hits-266-lower-than-forecast-2023-01-10/.

Harper, J., 2023. Inflation Gives Eastern European Currencies Wings. Deutsche Welle. https://www.dw.com/en/eastern-european-currencies-fly-high-on-rising-inflation/a-65564676.

Harris, M., 2021. Monetary War and Peace: London, Washington, Paris, and the Tripartite Agreement of 1936. Cambridge University Press, Cambridge.

Hayford, M., Pasurka, C.A., 1992. The political economy of the Fordney-McCumber and smooth-Hawley tariff acts. Explor. Econ. Hist. 29 (1), 30–50.

Hedges, C., 1993. Fortunes in Iraqi Bills Gone Overnight. New York Times.

Hegre, H., Oneal, J.R., Russett, B., 2010. Trade does promote peace: new simultaneous estimates of the reciprocal effects of trade and conflict. J. Peace Res. 47 (6), 763–774.

Hirsch, P., 2022. How Russia Rescued the Ruble. NPR Planet Money. https://www.npr.org/sections/money/2022/04/05/1090920442/how-russia-rescued-the-ruble.

Hummels, D.J., Ishii, Yi, K.-M., 2001. The nature and growth of vertical specialization in world trade. J. Int. Econ. 45 (1), 75–96.

Institute for Government, 2017. Non-tariff Barriers. https://www.instituteforgovernment.org.uk/article/explainer/non-tariff-barriers. (Accessed 16 June 2023).

Irwin, D., 2012. Trade Policy Disaster: Lessons from the 1930s. MIT Press, Cambridge, Massachusetts.

Kemoe, L., Mama, M.M., Mighri, H., Quayyum, S., 2023. African Currencies Are Under Pressure Amid Higher-for-Longer US Interest Rates. IMF Blog. https://www.imf.org/en/Blogs/Articles/2023/05/15/african-currencies-are-under-pressure-amid-higher-for-longer-us-interest-rates.

Kenton, W., 2022. International Currency Markets: Meaning, Overview. Investopedia. https://www.investopedia.com/terms/forex/i/international-currency-markets.asp.

Keohane, R., 1982. The demand for international regimes. Int. Organ. 36 (2), 325–355.

Keohane, R., Nye, J., 1977. Power and Interdependence: World Politics in Transition. Little, Brown and Company, Boston.

Komuves, A., 2022. Crown Firms After Central Bank Intervenes in Forex Market. Reuters. https://www.reuters.com/markets/europe/crown-firms-after-central-bank-intervenes-forex-market-2022-03-04/.

Kulikov, V., 2023. Economic Sanctions are Insufficient to Stop the War. Review of Democracy. https://revdem.ceu.edu/2023/03/24/economic-sanctions-are-insufficient-to-stop-the-war/.

Lechthaler, W., Mileva, M., 2018. Who benefits from trade wars? Intereconomics 53 (1), 22–26.

Lee, J.-W., Hyun, P.,J., 2009. Does Trade Integration Contribute to Peace? Asian Development Bank. Working Paper on Regional Economic Integration No. 24 https://www.adb.org/sites/default/files/publication/28499/wp24-trade-integration-peace.pdf.

Levy, J., Barbieri, K., 2004. Trading with the enemy during wartime. Secur. Stud. 13 (3), 1–47.

Lockett, H., Leng, C., 2023. The Renminbi's Share of Trade Doubles From 2 to 4.4%. Financial Times. https://www.ft.com/content/6d5bbdbc-9f5d-41b2-ba80-7d8ac3973cf3.

Magie, N., 2023. Regional Trade Networks. World History Project. OER Project. https://www.oerproject.com/OER-Materials/OER-media/PDFs/Origins/Era3/Regional-Trade-Networks.

Majaski, C., 2023. Devaluation: What It Is and How It Works. Investopedia. https://www.investopedia.com/terms/d/devaluation.asp.

Martin, P., Thoenig, M., Mayer, T., 2008. Civil wars and international trade. J. Eur. Econ. Assoc. 6 (2–3), 541–550.

McCormick, D., Pascoe, H., 2017. Sanctions and preventive war. J. Confl. Resolut. 61 (8), 1711–1739.

Mearsheimer, J., 1994–95. The false promise of international institutions. Int. Secur. 15 (3), 5–56.

Mitchener, K.J., O'Rourke, K.H., Wandschneider, K., 2022. The Smoot-Hawley trade war. Econ. J. 132 (October), 2500–2533.

Mulder, N., 2022. The Economic Weapon: The Rise of Sanctions as a Toll of Modern Warfare. Yale University Press, New Haven.

Oneal, J.R., Russett, B., 2000. Triangulating Peace: Democracy, Interdependence, and International Organizations. W. W. Norton, New York.

Ossa, R., 2014. Trade wars and trade talks with data. Am. Econ. Rev. 104 (12), 4104–4146.

Ossa, R., 2019. The costs of a trade war. In: Crowley, M.A. (Ed.), Trade War: The Clash of Economic Systems Endangering Global Prosperity. CEPR Press, London. https://cepr.org/system/files/publication-files/60137-trade_war_the_clash_of_economic_systems_threatening_global_prosperity.pdf.

Rana, W., 2015. Theory of complex interdependence: a comparative analysis of realist and neoliberal thoughts. Int. J. Bus. Soc. Sci. 6 (2), 290–297.

Resolution 661, 1990. Federation of American Scientists. https://web.archive.org/web/20000818054602/https://fas.org/news/un/iraq/sres/sres0661.htm.

Roberts, J., Bowden, J., 2022. The EU's Plans to Replace Russian gas: Aspirations and Reality. Atlantic Council. https://www.atlanticcouncil.org/blogs/energysource/the-eus-plans-to-replace-russian-gas/.

Rodgers, M., 2023. House Committee Approves Bill to Ban Russian Uranium Imports. American Nuclear Society. https://www.ans.org/news/article-5054/house-committee-approves-bill-to-ban-russian-uranium-imports/.

Rothgeb, J.M., 2001. U.S. Trade Policy: Balancing Economic Dreams and Political Realities. CQ Press, Washington, D.C.

Royal Geographical Society (n.d.). The Stone Age. https://www.rgs.org/CMSPages/GetFile.aspx?nodeguid=1809635c-3a57-4a4f-ac57-Clashbd4c218f33b8&lang=en-GB.

Ruble to Weaken Medium-Term Due to Declining Current Account Surplus – Commerzbank, 2023. FX Street Insights Team. https://www.fxstreet.com/news/usd-rub-ruble-to-weaken-medium-term-due-to-declining-current-account-surplus-commerzbank-202305091302.

Sadeh, T., Feldman, N., 2020. Globalization and wartime trade. Coop. Confl. 55 (2), 235–260.

Segal, T., 2021. Currency Fluctuations: How they Affect the Economy. Investopedia. https://www.investopedia.com/articles/forex/080613/effects-currency-fluctuations-economy.asp.

Sivabalan, S., 2022. Ruble Soars to 7-Year High Prompting Debate over Targeting Rate. Bloomberg. https://www.bloomberg.com/news/articles/2022-06-20/ruble-soars-to-seven-year-high-in-challenge-to-bank-of-russia#xj4y7vzkg.

Skok, Y., de Groot, O., 2022. War in Ukraine: Ukraine's Monetary-Financial Vulnerabilities. Center for Economic Policy Research. https://cepr.org/voxeu/columns/war-ukraine-ukraines-monetary-financial-vulnerabilities.

Sullivan, A., 2023. Russia's war economy staggers amid war chaos. Deutsche Welle. https://www.dw.com/en/vladimir-putin-power-and-regime-change-in-russia-depends-on-the-oil-price/a-66076602.

Syria Exchange Rate against USD: 1990-2023, 2023. CEIC Data. https://www.ceicdata.com/en/indicator/syria/exchange-rate-against-usd.

Tan, H., 2023. 5 Ways Russia's Been Sidestepping Western Sanctions and Keeping its Economy Alive, from Switching to the Chinese Yuan and Dabbling in Ghost Trades. Insider https://www.businessinsider.com/dedollarization-russia-ukraine-war-energy-oil-trades-sanctions-2023-5.

Thies, C.F., Baum, C.F., 2020. The effect of war on economic growth. Cato J. 2020 (Winter). https://www.cato.org/cato-journal/winter-2020/effect-war-economic-growth#references.

Wallerstein, I., 1979. The Capitalist World Economy. Cambridge University Press, Cambridge.

Warburton, C.E.S., 2009. War and exchange rate valuation. Econ. Peace Secur. J. 4 (1), 62–69.

What Are the Sanctions on Russia and Are They Hurting its Economy?, 2023. BBC. https://www.bbc.com/news/world-europe-60125659.

CHAPTER 7

Military contracting

At its simplest definition, military contractors are private organizations that are contracted by state militaries to provide services and supplies for military-related purposes. Military contractors have been part of war for many centuries, and they play a wide range of roles in international armed conflicts. While mercenary groups participated in international armed conflict long before modern standing armies, they still exist and are part of the picture in many military engagements, though often labeled differently. Beyond combatant roles, military contractors play roles that include manufacturing equipment and providing security, logistics, transportation, intelligence services, advising, training, and research services to combatant parties.

Policymakers have justified the use of military contractors as a step to bring about greater efficiency and flexibility in military functions, but no comprehensive data or study has been presented that proves this point. Others, such as the US Secretary of Defense, Donald Rumsfeld, championed the use of military contractors to permit military personnel to focus on the core war-fighting roles of the US military. Although the use of military contractors to provide services has permitted greater flexibility in meeting military needs, it comes at costs, financial and otherwise. Private military and security contractors have been used at times to prop up authoritarian regimes, such as in Liberia and Angola during their civil wars.

This chapter examines the development of military contractors and private military groups, as well as the recent change in the utility and function of both as a market. The subsequent discussion includes the following sections: the interactions between military contractors and private groups, and the political systems in which they operate; the impact of wars on defense companies; and the effects of military service providers on conflicts in which they take part. Furthermore, we delve into the human rights concerns associated with private military and security contractors, as well as efforts to regulate these actors. The chapter includes two case studies of the US experience with military contractors in wars in Afghanistan and Iraq and Russia's Wagner Group to show the current dynamics of private military markets and international conflicts. Finally, we conclude with a discussion

Markets and Conflict
https://doi.org/10.1016/B978-0-323-85525-9.00009-X

of lessons learned in the evaluation of military contractors and their impacts on society.

History of mercenaries and military contractors

While mercenaries have become taboo with the rise of modern, standing national armies in the past few centuries, fighting in wars for pay was considered to be an honorable profession in many societies for a far larger portion of human history. Mercenaries and mercenary armies have existed for over four millennia and were a regular feature of warfare. Large, permanent militaries are tremendously expensive, and rulers found themselves able to afford greater military capabilities if at least large portions were temporary mercenary forces. Such forces were used in many ancient societies, including Persia, Greece, Carthage, South Asia, and China to name a few. In both ancient societies and into the 17th and 18th centuries, there were both individual mercenaries and large companies that demonstrated an entrepreneurial approach toward those in charge of them. This included a wide range of situations, including loose arrangements, such as with privateers, formal purchases of fighting by mercenary bands, or large, independent companies that maintained their own militaries and essentially operated as contracted colonizers who sought profit, such as the Virginia Company and the British East India Company.

While mercenaries have played roles in supporting and strengthening kingdoms and early states at times, they also had the potential to threaten rulers and societies. This included out-of-work mercenaries extracting large ransoms from some city-states in Renaissance Italy, rogue mercenary units wreaking havoc during the 30 Years' War at times, and a large-scale mercenary rebellion in Ancient Rome (McFate, 2019). As modern state structures and institutions arose in the 17th and 18th centuries, they both permitted and normalized the large, modern administrative state. Military capabilities came to be increasingly common and integrated into modern expectations that place the monopoly on the legitimate use of force at the center of many definitions of a state. By the late 19th century, mercenaries were broadly seen as taboo and outlawed across most of the world.

Defining private military actors

While there is no universally shared definition of a mercenary, the term is generally used to refer to armed people, not in formal military service of a state, who are paid to carry out military operations in areas experiencing armed conflicts. Mercenaries could include people or groups actively engaged in combat operations, those providing armed security in conflict zones, or those hired to train military personnel in such a place. McFate (2019) identified five characteristics to distinguish mercenaries from terrorists, rebels, or soldiers in formal, state militaries. Profit-based motivation is perhaps the most important of these criteria, even if some mercenaries may also genuinely believe in the cause for which they are fighting. Toward this end as profit-seeking entities, mercenary groups are structured as private corporations, some of which have even been publicly traded. Additionally, they are distinguished from other security services in that they typically work outside their own countries, typically prioritize goals in their operations that are more similar to military rather than law enforcement organizations, and represent the lethal commodification of armed conflict. This typology holds even in cases where the mercenary groups are employed by states (McFate, 2019).

The terms private military contractor (PMC), private military and security contractor (PMSC), or private military firm (PMF) are often used today because the term mercenary has a negative connotation. Additionally, this emotionally charged term often distracts more than it helps to distinguish various actors in conflict zones and markets. Perhaps a more useful distinction could be that mercenaries are people working in this sort of capacity while PMCs, PMFs, or PMSCs are the companies that form a group under which the individuals operate. Private military firms are, in a sense, a modern, corporate version of mercenary organizations in which, rather than providing a military unit, modern PMFs provide a wide range of services that states, and other actors, can potentially utilize. One distinction between these private military actors and traditional mercenary groups is that many states today limit the roles that nonstate actors can play (Singer, 2005). Another way to potentially distinguish PMSCs from mercenary groups could be to consider PMSCs as moving into the realm of mercenaries when they are used as part of the core military efforts rather than to supplement core functions, such as war-fighting. In some cases, such as the use of Executive Outcomes in Sierra Leone or the Wagner Group in the Libyan Civil War or Ukraine, the lines have been blurred to the point that the label of mercenary force may be more appropriate (Swed and Burland, 2020).

Singer (2005) pointed out three forces that contributed in conjunction to the rise of these modern military firms in the 1990s. First, the end of the Cold War led states to decrease the size of their professional militaries, which both reduced the capacity of states and increased the availability of military operators, some of whom accepted lucrative opportunities to use their professional skills in the private market. Second, warfare in LDCs became more complicated and less professional on average, with many more forces employing child soldiers, and with wealthy countries being less willing to intervene in these messier situations. Third, advanced militaries in wealthy countries were at the same time coming to depend more heavily on private companies to maintain many of their functions, seeking to appear to have leaner governmental structures and perhaps internalizing neoliberal economic models. Due to this triangulation of factors, the world saw a new marketplace emerge that included private military firms coming to handle a range of functions that previously fell under state responsibilities (Singer, 2005).

Beyond the factors that Singer identified, many Western states revised their definitions of mercenaries to permit private military actors to, in many cases, play nearly any role other than the conduct of offensive operations. These legal changes aligned with a shift in norms to permit private actors to play a broader role in military operations. PMCs such as Sandline and Executive Outcomes actively promoted a revisiting of antimercenary norms in the late 20th century. While they were unsuccessful at fully legitimizing their roles or organizations, these and similar efforts played a role in enabling countries such as the United States and the United Kingdom, the leading employers of security contractors, to revisit their prohibitions on private military and security firms in the early 21st century (Petersohn, 2014).

The modern growth of military contractors

During the Cold War, many countries were in a constant state of military preparedness for various reasons. The US, USSR, many European countries, and others sought to deter a great power war or be prepared if such a war happened. They had built up large military arsenals for a war that never came. As the Cold War ended, the 1990s thus presented a confluence of factors that permitted the reemergence of modern military contractors, not only in the existing sectors of manufacturing and services but in a broad range of military and security services, including in armed capacities.

The breakup of the Soviet Union, liberalization of much of the former Soviet Bloc, and a gradual end to many civil wars, such as in Central America and parts of Africa, led to a perception that much smaller militaries were needed in many countries. Additionally, many states weakened as they lost the support of Cold War patrons. With the end of many prolonged conflicts and the Cold War, there was a surplus of both weaponry and former military personnel, many of whom needed jobs. Coupled with an ideological move toward liberalization and privatization in some countries as well as a move to end universal conscription in many countries, the stage was set for a reconsideration of the role of private military and security firms.

The 1990s revealed a shift in many countries in how they viewed both the legitimacy and utility of private military contractors compared to state military operators in performing a wide range of roles related to the military (Baum and McGahan, 2013). Around 1980, barely over 100 private military and security contractors (PMSCs) existed around the world. By 1990, this number had grown to nearly 300. By the year 2000, the number surpassed 500, peaking around 2012 at around 1200 PMSCs in operation. Most PMSCs are based in the US, the UK, South Africa, or China, with these four countries housing the headquarters of around 70% of PMSCs as of 2020, but PMSCs are headquartered in over 80 countries around the world (Swed and Burland, 2020).

With the Warsaw Pact dissolved and NATO countries largely moving to a peacetime footing, militaries declined in size. Due to pressures to maintain small militaries and a decline in regular conscription practices in many countries, the use of military contractors rose. While private companies have been used by the United States and other countries to produce military equipment for a long time, the regular use of contractors to provide military-related services, especially during peacetime, is a much more recent practice.

In the post-Cold War environment, the US military decreased its investment in support units within the military, prioritizing what it saw as core war-fighting roles. This shift necessitated the use of contractors to fulfill service roles that were previously performed by military personnel (Cancian, 2008). The DoD awarded its first Logistics Civil Augmentation contract to KBR (Kellogg, Brown, and Root) in 1992 for the company to provide laundry and dining services. Many noncombat service roles expanded dramatically following the US invasion of Iraq in 2003. Ultimately, a wide variety of contractors became involved in providing these services, greatly expanded by the 2003 war and in state-building missions in Iraq and Afghanistan (Gambone and McGarry, 2014). In FY 2021, the United States Department of Defense spent nearly $400 billion on military contractors, employing over a quarter million full-time equivalent positions in services provided on military contracts.

Today, approximately half of the US military budget is spent on contractor services. Military contractors play a large range of roles, including base construction, transportation, logistics services, base management roles, and some security functions. In the 21st century, Sweden has also expanded the role of contractors to support its military in various roles. This shift has been driven partially by its elimination of mandatory conscription in 2010 and a shift toward more liberalized economic policies (Berndtsson, 2014). Despite the reintroduction of conscription just 7 years later (Chandler, 2017), military contractors have continued to play major roles in Swedish defense. With Russia's invasion of Ukraine in 2022, Sweden has substantially increased its military budget (Milne, 2023), which has greatly bolstered military defense firms, such as Saab (Jungstedt, 2023).

The use of military contractors is often justified as a measure to decrease the costs and increase the quality of military goods and services, which benefits the public overall. These claims are, at a minimum, overstated and possibly wrong more often than they are right. For example, Peltier (2020) found that the high financial costs that the United States paid for the wars in Afghanistan and Iraq from 2001 to 2019, estimated at over $6.4 trillion, were inflated by payments to expensive military contractors. While military contractors are touted as forces that allow market-based efficiency measures to support military operations efficiently and effectively, contractors often lack the competitive pressures needed to minimize government costs. Many military contracts are awarded on a noncompetitive basis (45% of Pentagon contracts in 2019, for example), some contracts include lifetime service agreements with single suppliers, and competition is limited even in supposedly competitive bid processes.

Facing similar issues and cost overruns, the United Kingdom reformed some of its processes for defense procurement to create greater oversight of noncompetitive procurement and included measures aimed at improving the fairness, transparency, and efficiency of defense procurement systems and processes (Brooke-Holland, 2023). Many pieces of military hardware are so specialized that there is only one potential provider (Peltier, 2020). Even the basic market mechanisms do not provide the potential for effective market competition in many aspects of military contracts.

In other cases, militaries use private contractors because they do not have the ability to meet certain needs on their own. Some weak states use contractors to fulfill basic security, training, and logistics capabilities that they lack. Other states might be strong but seek deniability in their actions or have groups that can operate with looser rules, like the ability to recruit prisoners or foreign fighters. The Wagner Group played such a role even in a large-scale conflict on behalf of Russia in its invasion of Ukraine (Rampe, 2023). Even China, largely seen as an emergent power that can play a meaningful role in at least balancing against the United States, uses private contractors to augment its capabilities. In seaborne capabilities, the People's Liberation Army Navy relies heavily on private companies for assistance in naval logistics despite the substantial increases in China's naval capabilities. Based on recent exercises, China would need to use private ships to provide sufficient sealift capabilities in the event of a full-scale invasion of Taiwan (Honrada, 2023).

Military contractors as a market

Military material and service providers are often discussed in market terms, and in principle, the model is understandable and perhaps even desirable from the standpoint of governments. That said, for various reasons, military contracts do not operate in such a structure that we see market dynamics work effectively to boost efficiency and quality. Demand for goods and services produced by military contractors is relatively inelastic compared to most goods and services. Both the producers and consumers are limited in numbers, which limits the ability of the market to adjust and achieve equilibrium when prices become too high or too low. The limited number of producers and permissible consumers is due to a range of reasons, including national security concerns of governments in which contractors operate with highly specialized and sensitive programs. There are few companies (and sometimes only one) that can realistically provide the services or goods required in some cases. This is particularly the case in the development and production of complex weapons systems, and it is doubly so in the case of unique products developed by leading militaries to gain a strategic edge.

Furthermore, the time horizons do not allow for regular or frequent adjustments of consumption and production behaviors even when price signals would typically cause an adjustment by market actors. While many countries limit the length of military contracts, the largest military actors tend to have long development and procurement processes, especially for major weapons. While the largest militaries have a greater ability to dictate what weapon systems are developed, they often find themselves locked into these systems for long development processes and beyond. For example, major defense acquisitions by the US Department of Defense typically spend over a decade in development, and once a weapon system is slated for production, these weapons systems are in production with accompanying service contracts for years beyond the maximum contract length (*20 Years of Assessing DOD's Weapon Programs*, 2022).

Despite the US weapons manufacturers operating as private companies, they have much in common with Chinese companies that fulfill many similar roles. Both have little competition, have long time horizons, and often operate under cost-plus contracts, which limit incentives for efficiency (Curriden, 2023). US defense contractors are private, for-profit companies, but the defense industry has seen a consolidation that is similar to many other fields. Over the past few decades, military contracts have been concentrated in a relatively small number of countries. The top five arms contractors (Lockheed Martin, Boeing, Raytheon, General Dynamics, and Northrop Grumman) received about half of all DOD contracts in FY 2022. This concentration has left the Pentagon with limited choices, which decreases competition and increases exposure to potentially large price increases and decreases the ability of government officials to hold arms contractors accountable (Hartung, 2023).

Therefore, due to sunk costs and long lead time, even though government contracts in the US are limited to 5 years under the law (Contracts, 2023), the true commitments to weapons systems programs often extend many years beyond this period. When contract commitments are long, it creates a high level of stability for contractors, which plays a valuable role in getting them to commit to producing these systems, especially given governmental limitations in most countries on the export of weapons systems. While it is possible for manufacturers to sell weapons to foreign countries in some cases, such actions often require governmental approval. Additionally, changing major weapons systems, such as tanks or fighter jets, requires large additional costs after delivery as personnel are trained to use the new equipment.

Military contractors: Flexibility and entrenchment

While the role of military contractors as a tool to provide force flexibility is often discussed as a modern phenomenon, their use dates to ancient times. Prior to modern, professional militaries, rulers typically had relatively small standing forces. They used conscription to build their forces when larger ones were needed, but early rulers often used mercenary forces to expand their well-trained forces in times of conflict. While we often think of military contractors as a relatively modern phenomenon, rulers have long used them to accomplish a wide range of roles, including transport, food, logistics, and fighting. While direct combat roles for private forces became taboo in the modern state, many of these other roles persisted.

While certain types of military contractors project a steady presence, we can see boom and bust cycles of military contractors, often associated with a mixture of conflict prevalence and variations in legal structure and social expectations. In times of conflict, a military's needs can expand quickly, and training the necessary people within the military or bureaucratic structures takes time. Military contractors allow governments to potentially fulfill necessary roles quickly. In periods of extended conflicts where there is not a desire for large-scale military mobilization and where governments do not wish to move fully to a war footing, military contractors allow for the outsourcing of some roles that militaries might have played in the early to mid-20th century.

US military actions following the September 11th terrorist attacks offer a prime example of large-scale, long-term conflicts in which the government did not wish to institute a draft but nonetheless had a need to expand many military capabilities and resources rapidly. This case is discussed later in the chapter, but it serves as a prime example of a condition under which contractors can see a boom in demand, creating chaotic circumstances where oversight is slow to catch up. Even in circumstances of broad, societal mobilization, such as in the case of combatants during World War II, military contractors can either fill specialized gaps or play a valuable role in producing needed goods and expertise, especially in societies where nationalizing industries and running many large, state-owned enterprises may be undesirable.

Although military contractors are often promoted as a tool to permit force flexibility and decrease bloated governmental institutions, once their use is regularized, it can be difficult to stop using them. This entrenchment stems from multiple causes. First, contractors develop patterns of use by permanent government agencies that make it difficult for the military and others to operate without the contractors. Once a military role is outsourced, reinstitutionalizing it can be quite difficult. Second, once private contracts are established, especially within the borders of a country, they develop groups of people that depend on these contracts. Given this, eliminating them is not simply a budgetary matter but one that carries both primary and secondary economic impacts that can impact constituencies substantially.

Military industrial complex

In his farewell address, President Eisenhower warned about the influence that could be exerted over the policy and budgetary process by what he saw as the growing military-industrial complex. He saw the growing arms industry in the mid-20th century United States as creating a problematic influence on government. President Eisenhower argued that the military establishment plays a vital role in maintaining the peace by deterring potential aggressors. He viewed the increasingly influential arms industry as gaining, intentionally or not, a strong influence over legislatures at the local, state, and federal levels. While he recognized the need for weapons production, he nonetheless warned against the potential of this military-industrial complex to drive policy decisions and undermine democratic processes (Dunlap, 2011).

In his groundbreaking work, *The Iron Triangle*, Adams (1981) pointed to a driver of military spending that went beyond simple needs and policy interests. In the work, he argued that the industry made up of defense contractors exerts policy pressure on the government through a network of elected officials, bureaucratic agencies, and private firms in what he termed an iron triangle. More specifically, interest groups that operate on behalf of defense contractors interact with both members of Congress, especially on relevant defense and appropriations committees, and people working within the defense and oversight bureaucracy in ways that result in both Congress and the federal bureaucracy favoring defense firms, sometimes at the expense of the public.

Under the iron triangle model, interest groups provide electoral support to members of Congress through donations and PACs (in the modern era version). These same interest groups lobby Congress to support bureaucratic agencies and for legislation that ensures funding for and favorable regulation of defense contractors. This is accomplished through direct lobbying, actions taken by these interest groups in electoral politics, and in the manner that defense contractors build natural constituencies for themselves in the voting public (Adams, 1981). We can see similar mechanisms in the bureaucratic politics model applied by Jones (2001). Among other things, Jones pointed to the jobs that defense manufacturers bring to congressional districts as a powerful motivator for support of defense projects (Jones, 2001). Altogether, bureaucratic politics operating under the framework of the iron triangle model are credited with driving up defense spending in both the United States and beyond.

Many oversight experts are concerned about revolving door dynamics in which former government officials gain high-paying jobs in the private sector working for companies that lobby these same government agencies. These employees are seen as providing contractors with advantages in understanding government agencies, navigating bureaucratic structures, and negotiating effective deals for companies (Kenton, 2022). Many officials have retired from military or DOD civilian jobs and quickly gained high-paying jobs in the private sector working for defense contractors.

Oversight organizations often express concerns regarding these arrangements that include whether prospects of these jobs sometimes taint the decisions of officials in awarding contracts or provide an unfair advantage to the companies in gaining inside information or increased access to government officials and institutions. The General Accounting Office (GAO) has uncovered many worrisome patterns in the relationship between the DOD and for-profit companies, including a 2021 report that found that, between 2014 and 2019, over 1700 recently retired senior DOD and US military personnel, including many flag officers, working for 14 major arms manufacturers. The advantages brought to these companies through the revolving door tend to increase costs for the public, because these advantages allow companies to negotiate contracts that increase their profits (Summers, 2022).

The United States has faced increased pressures in the past few decades to privatize certain governmental functions and introduce elements of market competition into them. This same effect can be seen in defense contracting. Those desires, often at least as much ideologically driven as practically driven, don't always yield the benefits envisioned under a contracting system that was designed to encourage competitive bidding processes. Part of this is due to an increasing number of contracts being structured as cost-plus contracts, which shift all cost-related risks to the government rather than contractors, which lessens incentives for competition.

Additionally, there has been inadequate oversight and enforcement of contracts, including a frequent failure to use past performance evaluations in decisions to award or renew contracts. Part of the inefficiency is driven by a lack of adequate funding for these monitoring and compliance mechanisms, which is driven by the same desire to decrease the size of government functions as the push for using more contractors. Furthermore, contracting processes demonstrate preferential treatment for large, well-established firms that tend to have effective lobbying efforts (Berrios, 2006).

These iron triangle dynamics are found in varying shapes in many countries around the world, but the general findings are consistent and robust.

Other studies have found similar effects in a variety of countries. DeVore (2022) argues that the defense firms that are housed within a state tend to exercise distorting effects on political systems and decisions related to military procurement in the form of iron triangle dynamics that states can rarely escape. While DeVore (2022) argued that defense contractors do not make wars more likely as some of the most alarmist theories claim, iron triangle theories of the relationship between defense industries and governments have been robustly supported, though they do not always take precisely the same shape. Some of this variation depends on the institutions of regimes; the cultures of the countries; the size of defense contractors; and laws that regulate lobbying, interest groups, and defense firms (DeVore, 2022).

Importing weapons from other states makes sense as doing so creates competition among defense contractors for the business of those states, potentially increasing choices or decreasing prices due to competition. Despite these incentives, a high number of countries maintain domestic defense industries, even if not all have a wide range of products. Berman and Leff (2008) argue that countries support defense industries because they want to retain vital skills in their countries in case they need to increase production later, maintain the security of supplies, and sustain a comparatively higher level of adaptability than they might otherwise have.

In other words, countries, despite the knowledge of potential inefficiencies of maintaining domestic military production, support contractors in some cases as a hedge against potential future challenges. Sweden maintained a substantial weapons industry with many firms, in large part due to a wish to maintain its independence in neutrality. These industries have seen a renewed boost with increases in Sweden's defense spending in response to its worries about a security threat from Russia (Limmergard and Lindqvist, 2023), but even prior to this increase in spending, the Swedish government sought to maintain a strong defense industry despite occasional discomfort in parts of Swedish society with the notion of companies profiting from war (Jungstedt, 2023).

War and defense companies

Traditionally, defense stocks are seen as a safe haven and a great opportunity for investors during times of conflict for obvious reasons. With war and strategic uncertainty, countries are expected to increase their defense spending, and in the aggregate, wars do cause an increase in defense-related expenditures, including the use of private companies. After all, combatant parties need to purchase weapons, munitions, and nonlethal military supplies. Additionally, they must typically spend money to replenish their supplies that are drawn down during the war. A somewhat surprising negative effect for companies does come from the political ramifications of wars. While a defense company may see an increase in domestic and allied government demand for its products, wars are often accompanied by new export controls on military technology, even if a company's country is not directly involved. In addition, some actors may act more cautiously in long-term defense spending if they are concerned about the economic impacts of a war.

The military products and services of combatants are often the first targets of sanctions as these are seen as stoking conflict. Such trade restrictions cut off defense production and military service companies from sometimes lucrative revenue streams. Therefore, when evaluating investment opportunities associated with the threat and/or onset of war, firms and individuals are best served to take a cautious approach that considers a complex picture. The onset of war (especially a large war) tends to correlate with investors flocking to safer assets, which include well-established defense firms that are well positioned to benefit from the conflict and away from companies that face greater exposure to sanctions or other disruptions from the war (Zhang et al., 2022).

According to a study of US defense company performance during the post-Cold War era, stocks tend to see positive results from active armed conflicts, but they tend to see declines when conflicts end. Overall, defense stocks tend to have greater gains during periods of greater uncertainty with higher geopolitical volatility and a higher perceived likelihood of conflict onset or escalation. Budgetary announcements tend to be the point at which defense stocks see the most gains, pointing to stock prices responding more positively to news related to approved funding rather than speculative ones (Gurdgivev et al., 2022).

Russia's invasion of Ukraine shows complex ways in which defense markets can respond to a war. In the first 2 months following Russia's invasion of Ukraine, many major defense firms saw initial spikes in share values in the month following the war's start, but by the end of April, they decreased their financial forecasts and saw decreases in their stock values, which was largely attributed to sanctions and uncertainty (Goodkind, 2002). While the immediate picture for defense firms saw a slight decline in stock values and revenues, by the following year, many of the largest Western defense firms saw substantial increases in their revenues and stock share values, which were largely driven by the needs of the US and European militaries to replenish weapons and munitions that they had sent to Ukraine. By October 2023, many of these companies had lined up long-term contracts to increase production, especially to replace the vast numbers of artillery shells, missiles, and other munitions spent by Ukraine as well as to replace a wide range of equipment and vehicles sent from Western inventories to Ukraine (Stone, 2023).

A study of defense and aerospace firms found that Russia's invasion of Ukraine and the subsequent increases in defense spending increased the valuations of many defense firms in Europe and the United States. Within the first 2 months following Russia's invasion of Ukraine, major defense contractors in the United States saw increases in valuations of over 10% by the Fall of 2023, while the UK's BAE Systems, French Thalys, and German Rheinmetall saw share value gains of 22%, 48%, and 102%, respectively. Major, well-established defense contractors tend to see the greatest gains, especially those who are seen as best positioned to see increased demands for their products in the longer term because of the conflicts. Chinese and Indian weapons producers did not see similar large increases in share values, most likely because of the relatively neutral positions of their governments relative to the conflict (Zhang et al., 2022). Therefore while major defense companies in countries impacted by the onset of major conflicts often see benefits in share values the fastest, other firms will see profits and increases in share values once it becomes more certain how the conflict might impact them.

The United States and European countries have seen different results in their efforts to boost artillery shell production in response to the vast number of rounds that Ukraine has used in its war with Russia, depleting much of the stockpiles that these countries had to spare. Despite the broader prevalence of state-owned enterprises in most European countries compared to the US, the two countries have very different approaches to this sector than some might expect. The United States Army owns most of the artillery production facilities in the country and thus has a substantial ability to impact output levels with concerted effort and adequate funding.

In February 2022, the United States produced approximately 14,000 NATO-standard artillery shells per month. In December of that year, the army announced plans to increase production dramatically. In the 11 months since this announcement, the facilities have exceeded production rates targeted for the end of 2023 and have doubled production of 155 mm rounds. Based on early success, the US has increased its production goals, and if Congress approves the necessary funding, the army is confident that it can meet its goals of producing 100,000 artillery shells by the end of 2025, which is 2.5 times the original goal (Skove, 2023).

In EU countries, in comparison, these munitions are mostly produced by private firms. While European states can offer contracts to firms, they cannot order companies to invest in new facilities, increase automation, or operate facilities at increased hours or capacity. Additionally, according to a senior NATO military officer, the price of a standard 155 mm shell had risen four-fold from the start of the war to October 2023. The United States has not seen an increase in costs per unit on a similar scale (Skove, 2023).

The example of Western contractor response to the war in Ukraine pro-vides lessons on the fortunes and effectiveness of arms manufacturers. Wars do not necessarily lead to a rapid increase in the fortunes of defense contrac-tors. The processes by which defense production contracts are approved are slow, and war length is often far from certain. Once increased demand proves to create a long-term change in requirements, governments often respond by approving contracts to meet the needs presented by the conflict; however, a relatively small number of well-positioned, major companies can see rapid gains in the case of major wars.

In February 2022, most analysts did not anticipate that Russia and Ukraine would be locked in a prolonged, conventional conflict for well over a year. Once the shape of the conflict and the long-term security needs of the conflict became clearer, states responded by allocating contracts to meet the demands of the new security realities and expected futures. The Western responses to Russia's invasion of Ukraine, as well as Soviet production dur-ing World War II among others, point to advantages in state-driven efforts at increasing defense production rapidly and effectively with sufficient political will, and private arms manufacturers are not necessarily more efficient, espe-cially when there is not effective and centralized authority to compel actions of private actors.

Military service providers

Private military firms (PMFs) play a wider range of roles than many people realize, but these services can generally be broken down into three catego-ries: tactical military assistance, including direct combat roles; military sup-port firms, which provide services in support of direct military operations, including intelligence, logistics services, and technical and maintenance services; and military consulting services, which might provide strategic advice, training of military personnel, or social science research services

(Singer, 2005). Private military firms might play only one of these roles or all of them, depending on their structure and orientation.

While individual private military companies may vary in their intents, ethics, and accountability, the overall market for such services alters incentives for actors. Leander (2005) analyzed the PMC market to understand how the market for these actors impacts security and society in the world overall. She found that the use of private military actors does not build greater peace and security in the weakest African states that tend to use them. PMCs, like other actors and institutions, have a self-perpetuating tendency in which they tend to create processes where threats are redefined, and the roles of PMCs are expanded to meet these new strategic orientations (Leander, 2005). As with bureaucratic institutions within states, PMCs are prone to mission creep, not only due to the identification of new threats but as a reaction to perpetuate themselves.

Additionally, (Leander, 2005) found that the collective market for PMCs does not work to penalize bad actors in the sector as the most problematic behaviors are ultimately not seen as harmful by the actors (states and others) who employ them. Beyond the immediate impacts of these firms on altering security markets they enter and avoiding accountability, when states use private security firms, the more permanent state security apparatus is often undermined because of the perception of the relative effectiveness of these PMCs. This can lead to long-term dependence on these outside actors and a weaker state security apparatus Leander (2005). Overall, the weakening of state mechanisms tends to correlate with decreased public perception of legitimacy for the government and potentially for the regime, especially in the case of new regimes, which can create a dynamic that undermines the stability of the state in the long term. As states increasingly use private military firms, they must be careful that the expedient choice to employ private military firms does not create new problems.

PMSCs, human rights, and regulation

There are thousands of PMSCs operating around the world today. While they come from a wide range of countries, the most significant companies tend to originate from Russia, the United States, the UK, South Africa, or the People's Republic of China. Currently, no consistent international framework for regulating private military and security companies (PMSCs) exists. They are presumed to be accountable to the national laws of their host countries, and the host countries are presumed to be able to enforce these laws. PMSCs can escape accountability for at least two reasons: (1) PMSCs often operate within weak states and/or in places where the state's reach is limited, or (2) PMSCs may be employed under an agreement with an outside state whose interests do not always align with high levels of accountability for the PMSCs (Van Amstel and Rodenhauser, 2016).

Daumann (2022) found that, while the use of private military companies brings benefits to those who employ them, they can create negative externalities in the violation of national law and international humanitarian law in the countries where they operate, especially when their home country does not achieve effective regulation and control of such organizations. Regulation can come either in the form of rules applied to private military companies operating outside of the country, or such goals could be furthered through contracts made between security companies and those that employ them. For example, according to Tkach (2019), with the use of PMSCs in Iraq during the US occupation and its aftermath, the inclusion of performance incentives in contract structures tended to decrease the likelihood that contractors would use violence. To a lesser degree, the study found that competition tended to have a similar effect (Tkach, 2019).

While commercial military actors do not always commit offenses that harm civilian populations, any time that armed forces are operating among civilian populations there are concerns that violence will be used against civilians. Many have expressed concerns that commercial military actors are being used to commit atrocities against civilians on behalf of their clients, whether they are corporations, states, or other actors. In their analysis of CMAs, Penel and Petersohn (2022) found that firms systematically vary in the degree to which they comply with international norms on the treatment of civilians. They found that the variation is best explained by the degree to which the organizations face exposure to potential harm from international sanctions and the interest of the actors in maintaining the status quo of the current normative human rights order (Penel and Petersohn, 2022).

These findings complement those of Akcinaroglu and Radziszewski (2020), who found that military contractors in civil wars are less likely to commit human rights violations when the companies are publicly listed. According to their study, privately held companies are more likely to commit human rights violations than publicly traded companies, possibly because they can more easily reconstitute under a different name, such as Blackwater did in reforming as Xe following an infamous massacre by its operators in Iraq (Akcinaroglu and Radziszewski, 2020). Therefore, while the idea of people and firms trading stocks in PMSCs may create moral discomfort on its surface, publicly traded companies seem to be more likely to adhere to human rights norms than privately held companies.

In the 21st century, private military and security companies have become more visible, in part due to egregious human rights violations committed by actors in high-profile cases, such as civilian murders by Blackwater contractors in Iraq. Such incidents have led to the perception by some that such organizations are unaccountable in their operations. Efforts to regulate private military actors come in multiple forms, including national-level efforts, binding international agreements, and voluntary agreements. While efforts at binding international agreements, such as the UN mercenary convention, have not garnered the necessary support to formulate a formal agreement, voluntary international efforts, such as the Montreux agreement and the International Code of Conduct for Private Security Providers (ICoC), have found greater levels of success.

The Montreux Document arose from cooperation between the government of Switzerland and the ICRC to bridge the gap in practicality if not in formal legal code. The document clarified which existing laws apply to PMSCs, and it created a set of recommendations for states that employ PMSCs so they can ensure that these organizations are held accountable under international humanitarian law (Van Amstel and Rodenhauser, 2016). The International Code of Conduct for Private Security Providers (ICoC) was developed by the International Code of Conduct Association (ICoCA), which is an association made up of states, private security companies, and civil society organizations (*ICoC,* 2010).

The impact of private military contractors on societies and markets depends largely on the state in which or for which they are operating. While much of the earlier discussion involves the operation of military contractors in relatively wealthy states, military contractors play broad roles in less developed countries that are complex and potentially problematic. While private military and security companies can provide well-trained, professional forces for governments with comparatively weak states, this boost in state capabilities can potentially work to undermine the rule of law. UN working groups on the use of mercenaries found that such groups can destabilize countries and participate in human rights violations, including forced disappearances, sexual violence, unlawful detention, and extrajudicial killings (*Mercenaries, Private Military Contractors,* 2018).

Private military and security companies (PMSCs) are not only used by states and private companies to improve security. They are also used by IGOs and NGOs in humanitarian missions. While militarization of humanitarian missions may be necessary in some cases, it inherently involves the potential to undermine a sense of local ownership over peacebuilding efforts. The use of profit-driven PMSCs creates further complications (De Groot and Regilme, 2022). In their study of PMSCs in conflict zones, Akcinaroglu and Radziszewski (2020) demonstrated that companies that face higher levels of competition tend to be more effective. They argue that competition, along with being publicly traded, increases the perceived importance of reputation for private military and security companies. These self-interested incentives drive an increased sense of corporate professionalism, which in turn drives incentives for PMSCs to control corruption, improve effectiveness, and maintain higher levels of compliance with international humanitarian law and other laws regulating their operation. While the idea of people and institutions buying and selling stocks in private military and security companies may be unsettling, utilizing publicly traded companies more, compared to privately held ones, may help to improve the human rights records of PMSCs.

Military contractors in the US wars in Iraq and Afghanistan

The terrorist attacks of September 11th, 2001 shook society in the United States to the core. One of the most substantial aspects of the governmental response to these attacks was a dramatic expansion of military efforts overseas while not engaging the public in the type of large-scale mobilization that one would traditionally see during wartime. Given the dangerous environment in which these contractors operated in Iraq, they developed their own security forces. Additionally, the United States hired some contractors in security roles (Gambone and McGarry, 2014). At the height of contractor use in FY 2009, over 20,000 private military and security contractors were employed by the United States in Afghanistan and Iraq (Peters, 2021). These contractors included local nationals, US citizens, and citizens of third countries.

In the drive to insulate itself from costs and to obtain flexibility in military expenditures, the United States government expanded its use of military contractors to provide a wide range of services. In the long term, it is unclear whether the use of military contractors leads to the cost savings policymakers may have hoped to achieve. From 2001 to 2019, US defense spending on military contractors grew by over 160%, from $140 billion to $370 billion (*Corporate Power, Profiteering, and the "Camo Economy"*, 2021). A report from the Project on Government Oversight found that, in FY 2010, the

Department of Defense spent nearly three times as much on people employed by private firms to perform similar jobs compared with civilian DoD employees (Amey, 2012).

The greatly expanded use of military service providers allowed the United States to expand its capabilities quickly as companies could draw on a global pool of resources and expertise; however, this came at a cost. While doing so arguably increased the effectiveness of military forces somewhat, it came with a cost in terms of accountability and arguably to the values that the US and others hold as important. This could, at times, harm mission effectiveness. Actions by some PMSCs in Iraq and Afghanistan contributed to local corruption as these organizations paid bribes to local officials, helped to fund the Taliban and other groups, and committed human rights abuses that were both intrinsically bad and in practical terms were detrimental to efforts to build a sense of local buy-in to US goals (Avant and Nevers, 2011).

In its operations in Afghanistan and in the occupation of Iraq following the 2003 invasion, the United States heavily used private military contractors to play a wide variety of roles, including the security of government officials and installations, escorting supplies, providing services to US bases in the country, building installations, and many more things. The expansion in the use of contractors for this operation was so fast and unprecedented that the US government was unable to effectively oversee the contractors and hold them accountable consistently. Many attempts to quantify the amounts lost through ineffective oversight of contracting processes were undertaken by the various agencies within the US government. The Commission on Wartime Contracting analyzed contracts in Iraq and Afghanistan and found that, as of August 2011, somewhere in the range of $31 billion to $60 billion had been lost due to fraud and waste (Schartz and Church, 2013).

Beyond money lost to fraud, inefficiencies, and contractor profits, contractor use undermined US strategy in the countries and helped to fuel the recruiting efforts and arguments of anti-American insurgents. Abuses by contractors included mistreatment and abuse of local nationals in Iraq and Afghanistan. These actions included notorious cases of murder, torture, and abuse in both countries. While there have been abuses by military personnel directly, professional norms are clearer, and military justice systems allow for clear mechanisms for punishing offenders, imperfect though they may be. Perhaps the most notorious of these incidents was the prisoner abuse scandal at the Abu Ghraib prison in Iraq (Schartz and Church, 2013). Beyond the problems in terms of public relations, contractors caused strategic problems for US objectives at times. For example, contractors and subcontractors are known to have paid the Taliban and other insurgent groups for protection in parts of Afghanistan that were insecure (Schartz and Church, 2013).

By 2007, contracting had grown so large and was riddled with such problems that Senators Jim Webb and Claire McCaskill introduced a bill to create a commission to oversee wartime contracting in Iraq and Afghanistan. The creation of this committee was included in the National Defense Authorization Act for Fiscal Year 2008, which passed through Congress and was signed into law by President Bush in January 2008. The law also included the creation of the Special Inspector General for Afghanistan Reconstruction (SIGAR) and the Special Inspector General for Iraq Reconstruction (SIGIR) to provide independent oversight of reconstruction projects in Afghanistan and Iraq, respectively.

The commission carried out activities over the next few years in which time it sought to identify problems in military contracting and recommend reforms to address these shortcomings. In June 2011, the commission issued its final report (*Commission on Wartime Contracting,* 2011). In the report, the commission produced a thorough overview of the use of military contractors in Iraq and Afghanistan, and it issued a set of recommendations to correct flaws that it found in the system. The commission found that these problems stemmed from a lack of communication among agencies, a failure to consider the long-term implications and costs at the start of contracts, limited competition for contracts, and inadequate oversight and enforcement mechanisms (*Transforming Wartime Contracting,* 2011).

The aftermath of this increased scrutiny on military contracting demonstrated some of the difficulties. Attached to the defense appropriation bill for FY 2008, President Bush issued signing statements in which he sought to ensure that executive authority and flexibility were not lost beyond what was required under the law and permitted under the US Constitution (Froomkin, 2008). SIGAR increased scrutiny; issued comprehensive reports on many contractor activities; and made many robust recommendations to improve efficiency, effectiveness, and accountability. In many ways, the organization operated as it was envisioned, and those within it performed their work admirably, but SIGAR had no mandate to make changes directly.

While the organization made recommendations to the DOD, other executive organizations, and Congress, the responses were limited. Many of the most important problems identified by SIGAR did not involve contractors; however, the organization found that contractors' actions exacerbated existing problems, including corruption and ethnic tensions. Moreover, SIGAR found that advisers were often poorly trained or inexperienced and that U.S. logistics, training, and weapons procurement policies were counterproductive to building an effective and self-sustaining military or police force in Afghanistan (Sullivan, 2023).

While the reports were detailed and thorough, and they identified problems in the reconstruction and war-fighting efforts, Congress did not use its legislative powers to effectively hold the executive branch accountable. While the speed of the collapse of the Islamic Republic of Afghanistan in the wake of the Taliban advance stunned many people, the seeds of the state's weakness and eventual failure were far from unpredictable, and perhaps an effective inspector general early in the state-building process with cooperating policy partners could have created a different story. Perhaps this experience can provide lessons for future postconflict reconstruction projects (Sullivan, 2023).

Wagner Group

In examining the rise and fall of the Wagner Group, it is hard to tell whether its example will do more to encourage or discourage state use of private military and security companies in the future. The infamous group has seen action in combat in a wider range of theaters, including Mali, the Central African Republic, Syria, Ukraine, and other countries. At its height, during Russia's invasion of Ukraine, the Wagner Group was estimated to have approximately 50,000 fighters engaged in the Ukraine war alone. Yevgeny Prigozhin, the former head of the organization, eventually became a vocal critic of Russia's execution of the war. These events escalated during the assault on the Ukrainian city of Bakhmut in the summer of 2023, which culminated in a depleted Wagner Group carrying out actions that many equated to a failed coup (Dunigan, 2023).

Due to Russian laws that formally outlawed PMCs, the Wagner Group existed in somewhat of a murky area for many years. Some viewed private armies of this type as potential threats to the security of the Russian state, while others tacitly acknowledged that private armies already existed in effect in the forms of private security forces already permitted for firms such as Gazprom. That said, despite the technically illegal nature of PMCs during the 2010s in Russia, employment of the Wagner Group outside of the country allowed Russia to conduct certain operations with a veil of plausible deniability (Marten, 2022). The organization, like other Russian PMCs, has operated in something of a private-public partnership with the Russian state (Bowen, 2023). The Wagner group in many ways operates as a mechanism of the Russian state with close ties to the GRU, and it has often recruited and trained Russian military veterans and, at times, operated Russian Air Force planes (Marten, 2022).

The Wagner Group was established by Yevgeny Prigozhin and Dmitry Utkin (a former officer in GRU (Russia's military foreign intelligence service). By 2014, the Wagner Group had formally emerged from a previous mixture of private predecessor organizations. In its first formal year of existence, it operated in Crimea as part of the operation to take control of the Peninsula and stir up insurrections within Ukraine. In the same year, the organization expanded operations in Syria that were started by a predecessor group, Slavonic Corp (Wagner Group: Organizational Overview, 2023).

Operations by the Wagner Group in Ukraine and Syria during 2015 and 2016 demonstrate a close relationship between the organization and the Russian military, including the group receiving Russian air support during operations in Syria. Wagner Group troops were often used in the most difficult fighting in the operation to retake Palmyra from ISIS, and they played important roles in military operations in the Donbas region of Ukraine. By using the group, Russia gained a few advantages. The Russian government could direct involvement in military operations inside Ukraine more easily; create a level of deniability related to war crimes in Syria; and perhaps most importantly, limit official Russian casualty figures in military operations (Marten, 2019). The organization managed to skirt PMC regulations in Russia by using a complex set of companies and other organizations in a complex structure. In fact, from 2014 to 2022, there was no entity formally registered as the Wagner Group (Wagner Group: Organizational Overview, 2023).

Throughout its history, the Wagner Group has generally operated as a tool for the Russian state to pursue its interests. While the Wagner Group has earned substantial profits from its activities, they generally align with the wishes of the Russian government in most cases. Its actions at times even draw comparisons to the notorious booty futures that shady private companies used in which they armed rebel groups to take valuable resources that the rebels would grant the companies contracts to exploit. For example, one of Wagner's affiliates earned a percentage of the profits from oil fields that it recaptured in Syria. In the Central African Republic, Prigozhin's commercial mining companies gained mining rights in exchange for Wagner's military services. In the years since 2018, the Wagner Group has come to play a significant role in many countries in Africa, including the Central African Republic, Madagascar, Mali, Mozambique, Libya, and Sudan (Rampe, 2023).

Beyond direct combat operations, the Wagner Group has been used as a channel by the Russian government to support groups with a level of plausible deniability. The organization has been used as a flexible organization that can effectively deliver logistical capabilities and act as an expeditionary force for Russia or other governments. The Wagner Group provides advice to governments, trains forces on the ground where required, and participates in security and combat operations directly (Blazakis et al., 2003).

The organization grew effectively by closely affiliating itself with the Russian state and becoming an organization that both generated substantial profits and served as an effective tool of Russian foreign and defense policy. In some cases, like in Syria and Ukraine, the Wagner Group even coordinated combat operations with the formal Russian military. The two built a close relationship in which the Wagner Group served as a continuous contractor, and arguably as an informal part of the Ministry of Defense. This has provided advantages in effectiveness for both parties, but it has also exposed Wagner and Prigozhin to sanctions from the United States and other countries (Bowen, 2023).

Russia's invasion of Ukraine saw the Wagner Group grow quickly to unprecedented heights. At its height, the group is estimated to have had over 50,000 fighters engaged in the war in Ukraine (Dunigan, 2023). It did so in part by recruiting convicted people from Russia's prisons and enlisting them to fight in exchange for their freedom. Wagner mercenaries engaged in much of the most difficult fighting, especially in the Donbas region. While the Wagner leadership seemed satisfied with using their personnel in much of the most dangerous duties, during the battle for Bakhmut in 2023, Prigozhin became increasingly and publicly critical of the Kremlin's conduct of the war, including alleging that Russian leadership was withholding artillery support from his troops. In mid-June, the Russian government became increasingly worried about its ability to control the Wagner Group fighters, and it demanded that they all sign contracts with Russia's Ministry of Defense and become formally and fully under military command. Following this demand, Prigozhin only increased the intensity of his attacks on Russian military leadership (Yaffa, 2023).

On June 23rd, the Wagner Group started what Prigozhin called a "march for justice" in which he led the remaining forces (about 25,000) on a march into Russia where they occupied the regional headquarters in

Rostov-on-Don and demanded that Shoigu (Defense Minister) and Gerasimov (military head of Russia's armed forces) be brought to him to face justice. The mercenary group began to march toward Moscow, shooting down two Russian military aircraft along the way. Prigozhin had insisted during the course of the uprising that their actions were not against the regime in Russia, but President Putin denounced Wagner's actions as treason. On June 24th, Putin publicly denounced the uprising as an act of treason against the Russian state. Shortly afterward, Prigozhin accepted a deal in which he and his remaining fighters would leave Russia and move to Belarus. Some of the organization's fighters eventually joined the formal Russian military, and others continued to operate under the Wagner Group in various countries. Prigozhin and Utkin, the founders of the Wagner Group, died in an August plane crash in Russia that seems likely to have been caused by a bomb within the plane (Bagaeva et al., 2023). The Wagner Group provides a cautionary tale against overreliance on a large defense contractor. While the organization will likely continue to operate in some form in other countries, the Russian government is unlikely to experiment with such a large, independent military force soon.

Conclusions

Military contractors play a substantial role in modern warfare by providing a wide range of products and services, primarily to state actors but also to others in conflict zones. Military equipment manufacturers are used heavily in the development and production of weapons. In the late 20th century, many states began to increasingly use military contractors to provide non-combat services in a wide range of areas, including construction, food and laundry service, maintenance, education, translation, intelligence, and many other areas. Beyond these, private military and security are used by states in a wide variety of roles and places. States with strong militaries often use armed private military and security contractors in their foreign operations. Doing so provides them with a politically viable route to procure flexible and expandable resources that they utilize. Weak states use private military and security contractors to augment their weak capacity with a force that has internal structures and training already established. In the past decade, the world has seen more frequent use of PMSCs in a manner that has come to resemble the old roles of mercenary groups (Swed and Burland, 2020).

Military contractors often make fortunes from both war and the preparation for war. While contractors can profit from wars, conflicts are unpredictable in scope, shape, and length. In many cases, if they profit from wars, it is once the shape of the conflict is more known. Many wars last only a short time or operate at a low level, and therefore such conflicts do not have substantial impacts on military contractors directly. Defense firms can see substantial boosts in their stock prices with the onset of major conflicts, especially if they are viewed as well positioned to profit from a war. In the case of the Ukraine war, many defense contractors saw a short-term spike in share values, followed by a substantial return downward toward normal share prices, and once long-term contracts were approved and profits started to come in, they saw their share values steadily increase. This example demonstrates the principle that, while speculation can create profits for early investors in the short term, these initial spikes can fade, and it is only once large contracts that impact the earnings picture are locked in that more substantial profits are realized. In most cases, long-term contracts generate far more revenue. A large portion of military budgets are spent on strategic balance, deterrence forces, and planning for wars that do not happen. These military expenditures are far more reliable and steadier than wars themselves. Therefore military equipment manufacturers tend to see a lagged effect in profits from wars and benefit far more from steady, peacetime contracts on average, especially given the substantial decline in large, interstate wars in the past half-century or more.

Private military contractors can gain substantial revenues from wars, but they are far better served if they can provide long-term services to relatively permanent military installations and functions. These companies provide many long-term services that include education, training, construction, logistics, food and laundry services, information technology support, and many more functions. Even in companies that provide security-related services, they earn more in most cases from long-term missions. PMSCs were not highly involved in the active war-fighting stages in Afghanistan in 2001 or Iraq in 2003, but they were highly involved in state building efforts where the occupation forces faced insurgencies.

Various actors must understand how military contractors function individually and how they work collectively as a market. The use of military contractors creates an additional step of removal from the ultimate agents, which creates the inherent risk of agency loss. The hope is that the use of contractors will produce gains in efficiency or improved qualities that will offset any potential loss. Even in cases where there is sufficient competition in a specific market to potentially achieve such gains, the use of contractors may result in an erosion of state capacity in the long term, especially true in the case of relatively low-capacity states that employ private military and security companies to perform basic security functions that are seen as essential state roles. The use of such companies decreases the incentives and likelihood for the state to develop such capacities. Additionally, it runs the risk of undermining the legitimacy of the state in the eyes of its people. Particularly if underlying grievances of conflicts are not addressed, the appearance of foreign contractors propping up the state, especially if they are involved in activities that are seen as exploitative, increases the ability of rebel groups to recruit new people to their cause.

States often justify the use of contractors as either a necessity or as a route to improve the efficiency and flexibility of military functions. Private military manufacturers may be preferable from the standpoint of ideology and an interest in avoiding bloated state-owned enterprises, but they are not always more efficient economically, especially in situations where competition is limited and there are few actors in the market. Moreover, state-directed efforts (whether through SOEs or the power to compel production in private industry) have advantages in making rapid shifts in production, given sufficiently strong and coordinated institutions with political will. PMSCs offer states flexibility and the ability to carry out military and security operations at a lower political cost with ready-trained personnel; however, they come at a cost, which can include results that involve waste, human rights abuses, and actions that undermine mission effectiveness or the state itself.

Military contractors are a large and ever-increasing part of modern conflicts. They create substantial challenges to governments as states seek to maintain their power and navigate how best to use military contractors to their advantage. Defense production firms offer substantial products to help states advance their security interests, but oversight and regulation of this sector are important to achieve efficient outcomes and maintain accountability of both the firms and government officials. The complicated sets of interests for states, and the limited numbers of highly specialized firms, can frustrate the ability of military-industrial production to operate as an efficient market. While private firms provide states with the ability to supplement their military capabilities, gain flexibility in operations, and distance themselves somewhat from the consequences of their decisions, the use of these actors comes at a cost. As states employ private military and security contractors, they run into a classic principal-agent problem in which the agent has the potential to harm the goals of the principal or be inefficient. Finally, regulation of contractor effectiveness and adherence to human rights norms are a major challenge for states and other international actors which remains to be addressed. While the use of military contractors may be an unavoidable part of modern warfare, states and other actors must pay attention to the realities and implications of the use of private military firms so that they can make fully informed decisions.

References

20 Years of Assessing DOD's Weapon Programs Shows the Importance of Having the Right Information Before Making Investment Decisions. 2022. U.S. Government Accountability Office. https://www.gao.gov/blog/20-years-assessing-dods-weapon-programs-shows-importance-having-right-information-making-investment-decisions.

Adams, G., 1981. The Iron Triangle: The Politics of Defense Contracting. Transaction Publishers, New Brunswick. In press.

Akcinaroglu, S., Radziszewski, E., 2020. Private Militaries and the Security Industry in Civil Wars: Competition and Market Accountability. Oxford University Press, New York.

Amey, S., 2012. DoD contractors cost nearly 3 times more than DoD civilians. In: Project on Government Oversight. https://www.pogo.org/analysis/dod-contractors-cost-nearly-3-times-more-than-dod-civilians.

Avant, D.D., Nevers, R., 2011. Military contractors & the American way of war. Daedalus 140 (3), 88–99.

Bagaeva, A., Shumskaia, N., Osborne, M., 2023. Bodies from Yevgeny Prigozhin Plane Crash Contained 'Fragments of Hand Grenades,' Russia says. ABC News. https://abcnews.go.com/International/bodies-yevgeny-prigozhin-plane-crash-contained-fragments-hand/story?id=103762202.

Baum, J.A.C., McGahan, A.M., 2013. The reorganization of legitimate violence: the contested terrain of the private military and security industry during the post-cold war era. Res. Organ. Behav. 33 (1), 3–37.

Berman, E., Leff, J., 2008. Light weapons: products, producers, and proliferation. In: Small Arms Survey 2008. Cambridge University Press, Cambridge.

Berndtsson, J., 2014. Realizing the "market-state"? Military transformation and security outsourcing in Sweden. Int. J. 69 (4), 542–558. https://doi.org/10.1177/0020702014542813. In press.

Berrios, R., 2006. Government contracts and contractor behavior. J. Bus. Ethics 63 (2), 119–130.

Blazakis, J., Clarke, C.P., Chowhury Fink, N., Steinberg, S., 2003. Wagner Group: The Evolution of a Private Army. The Soufan Center Special Report. https://thesoufancenter.org/wp-20 yearcontent/uploads/2023/06/TSC-Special-Report-The-Wagner-Group-The-Evolution-Of-Putins-Private-Army.pdf.

Bowen, A.S., 2023. Russia's Wagner Private Military Company (PMC). Congressional Research Service. https://crsreports.congress.gov/product/pdf/IF/IF12344.

Brooke-Holland, L., 2023. Defence Procurement Reform: The Single Source Contract Regulations. House of Commons Library. https://researchbriefings.files.parliament.uk/documents/CBP-9645/CBP-9645.pdf.

Cancian, M., 2008. Contractors: the new element of military force structure. Parameters 38 (3), 61–77.

Chandler, A., 2017. Why Sweden Brought Back the Draft. The Atlantic. https://www.theatlantic.com/international/archive/2017/03/sweden-conscription/518571/.

Commission on Wartime Contracting in Iraq and Afghanistan. 2011. https://cybercemetery.unt.edu/archive/cwc/20110929222001/http://www.wartimecontracting.gov/docs/CWCoverview.pdf.

Contracts, 2023. Federal Acquisition Registration. https://www.acquisition.gov/far/17.204.

Corporate Power, Profiteering, and the "Camo Economy". 2021. Watson Institute for International & Public Affairs. Costs of War https://watson.brown.edu/costsofwar/costs/social/corporate.

Curriden, C., 2023. The Chinese Acquisition Process. Testimony presented before the U.S.-China Economic and Security Review Commission. https://www.rand.org/content/dam/rand/pubs/testimonies/CTA2600/CTA2691-1/RAND_CTA2691-1.pdf.

Daumann, F., 2022. Potential Negative Externalities of Private Military Entrepreneurs from an Economic Perspective. Defense and Peace Economics.

De Groot, T., Regilme, S.S.F., 2022. Private military and security companies and the militarization of humanitarianism. J. Dev. Soc. 38 (1), 50–80.

DeVore, M.S., 2022. Military-industrial complexes and their variations. Politics. In: The Oxford Encyclopedia of the Military in Politics. Oxford University Press, Oxford.

Dunigan, M., 2023. The Wagner Group Will Live to Fight Another Day. Frand Corporation. https://www.rand.org/pubs/commentary/2023/06/the-wagner-group-will-live-to-fight-another-day.html.

Dunlap, C., 2011. The military-industrial complex. Daedalus 140 (3), 135–147.

Froomkin, D., 2008. Bush Thumbs Nose at Congress. The Washington Post.

Gambone, M.D., McGarry, J.J., 2014. A wolf by the ears: U.S. policy failures, reform, and the necessity of private military security contractors, 2003-2013. Yale J. Int. Aff. 9 (1), 25–39.

Goodkind, N., 2002. Defense Companies Aren't Getting a Boost from Russia's War with Ukraine. CNN. https://www.cnn.com/2022/04/28/investing/defense-stocks-russia-ukraine/index.html.

Gurdgiev, C., Henrichsen, A., Mulhair, A., 2022. The budgets of wars: analysis of the U.S. defense stocks in the post-cold war era. Int. Rev. Econ. Finance 82 (November), 335–346.

Hartung, W., 2023. New Revelations Underscore Need To Curb Defense Revolving Door. Forbes. https://www.forbes.com/sites/williamhartung/2023/05/03/new-revelations-underscore-need-to-curb-defense-revolving-door/?sh=32c6c50562a0.

Honrada, G., 2023. China Would Use Commercial Ferries to Invade Taiwan. Asia Times. https://asiatimes.com/2023/10/china-would-use-commercial-ferries-to-invade-taiwan/.

Jones, C.M., 2001. Roles, politics, and the survival of the V-22 osprey. J. Political Mil. Sociol. 29 (Summer), 46–72.

Jungstedt, C., 2023. Sweden's Saab Comes In From Cold as Investors Return to Defense. Bloomberg. https://www.bloomberg.com/news/articles/2023-05-31/sweden-s-saab-comes-in-from-cold-after-putin-invaded-ukraine#xj4y7vzkg.

Kenton, W., 2022. Revolving Door: Definition in Business and Government. Investopedia. https://www.investopedia.com/terms/r/revolving-door.asp.

Leander, A., 2005. The market for force and public security: the destabilizing consequences of private military companies. J. Peace Res. 42 (5), 605–622. https://doi.org/10.1177/0022343305056237. In press.

Limmergard, R., Lindqvist, J., 2023. Swedish Defence-Instrial Capabilities Shine Bright. European Security & Dence. https://euro-sd.com/2023/06/articles/31839/swedish-defence-industrial-capabilities-shine-bright/.

Marten, K., 2019. Russia's use of semi-state security forces: the case of the Wagner group. Post-Sov. Aff. 35 (3), 181–204.

Marten, K., 2022. Russia's Use of the Wagner Group: Definitions, Strategic Objectives, and Accountability. Testimony before the Committee on Oversight and Reform, Subcommittee on National Security. United States House of Representatives. https://docs.house.gov/meetings/GO/GO06/20220921/115113/HHRG-117-GO06-Wstate-MartenK-20220921.pdf.

Mercenaries, Private Military Contractors Can Destabilize Rule of Law, Expert Tells Third Committee, amid Calls to End Racism, Respect Migrant Rights. 2018. Meetings Coverage and Press Releases, United Nations. https://press.un.org/en/2018/gashc4246.doc.htm.

McFate, S., 2019. Mercenaries and War: Understanding Private Armies Today. https://ndupress.ndu.edu/Portals/68/Documents/strat-monograph/mercenaries-and-war.pdf. (Accessed 21 October 2023).

Milne, R., 2023. Sweden to Boost Defence Spending Next Year by Almost 30%. Financial Times. https://www.ft.com/content/d1afa268-a59b-4299-9b27-b8d716819417.

Peltier, H., 2020. The Growth of the "Camo Economy" and the Commercialization of the Post-9/11 Wars. Costs of War. Watson Institute for International & Public Affairs. Brown University. https://watson.brown.edu/costsofwar/papers/2020/growth-camo-economy-and-commercialization-post-911-wars-0.

Penel, C., Petersohn, U., 2022. Commercial military actors and civilian victimization in Africa, Middle East, Latin America, and Asia, 1980-2011. J. Glob. Secur. Stud. 7 (1), 1–19.

Peters, S.V., 2021. Department of Defense Contractor and Troop Levels in Afghanistan and Iraq: 2007-2020. Congressional Research Service. https://sgp.fas.org/crs/natsec/R44116.pdf.

Petersohn, U., 2014. Reframing the anti-mercenary norm: private military and security companies and Mercenarism. Int. J. 69 (4), 475–493.

Rampe, W., 2023. What is Russia's Wagner Group Doing in Africa? Council on Foreign Relations. https://www.cfr.org/in-brief/what-russias-wagner-group-doing-africa.

Schartz, M., Church, J., 2013. Department of Defense's Use of Contractors to Support Military Operations: Background, Analysis, and Issues for Congress. Congressional Research Service, pp. 7–7500.

Singer, P., 2005. Outsourcing war. Foreign Aff. 82 (2), 119–132.

Skove, S., 2023. Army Spending $1.5B on 155mm Rounds to Feed Ukrainian Artillery. https://www.defenseone.com/threats/2023/10/army-spending-15b-155mm-rounds-feed-ukrainian-artillery/391040/. (Accessed 18 November 2023).

Stone, M., 2023. Ukraine War Orders Starting to Boost Revenues for Big US Defense Contractors. Reuters. https://www.reuters.com/business/aerospace-defense/ukraine-war-orders-starting-boost-revenues-big-us-defense-contractors-2023-10-27/.

Sullivan, P.J., 2023. Auditing Failure: The Special Inspector General for Afghanistan Reconstruction, 2012-2021. https://hdl.handle.net/11264/1462.

Summers, R., 2022. The Pentagon's Revolving Door Keeps Spinning: 2021 in Review. Project on Government Oversight. https://www.pogo.org/analysis/the-pentagons-revolving-door-keeps-spinning-2021-in-review.

Swed, O., Burland, D., 2020. The Global Expansion of PMSCs: Trends, Opportunities, and Risks. https://www.ohchr.org/sites/default/files/Documents/issues/Mercenaries/WG/OtherStakeholders/swed-burland-submission.pdf.

The International Code of Conduct for Private Security Service Providers (ICoC). 2010. https://observatoire-securite-privee.org/en/content/international-code-conduct-private-security-service-providers-icoc.

Tkach, B., 2019. Private military and security companies, contract structure, market competition, and violence in Iraq. Confl. Manag. Peace Sci. 36 (3), 291–311.

Transforming Wartime Contracting: Controlling Costs and Risks. 2011. Commission on Wartime Contracting in Iraq and Afghanistan. Final Report to Congress https://cybercemetery.unt.edu/archive/cwc/20110929213820/http://www.wartimecontracting.gov/docs/CWC_FinalReport-lowres.pdf.

Van Amstel, N., Rodenhauser, T., 2016. The Montreux Document and the International Code of Conduct: Understanding the Relationship Between International Initiatives to Regulate the Global Private Security Industry. https://www.montreuxdocument.org/pdf/DCAF-PPPs-Series-Paper_The-MD-and-ICoC-Understanding-the-Relationship.pdf.

Wagner Group: Organizational Overview, 2023. Mapping Militants Project. Stanford Center for International Security and Cooperation. https://cisac.fsi.stanford.edu/mappingmilitants/profiles/wagner-group#_ftn9.

Yaffa, J., 2023. Inside the Wagner Group's Armed Uprising. The New Yorker. https://www.newyorker.com/magazine/2023/08/07/inside-the-wagner-uprising.

Zhang, Z., Bouri, E., Klein, T., Jalk, N., 2022. Geopolitical risk and the returns and volatility of global defense companies: a new race to arms? Int. Rev. Financ. Anal. 83 (November).

CHAPTER 8

Natural resources

While most people reading this book are fortunate enough to not directly see the interplay between natural resources and war in their daily lives, in looking at the historical record and modern landscape, one can see intimate and inseparable linkages between natural resources and war. Scarcity and abundance of natural resources, as well as access to them, have fueled conflicts in the past; we can expect them to be a relevant piece of the picture, albeit differently, in future conflicts. Between the globalized supply chains and anticipated impacts of climate change, we can expect natural resources to be intimately connected with and impacted by war for the foreseeable future. While energy resources and agriculture are certainly at the heart of natural resources in a modern economy, these are sufficiently important to warrant their separate chapters. For that reason, this chapter focuses primarily on natural resources outside of the energy and agricultural sectors.

While modern markets and trade relationships have altered the need for states to physically control natural resources in most cases, these resources still contribute substantially to many conflicts. Even if states are not concerned with physically occupying and controlling lands with key natural resources, they may want to ensure access to these resources, even if through trade, or they may want to ensure the free flow of goods into global markets. States also might concern themselves with denying actual or potential rivals access to resources that could potentially increase their relative power in the international system and thus make themselves more vulnerable. For example, Iraq's invasion and annexation of Kuwait threatened to disturb the balance of power in a region that was vital to global supplies of one of the vital natural resources in oil.

This chapter begins by discussing the historical and modern relationship between resources in wars, followed by a brief overview of commodity markets and a discussion of how wars affect material prices and extraction. The next section will evaluate the relationship between civil wars and raw materials, followed by a brief discussion of how terrorism and natural resources interact. To illustrate the impacts of international war, this chapter then discussed two case studies of World War II and the Russian invasion of

Markets and Conflict
https://doi.org/10.1016/B978-0-323-85525-9.00002-7

Ukraine. Finally, it concludes with a discussion of overall lessons on the relationship between resource management and war for governments, companies, and investors.

Historical relationship between resources and war

The need for access to natural resources has driven many wars over the centuries. In ancient societies, physical control over key resources could drive the strength of early kingdoms and empires, including salt, gold, arable land, and other resources. Early wars included efforts to control vital and powerful resources as well as to control or access lucrative trade routes. European colonization of the Americas was driven largely by an attempt to control and extract natural resources, including gold and silver especially. Similarly, the drive to conquer and colonize Africa was driven heavily by an effort to control and extract natural resources, including gold, ivory, diamonds, and timber, among other resources.

While war requires an expenditure of substantial resources on behalf of the party waging the war, kingdoms and states have often waged war to control scarce and valuable resources. Early empires were often driven by cycles of expansion, consolidation over acquired lands, and contraction in which the empires declined and fell, whether due to internal pressures or external forces (Findlay and O'Rourke, 2010). The waves of expansion by various empires were often driven by the desire to control valuable natural resources of various types, whether to derive the wealth themselves or to prevent potential rivals from gaining them.

European empires were driven to wage wars of expansion in part due to a rush for resources at multiple points in history, including the colonization of the Americas and 19th century scramble to conquer Africa (Findlay and O'Rourke, 2010). Even as trade has seemingly become a more viable and presumably more attractive route to acquire valuable goods in the modern era, natural resources are integrally entangled with war. Especially given the interdependence of modern economies and resource distribution networks, it is important to understand how war both impacts and is impacted by natural resources.

Resources and war in the modern era

In an increasingly global marketplace, the supply and distribution of natural resources is vitally important and is subject to substantial disruptions and opportunities as a result of international armed conflict. Businesses, governments, and societies see their expectations, activities, and opportunities altered by war. This can include disruptions to access of natural resources, increased exploitation of natural resources to support war efforts, variations in costs and availability, and employment. Moreover, government interventions in the face of these challenges can further distort markets, and criminal and rebel activity can create new players in markets. For example, increased consumption of key strategic commodities in the defense industries can substantially raise prices for civilian consumption; aside from agriculture and energy sectors, this includes materials such as steel, rubber, and REMs (rare earth minerals). Beyond these short-term disruptions to prices, occasionally wars signal longer-term shifts in investments and priorities, whether for governments, the private sector, or both.

Many raw materials are vital to the functioning of economic well-being or even the basic survival of modern societies. In such cases, we see the drive to obtain access to these resources as a potential trigger for armed hostilities. While states and societies generally prefer to and typically do obtain these necessary resources through nonviolent means, we see wars and potential for wars often driven by natural resource access. For example, it is hard to imagine that Egypt would allow Sudan or Ethiopia to obstruct or alter the flow of the Nile given how vital its waters are to Egyptian society, from electricity generation to agriculture to the provision of drinking water (Klare, 2001). Access and rights to water have been major sticking points in resolving conflicts between Israel and Syria (Ma'oz, 2005). While there are ample obstacles to a two-state or other solution to the problems of Palestinians in the occupied territories, Israeli settlements not only strip territory and perceptions of security from Palestinians; they also block the development of agriculture in the West Bank and impede effective access to water resources (Owda, 2023).

Wars disrupt supply chains by increasing transportation risks and costs, making it harder or impossible to transport along certain routes, and resulting in shifts in distribution routes and mechanisms. This impacts the price and consumption patterns and levels of raw materials, and it has secondary or tertiary impacts on the industrial production of finished goods. When wars strike, supply chains are often impacted in one way or another, whether due to blockades, embargoes, sanctions, rerouting of resources, or something else.

During war, production, and access to, commodities can be disrupted and/or diverted, which creates inflationary pressures, both for the resources themselves and for other products that depend on these materials. For example, increases in the price of steel increase the costs of automobiles, tools, and many consumer goods. Inflationary pressures in this case are driven in war by a scarcity of supply or concern about future supplies of the material. This can be created due to the severing or restricting of trade relations, speculative buying of commodities in physical form, or through commodity markets.

Wars contribute directly to the destruction of natural resources and ecosystem degradation and often divert public resources away from the management of public goods broadly speaking. During wars, resources shift from many other state functions toward defense, including parks, environmental preservation efforts, and natural resource conservation. Additionally, public areas are often damaged or polluted, and some are converted to military use. Public investment in resource management typically decreases during wartime. This includes decreased efforts to protect parks and punish improper exploitation of natural resources. In places with valuable animal life, wars tend to lead to increased poaching activities, whether from decreased government antipoaching activities or due to people who are out of work capturing and selling animals on the black market or killing them for food. During its civil war, Mozambique saw a curious case in which tuskless elephants became more prevalent. Such elephants had an evolutionary advantage as they were not hunted for their ivory by poachers who operated unchecked in many parts of the country during the war. Therefore not only were elephant populations depleted but many of those that remained were fundamentally different because of war (Stokstad, 2021).

The potential for armed conflict, and even the presence of militaries during peacetime, causes substantial environmental damage. During a typical year in recent years, militaries around the world are responsible for about 5% of global greenhouse emissions (Depledge, 2023). This estimate, while made with substantial missing data, does not account for rebel and other armed military and paramilitary groups. Militaries also take up large portions of land, including in many ecologically sensitive areas (Weir, 2020). Even in peacetime, militaries cause damage to natural resources through emissions, the use of weaponry on firing ranges and proving grounds, and the generation of waste in many ways through a wide range of activities.

During high-intensity conflicts, damage escalates tremendously. Wars lead to increased CO_2 emissions, and deployment and movement of personnel, vehicles, and other equipment damage landscapes and ecosystems by killing animals and destroying vegetation, including vast swathes of forest in some cases. Explosive weapons create tremendous ecological damage by causing high levels of air, land, and water pollution, creating rubble. Scorched earth strategies destroy infrastructure that is vital to extracting, treating, and distributing water. Wars also can make seaways hard to navigate and damage fisheries through pollution caused by wrecked and damaged ships as well as explosive ordinance. It can take some time for marine habitats to recover, even after the visible damage has been removed (Weir, 2020).

Evidence on the impacts of war on deforestation is surprisingly mixed. While public resources dedicated to the protection of forests and reforestation are harmed during wars, the picture beyond this becomes rather complicated. During Yemen's current war, firewood gathering has increased tremendously, especially given the fuel crisis in the country (Aldagbashy, 2019). Contrary to expectations, in the case of many civil wars, wars slow rates of deforestation. For example, following the end of the civil wars in Nepal, Sri Lanka, Ivory Coast, and Peru, rates of deforestation increased by a rate of 68% on average. During the wars, guerillas used forests and jungles as cover for their bases. The exploitation of timber resources consequently becomes dangerous and thus decreases activities of harvesting trees (Grima and Singh, 2019).

Basics of commodity markets

While some natural resources do not generally operate within the framework of commodity markets, such markets are vital to understanding how raw materials in society function. Commodity markets are places in which traders can exchange raw materials. Within the framework of commodity markets, raw goods, such as agricultural goods, fossil fuels, timber, iron, gold, rare earth minerals, or other materials, are traded, both in physical form and speculative form. At the heart of commodity markets are agreements between sellers and buyers on contracts in which the commodities will be delivered in the future at agreed-upon prices. While such contracts can and do take place through direct mechanisms, commodity markets include platforms through which such transactions are facilitated at rapid speeds due to the existence of a multitude of buyers and sellers in the market at any given time. Through such mechanisms, we see the typical market dynamics at work in which buyers and sellers drive prices through their collective willingness to sell and buy products at given prices. In the framework of these markets, the prices that buyers are willing to pay, and thus sellers can charge, are driven by a wide variety of factors, including levels of supply and demand of the products, geopolitical events, government interventions in markets, and natural events (Hayes, 2021).

Commodity markets provide advantages in that they allow producers and consumers to gain access to raw materials in a centralized marketplace that is highly fluid. While commodity markets were traditionally the domain of professional traders, expanded options for participating have led to the involvement of a much wider range of actors. This has led to increases in the financialization of commodities and an expansion of futures trading in the area of commodities. This has resulted in more fluid and adaptive markets that tend to adjust and find new equilibrium points more effectively and quickly. As the markets have become more liquid, we have also seen increasing volatility in the markets overall as investors respond more heavily and quickly to future expectations of commodity prices (Cheng and Xiong, 2014).

Of course, not all raw materials are sold in commodity markets, and they are subject to varying levels of government involvement. Many materials are sold in specialized markets where they may have varying levels to which they are subject to the dynamics in commodity markets. Nonetheless, unless otherwise prohibited or impractical, most material prices are subject to normal supply and demand dynamics, which generally drive prices. Even if some of these markets are not nearly as financialized as commodity markets, they sometimes become financialized indirectly through the operations of publicly traded countries engaged in extracting and selling these resources.

Material prices in war

Wars tend to increase volatility in the prices of commodities for various reasons. Wars can lead to disruptions in supply chains for commodities, decrease access to markets, interrupt harvesting of raw materials, interfere with transportation, and destroy facilities and infrastructure used in both extraction and transportation. For all of these reasons as well as the increased uncertainty that wars bring, we tend to see strong speculative pressures when the clouds of war gather, when wars start, or when there are major shifts in the tides of war. In most cases though, these overhyped price shifts tend to fade before too long, and the fundamentals of supply and demand relationships tend to win out in the long term, provided that the war in question hasn't fundamentally reshaped some aspect of these relationships.

Government actions during wars often disrupt commodity prices through a wide variety of mechanisms. We have already addressed the potential for wars to destroy commodities, production/extraction facilities, and infrastructure to transport commodities, thus diminishing levels of supply. Beyond the physically destructive aspects of wars, wartime governments can and do affect market dynamics in many ways that we see in commodity markets. Governments during war increase their demand for commodities that are important to the war effort and decrease their demand for other commodities. Governments may increase taxes on society, thus making commodities and their production more expensive. Both combatant and noncombatant states often alter the rules of trade during war, including embargoes, export controls, and other forms of sanctions, denying market access in one or more areas in both directions. Governments sometimes seize control of or increase control over industries that are considered vital to the war efforts. In rare cases, governments implement price controls and potentially ration the levels at which people in society can access key resources. While this is far from an exhaustive list, it provides an overview of the vast and sweeping roles that governments play during wars that can impact commodity markets.

Making peace at the end of wars often has a downward pressure on commodity prices due to a lowered demand and decreased costs in extracting and distributing raw materials in a market. In wars of mass mobilization, commodity prices sink and sometimes collapse with the arrival of peacetime when demand subsides. Coupled with decreased levels of government spending and sometimes downward pressure on wages as former combatants reenter the workforce, we often see decreases in prices of materials that were used heavily in wartime but are less valuable during peacetime. In essence, we see a shift in market value from one set of materials to another. Meanwhile, both domestic and international markets for commodities tend to be more stable once peacetime operations have become normalized.

Natural resources and materials can play a valuable political role in facilitating peace in the wake of war as well. While it was years later, the common management of Coal and Steel in the European Coal and Steel Community led to greater levels of trust, expanded levels of cooperation, and played an important role in promoting positive and peaceful relations among Western European states, ultimately expanding geographically and functionally, becoming the European Union which spans most of Europe's land, including 27 member states. We see this even more acutely in the wake of civil wars as natural resources can play a key role in sparking and sustaining wars as well as in building peace (Halle, 2009).

Investment in raw material production and extraction

Wars can strongly impact investment in the production and extraction of raw materials as well as the distribution of such resources. They impact the access of markets to capital, both domestically and from foreign sources for the simple reason that wars either make it so that resources are not harvestable or at a minimum require investors to price in risk such that the investment may be less desirable or undesirable altogether. Even the risk of armed conflict often makes potential investors get nervous and look elsewhere for opportunities. Any political risk analysis data includes multiple variables that seek to assess the risk of various forms of armed conflict. For example, the International Country Risk Guide dataset and country profiles include multiple dimensions that account for the risk of armed conflict from interstate war, civil war, terrorism, and other forms of violence and unrest ("Guide to Data Variables," 2023). The data, generated for about 40 years, guides companies in assessing political risk when making investments. While war disrupts investment in production in war zones, it boosts efforts to increase efficiency, and it can provide incentives for market actors to boost efforts at exploration, extraction, and efficiency, making the global impacts complex and variable.

Peace, conversely, tends to correlate with a lower level of risk for investments and economic involvement, all things being equal. Therefore it tends to lead to a greater likelihood for companies to increase efforts to invest in resource extraction, all things being equal. The likelihood of seeing such patterns postconflict largely requires effective peacebuilding efforts, including infrastructure reconstruction among other things. In cases where resource extraction efforts contributed to grievances that led to conflict, resumption often depends on whether the peace deal effectively addresses the underlying causes of the conflict.

Resources and civil wars

The presence of natural resources as a substantial part of a country's economy can potentially contribute to civil wars in several ways. They can potentially provide incentives for resource-rich regions to form independent states or provide incentives for the central government to seek to control such regions more closely through coercive measures. The presence of substantial natural resources in a country (especially lootable ones) can provide a source of financing for rebel groups that helps to sustain operations and can provide an incentive to continue wars on the part of rebel leaders.

Collier and Hoeffler (2004) found that the presence of exploitable resources correlates significantly with the likelihood of civil war onset. While they don't deny the contributory effect of grievances to conflict occurrence, they found that models focusing primarily on grievances added little explanatory power to predicting the likelihood of civil war onset. They found that the presence of viable sources of finance that potential rebels can use plays an important role in creating circumstances that are favorable to a viable and sustainable rebellion. While this can come from other sources, such as a foreign benefactor or a diaspora that remits money to fund rebellion, the presence of primary commodities as a high portion of exports correlates significantly with the onset and length of civil wars.

While the presence of natural resources alone does not make civil war likely to occur, when it is coupled with other factors, such as weak states, geographic dispersion, ethnic fractionalization, and other factors, can both drive domestic conflict and cause it to last longer as financial interests of those in leadership positions of rebel groups can become intertwined with control of valuable resources. Inequitable wealth sharing and environmental degradation related to the exploitation of natural resources add a potential spark for a civil war given the presence of other factors (Halle, 2009).

Lujala et al. (2005) found that in the case of diamonds, secondary diamonds, such as alluvial diamonds found in riverbeds, that are easier to exploit, correlate significantly with civil war onset. The same is not the case with primary diamonds, such as those harvested from underground mines, that require a much more substantial effort and operation to exploit. This is because rebels can control the area and quickly and fairly easily harvest the resources to fund their rebellion with secondary diamonds (Lujala et al., 2005). They hypothesized that this was due to the ease of extracting the resources with limited investment as well as the prospects for seizing and exploiting the resource ahead of time (Lujala et al., 2005). For example, Charles Taylor funded the RUF in Sierra Leone's civil war partly due to a calculation of their likelihood to be able to seize and control alluvial diamond deposits that could be quickly harvested and then sent to Liberia and sold on global markets (Siberfein, 2004).

In the Democratic Republic of Congo (DRC), conflicts in the Eastern part of the country have been fueled by various groups competing with one another and the government for control of mineral wealth in the country, including coltan and tungsten. The revenue that rebel groups have gained from selling these resources has both funded their continued activities and entrenched interests in the conflict continuing. While the country's vast natural resource wealth could be used to provide stable government revenues and economic opportunities for its people, these resources have become a curse in a true sense as rebels use them to support their operations, and incentives provided by control over these revenue sources provide incentives to continue the conflict. While the United States and many outside countries have passed legislation in an attempt to stem the flow of conflict minerals, complex supply chains have made it difficult for buyers to ascertain the true origins of the materials, often sold secondhand by merchants. This has driven many multinational corporations to avoid purchasing minerals from the DRC altogether to avoid criminal action, which has artificially harmed some mining operations, leading to some miners losing work and, in some cases, joining rebel groups to support themselves in the absence of legitimate work (Center for Preventive Action, 2023).

Many specific cases point to natural resource exploitation as an important source of rebel group funding. Armed rebel groups, like any venture, must obtain resources to purchase equipment, pay salaries, maintain necessary infrastructure, and generally operate. This can lead to a need to control territory to facilitate effective resource extraction, which incentivizes rebel groups to seek control of territory with valuable resources and develop quasi-state organizations to manage the territory and oversee resource harvesting (Haas, 2021).

Beyond the impact of exploitable natural resources on rebel groups' incentives and opportunities, we see that extractive industries can create tensions between central governments and people within various regions of the countries. Poor engagement with communities and stakeholders related to extractive industry products can lead to violent responses, such as in the case of the Bougainville War in Papua New Guinea (*Extractive Industries and Conflict,* 2012). In this case, large copper deposits were discovered in the North Solomon Islands province of Papua New Guinea. Exploitation of these deposits generated substantial social and environmental consequences. The mining operations heavily involved primarily outside labor that included many white Australians as well as Papua New Guineans, who were also different ethnically from the natives of Bougainville Island. From the 1960s to the 1980s, ethnic tensions fueled by local populations not being substantially consulted in the resource extraction, as well as environmental damage caused by the consequences of the mining operations, led to high levels of tension between the local population and the mining operation, supported by the central government of Papua New Guinea. When Bougainvillean concerns were not adequately addressed by the company, Rio Tinto, or the government of Papua New Guinea, earlier nationalist aspirations that preceded Papua New Guinea's independence were reignited with an outbreak of violence in 1989, first with acts of sabotage against the mining operation that forced its closure. When the government sent military troops to restore order, local organizations responded defiantly and violently. This led to the Bougainville Revolutionary Army's decade-long secessionist struggle, which left thousands dead and ended in a peace agreement under which Bougainville became an autonomous region of Papua New Guinea in 2001 (*Extractive Industries and Conflict*, 2012).

The Panguna copper mine, with deposits valued at approximately $60 billion, remains closed to this day, and its association remains mired in Bougainville's musings over a potential independence referendum (Harding and Pohle-Anderson, 2022). The mine is symbolically and historically tied to aspirations for independence, and its attachment to the pain caused to the people of Bougainville made it difficult to navigate the reopening of the mine. At the same time, the Panguna copper mine offers Bougainville a powerful resource to become a prosperous and independent country (Wilson, 2022). In 2022 the autonomous government announced an agreement with local landowners to reopen the mine. Nonetheless, the costs of reconstructing the mine and restarting the harvesting of copper ore present a barrier. Rio Tinto relinquished its interest in the mine in 2016, and Bougainville has yet to find an investor or aid partner to provide the necessary funds to restart mining operations. If the legislature of Papua New Guinea ratifies the agreement for Bougainville independence agreed to in 2021 following the nonbinding independence referendum in Bougainville in 2019, the Panguna mine and a new republic will likely find themselves thrust into geopolitical competition among the two Chinas and the global superpowers as it seeks funds to restart mining and realize national ambitions of prosperity, all the while trying to avoid the same problems that led to a violent final decade of the last century (Peake and Pohle-Anderson, 2023).

The prelude to and aftermath of the Bougainville Conflict teaches us some valuable lessons about risk in commodity extraction. Engagement of commodity extraction companies with local areas involves multiple levels of interaction. For these companies to operate effectively and with high levels of stability, they must engage stakeholders at multiple levels in the societies where they operate. While projects that ignore local concerns may gain approval in some instances without substantial difficulty, such actions can expose extractive efforts to risks. While widespread violence and effective destruction of the venture are not the typical outcome, other disruptions short of a full-blown secessionist movement can prove detrimental to local operations. Given the increased sensitivity by many governments to local concerns in extractive industry ventures, community buy-in has become increasingly important to consider as litigation, protests, and other forms of political pressure have stopped, delayed, or increased costs of mining and related development efforts.

Natural resources can make civil wars more likely to start and continue. They offer an opportunity for rebel groups to fund their rebellions, provide incentives to control territory, and potentially entangle the financial well-being of combatants with the continuation of civil wars. Governments and firms must consider local stakeholders in making decisions on resource extraction, especially in societies with high levels of ethnic, religious, and/or regional fractionalization. Other aspects of the relationship between resources and civil wars are more difficult to use for governments to form practicable policy approaches. It is important to be aware of the opportunities and incentives different types of natural resources create relative to armed conflict. Firms and investors must consider the potential for certain types of resources, coupled with other civil war risk factors when making choices in investments.

While natural resources are important in understanding civil wars, they also are vital to understanding peace in the aftermath of wars. Natural resources can provide valuable resources to fund reconstruction, provide revenue for government institutions, and fund public goods more effectively (Halle, 2009). They also can allow opportunities and resources for economic development, including employment for former combatants and those whose lives were disrupted by war. Used properly, natural resources can help shift incentives toward peace and facilitate many key peacemaking activities, including the reintegration of former combatants. Effective management in common of the environment and natural resources can provide the basis for former warring parties to work in common and potentially build trust while managing resources, in some cases, were at the heart of the conflict itself (Halle, 2009). None of this is a given, but considering the role of natural resources in postconflict societies is an often neglected but important part of successful peacebuilding efforts.

Terrorism and natural resources

Investments in resource extraction often involve substantial disruptions to local lands and ecosystems. The largest such projects often take place in remote areas in less developed countries. In cases where this overlaps with high levels of ethnic, religious, and/or regional fractionalization, resource extraction efforts can provide fuel to a combustible situation. If local populations feel additionally marginalized and/or victimized in the conduct of resource extraction activities and effective legal remedies are not available, we sometimes see violence. This can include the use of terrorism as a tool to draw attention to the situation and alter economic and political calculations of actors involved in resource extraction and what is often seen as exploitation of the local populations (Dreher and Kreibaum, 2016).

The prevalence of terrorist attacks in regions with valuable natural resources increases the risks associated with extraction and can act as a deterrent to developing, harvesting, or extracting the resources. Terrorist attacks can increase uncertainty, thus decreasing investments in extraction and distribution efforts and infrastructure. This can be an effective route to disrupt FDI which is often vital to extracting natural resources in developing and underdeveloped countries. Even when such projects proceed, costs increase due to costs of security and insurance, resulting in lower profits and lower returns on investment; therefore, the utility calculations for resource exploitation can be negatively impacted by activist terrorist movements in areas with valuable natural resources (Lassoued et al., 2016). The relationship between terrorism and natural resources follows a very similar logic to that in the case of civil wars. We don't tend to see the greatest effects on natural resource destruction and commodity price disruption not from the terrorist attacks themselves or from the market responses directly. The greatest effects come when states have an outsized response to these attacks, especially when a military is employed as part of the response, as opposed to approaches that are more oriented toward law enforcement agencies. In cases where states use terrorist attacks to justify military strikes or prolonged wars, we can see indirect effects that tie into previous categories of the impacts of war on commodities and other natural resources.

World War II as a case study

World War II was the deadliest and most far-flung conflict in human history. As such, it allows the opportunity to look at how an extensive war across most of the world might impact resources and their management as it caused substantial disruptions to markets in many ways. The governments that were involved in war had a tremendous increase in demand for raw materials including oil and agricultural goods but also steel, aluminum, copper, rubber, tin, and many more goods.

The increased governmental demand for raw and finished materials had a tremendous impact on systemic demand and prices. Governments from both sides of the war rationed vital materials, including petroleum products, metal, rubber, agricultural products, and many more items. Many societies dramatically increased their recycling programs in response to general scarcity and the need for wartime production.

Sanctions in the early years of World War II are often dismissed as abject failures and largely counterproductive, but the picture is a bit more complicated. The most robust sanctions in some ways were those imposed on Italy following its invasion of Ethiopia in 1935. Following the invasion, the League of Nations quickly identified Italy as the aggressor, and 52 of its 58 member states imposed sanctions on Italy. The measures varied from imposing strict export controls on vital goods, such as vital raw materials, including strategic metals, to banning imports from Italy entirely. The sanctioning states also sought to cut off Italy's ability to access foreign exchange systems of the day. While Italy's offensive was more effective than anticipated, it suffered heavily from the sanctions, and it only survived them due to strict control measures domestically to keep order and distribute resources sufficiently for essential purposes (Mulder, 2022). Had the Italian military become bogged down as Russia was in Ukraine, it is possible that the sanctions could have started to bite into Italy's capacity and will to wage war sufficiently that it might have relented in its assault on Ethiopia.

Many governments intervened directly to ensure that vital war materials were extracted and managed to promote the perceived national needs. This led to both short- and long-term nationalizations of key extractive sectors in many countries, including the temporary nationalization of coal mines in the United States. Furthermore, because labor to extract such resources was considered vital to national security, even the most liberal economies saw governments intervene in labor disputes, ruling strikes invalid and/or forcing corporations to settle labor disputes. In the case of the United States, a widespread strike by coal miners in 1943 led to President Franklin Roosevelt issuing an executive order to nationalize coal mines. Under these conditions, coal miners were able to continue to press for better pay and conditions, ultimately winning major concessions during the war (Kratz, 2018).

The United States was a major global exporter of key industrial and military goods, including oil and various metals. Following Germany's invasion of Poland in 1939, President Roosevelt received a revision to the Neutrality Acts that permitted him greater flexibility in managing trade relations. He placed a cash and carry requirement on the export of goods to the warring parties, creating a near de facto embargo on Germany. Following Japan's increased aggression in Indochina in 1940, the United States imposed a limited embargo of aviation fuel and high-grade scrap iron on Japan. Following Japan's further expansion of its military campaign, the United States ultimately placed an embargo on the shipment of a wide variety of materials to Japan including oil and many strategic metals such as iron, copper, and steel. Following the UK and Netherlands joining the oil embargo, Japan chose to expand its conquests, ultimately declaring war on all three and seizing control of the Dutch East Indies and its rich oil and rubber resources, as well as various UK and US territories in East Asia and the Pacific. While the US and its allies perhaps planned to deter Japanese aggression through sanctions, these actions yielded the opposite effect, causing Japanese leaders to make the calculation that they must expand the war to continue its other campaigns, such as the war in China. Also, by taking control over oil production in the Dutch East Indies, Japan hoped to cut off a vital resource for its opponents in China (Golden, 2022).

Although World War II caused tightness in many commodities, it caused gluts in others at times, both during the war and in its aftermath. British and American embargoes against the Axis powers caused a glut of many commodities from the colonies of the UK and now-conquered continental European countries as well as allied states. This was largely because, with the German conquest of Western Europe, these exporters had lost access to European markets altogether. The lack of export markets for these primary commodity producers led the US and UK to rush to create a price stabilization mechanism to maintain support in Latin America and avoid revolt in British and European overseas colonies (Martin, 2021).

World War II provides a picture of a relatively maximalist view of how war can reshape natural resources and commodities. Commodity prices of many key goods soared and remained high throughout the war in most cases. This led even the most liberal market societies to introduce rationing and strict price controls, intervene in labor disputes in key industries, and nationalize key sectors, even if temporarily and/or in part. The war included cases where governments intervened in extraordinary ways, including rationing across most countries actively engaged in combat.

Russian invasion of Ukraine as a case study

On February 24, 2022, Russia launched a full invasion of Ukraine with the intent of seizing Kyiv and replacing the current government with a more favorable one. This sort of war is an unusual one in the modern era given the size of the countries involved and the substantial size and length of this interstate war, but it provides a useful example of the impacts that wars can potentially have on raw materials. In this section, we will review the impacts of the first 13 months of the war on primary commodities. While much of the coverage of how the war has affected material prices focuses on energy (oil, gas, and coal) and agriculture (wheat, soybeans, sunflower oil, etc.), the war has impacted other commodities as well, including many metals and fertilizers (Baffes and Nagle, 2022).

While sanctions against Russia have been far more sweeping than most initially expected, they have been more limited than one might expect based on the public narratives related to them. US sanctions in the energy sector have been quite robust, including bans on the import of oil, coal, and liquified natural gas from Russia, as well as US firms investing in most Russian energy firms. It also froze Russian foreign reserves held in the United States and, along with its allies, froze Russia out of the SWIFT interbank messaging system. For example, sanctions have not targeted the nuclear sector, and the US and countries participating in the sanctions have continued to import uranium from Russia (Berman and Siripurapu, 2023). The EU and Canada have banned the import of finished steel products from Russia, and imports to the US have fallen to such an extent that they are negligible (Asenov, 2022). Various countries targeted other materials such as aluminum but given Russia's large place in key commodities such as precious metals and diamonds, many of these sectors remained directly untouched. Additionally, they do not have the outsized role of energy products in Russian exports, which made up over 60% of Russian exports prior to the war (*Russia Exports,* 2023). That said, other financial and banking sanctions made it more difficult for Russia to export some of these materials at previous levels, and many individual firms in G7 and EU countries have made decisions to forego business relations in or with Russia and companies within it. Additional sanctions included ones targeted at individuals associated with the regime or sanctions targeted at denying Russia access to vital materials for the military campaign.

When Russia invaded Ukraine, we saw a disruption of raw material extraction efforts in parts of Ukraine. For example, coal production in Ukraine fell by over 50% in 2022, largely due to the inability of companies to operate in much of the country and the fact that most of Ukraine's coal deposits are located in the Donbas region, which has been at the center of much of the fighting. While the war has largely not been fought on Russian soil and thus hasn't created the same types of disruptions to natural resource production and extraction, international sanctions impacted Russian commodity exports by largely closing the markets of G7 countries as well as much of the EU and some other countries around the world. These sanctions blocked a large portion of Russian exports of materials to G7 countries, most of the EU, and some other countries, impacting the ability of Russia to use its normal export routes. Furthermore, it complicated the picture of Russia's sale of key commodities to overseas markets. Additionally, it created similar complications in how companies in countries sanctioning Russia replaced these familiar suppliers.

In the case of the Russian invasion of Ukraine, we saw a tremendous spike in commodity prices in the short term (Baffes and Nagle, 2022), but many of these settled down before long. While some of these commodities for which Russia and/or Ukraine are heavy producers saw large but short spikes (such as palladium), other commodities settled down to prewar price levels after many months (such as fertilizers), and others became relatively more stable but took longer and have not fully returned to prewar levels (such as oil). The war illustrated useful lessons related to the impact of sanctions on commodity prices. It showed that short-term shocks in commodity prices are often the result of speculative fears rather than effective market predictions. Therefore, like with other price shocks due to news-led speculation, such events create opportunities for savvy investors with steady hands. Furthermore, it demonstrated a limited impact of sanctions when they don't include major players in the global economy. Sanctions on the exports of many Russian commodities have caused increased costs for Russian exporters as they must often use more expensive supply routes by shipping to China and India rather than Europe, for example, and at times must offer price discounts to these new markets. This will likely make Russia more dependent on China and others politically and economically for years to come. Non-Russian firms that normally sold oil, gas, steel, or other commodities to China shifted their sales to other targets in many cases. Thus the supply levels of these commodities were not negatively impacted either at the global level or even in the economies of countries that have participated in sanctions against Russia.

According to World Bank reports on commodity price reports, the first quarter of 2022 saw substantial increases in many commodity prices as a result of the war. For example, potassium chloride prices increased by about 150%, while the price of nickel increased by about 50% in this period. Commodity prices increased for an expected set of reasons. Russia's navy imposed physical blockades on the export of goods from Ukraine by sea. While the agricultural deal brokered by Turkey helped to ease these problems in the areas of food and fertilizer, it did not impact the ability of Ukraine to export other commodities or reverse damage to physical infrastructure that the war caused. Given the diversion of much rail traffic to facilitate civilian evacuation in the early months of the war and the tremendous tonnage shipped out by Ukraine through its seaports, sufficient adaptation to transport commodities by land was not possible. Nonetheless, the impact of the decrease in Ukraine's extraction and export of commodities does not have a tremendous impact on global markets, especially when accounting for nonagricultural goods.

The resilience of the global commodity markets in the case of the Russo-Ukrainian War presents a valuable lesson to policymakers, firms, and investors. While the impact of the war on commodity prices is less than many initially predicted, it is far from immaterial, and it drove a substantial restructuring in the flow of commodities. For the most part, flows of basic commodities such as steel and oil that previously went to Europe or the United States were redirected to other markets, such as India, China, and Turkey. Aggregate supply and demand for basic commodities haven't changed globally for the most part as other countries were often eager to import increased levels of oil, steel, gold, and other materials from Russia that now were subject to EU sanctions. In many cases, Russia had to sell these materials at a discount and/or pay more in transportation costs, slightly limiting profits, but this did not have a tremendous impact on the global commodity price picture in most instances in the longer term.

The war caused tremendous worries in the production and supply of noble gases, including neon, xenon, and krypton. In typical years, Russia and Ukraine have supplied about half of the global supply of neon and about a quarter of the global supply of xenon and krypton. Much of the neon supply was generated as a by-product of steel production within Ukraine. These gases are vital to many industries, including semiconductor production, used in window glazing, and as propellants, among other things. The rare gases produced in Russia and Ukraine are largely drawn from air-separation plants built at steel mills in the 1980s. Rare gases extracted were sent to Ukraine for purification, which is important for most industrial uses. While these shipments continued following Russia's annexation of Crimea, they stopped with the invasion in February 2022. Ukrainian steel mills have operated at a small percentage of previous capacity since the invasion, thus further diminishing the production of the by-product gases. While prices of these rare gases surged following Russia's invasion of Ukraine more than sixfold, industries weathered these disruptions and adapted in surprisingly effective ways. Chipmakers drew upon their neon reserves and invested in gas recycling technologies. In other cases, manufacturers have replaced rare gases with alternative materials. Russia diverted its rare gas production to China, which then exported its production which had a surplus at the time of the war. Others have made long-term efforts to diversify their supplies and to boost production and efficiency of rare gas production (*How Rare-Gas Supply Adapted to Russia's War*, 2023).

Given that sanctions restricted or banned the import of certain commodities from Russia in most EU, G7, and other countries that have joined efforts to sanction Russia, flexibility in global commodity markets will be limited in the future. This could cause greater difficulty in markets adjusting to future disruptions or effectively reaching price equilibrium as market actors are limited from the standpoint of investors, buyers, and sellers (Saefong, 2023).

The war has impacted longer-term investments in mining industries in Russia, both by the central government and by outside investors. The Russian government has diverted much attention and resources toward the war effort, making it difficult to concentrate as fully on the development of long-term projects. Outside firms, especially those located in Western countries, have largely reconsidered their approaches to Russia. Uncertainty created by the war and subsequent sanctions may have a longer-term impact on natural resources that is yet to materialize. Many Western firms are hesitant to invest in Russia currently, either because of current sanctions, concerns about bad press, or due to high levels of uncertainty. This has led to a decrease in mineral expansion in Russia relative to plans that existed even mere weeks before the invasion. For example, domestic plans for a $15 billion investment in two new copper mines were put on hold while resources were shifted toward military industries (Casey, 2023).

A longer-term impact of the war may be the European Union's move toward energy independence and a reduction in hydrocarbon use in general. In May 2022, the European Commission released a plan to end the EU's dependence on Russian hydrocarbons by the end of 2027. This includes a substantial boost to renewable energy. The European Commission previously planned to boost renewables in final energy consumption to 40% of total energy consumption by 2030. Due to the war, the commission boosted this goal to 45%. The International Energy Agency expects EU renewable electricity generation to double from 2022 to

2027 alone (*Russia's War on Ukraine,* 2023). These ambitious targets will generate tremendous demand for many vital commodities, including aluminum, lithium, graphite, cobalt, manganese, arsenic, gallium, germanium, indium, tellurium, and various rare earth elements (*Critical Mineral Commodities in Renewable Energy,* 2019). We are likely to see upward price pressure on some of these key minerals as a result of increased demand unless there is a corresponding increase in supply. One side effect could be increased leverage in geopolitics for the countries that hold substantial reserves of these materials. China is the leader in reserves, production, and refining of these vital rare earth elements, followed by Russia and Vietnam (Leruth and Mazarei, 2022). Barring the discovery of large deposits elsewhere, it remains unclear how these powers might gain and use influence from their dominance in this vital area.

While the commodity prices have not remained high as many expected at the outset of the war, limited sanctions in some areas and adaptations in Russian export directions and relationships have largely allowed most non-agricultural commodity prices to revert to or below their prewar levels. It is hard to say what impact the sluggish Chinese economic recovery from the COVID-19 pandemic has had in preventing a greater rise in commodity prices. China's economy in 2022 posted its slowest growth rate in decades with its GPD growing by about 3%, or half the forecasted growth rate (Helbling, 2023). Commodity prices are likely to see the full effects of the war later and in more subtle ways than initially expected. First, deferred investment by Russia domestically and increased caution in external investment in the Russian market may lead to an underinvestment in resource development in Russia and tighter resource supplies in the future. Second, it will likely be years at a minimum before European and G7 demand for Russian goods returns to prewar levels, and it will probably return with greater caution. Third, the war seems to have resulted in a shock to the system of European energy imports. Not only will most European countries be resistant to the idea of returning to Russian gas and oil supplies, but the experience is likely to have a lasting impact that will drive European energy markets toward reducing dependence on natural gas and especially oil in general long term. The war and Russia's assumptions regarding, and attempts to wield, its energy resources as a weapon to keep European states subdued have given these states a substantial push toward efforts to wean themselves off of Russian energy, and it has given a substantial push to efforts to move toward a lighter use of hydrocarbons in general.

Conclusions

If there is one overarching lesson about the relationship between resource management and war, it is that there is great value in taking the long-view, big-picture approach whenever possible. This applies equally though in different ways to governments, firms, and investors. The job for governments is perhaps the most difficult as they have the most angles to consider. Firms can insulate themselves from the short-term price shocks that can accompany wars without signaling a long-term shift in market demands, especially when the disruption comes from speculation driven by expectations related to sanctions. If the sanctions do not involve broad global involvement, markets will likely adjust, and commodity prices will recover from initial price shocks. Therefore firms can limit their exposure to the risk of war-related disruptions by not only diversifying their supply chains but also building greater stockpiles of supplies and raw materials so that they can ride out short-term supply disruptions.

While wars themselves make substantial demands on commodities, post-war reconstruction efforts potentially provide a greater challenge and demand. Societies coming out of war often see a marked increase in demand for materials to rebuild homes, businesses, and infrastructure. Furthermore, a return to normal economic activity can see an increase in demand for civilian goods and a decrease in demand from the public sector. Therefore firms often find themselves shifting rapidly to serve a very different market. While many high-demand materials overlap between wartime and peacetime (copper, steel, etc.), others differ. Peacetime reconstruction tends to see an increase in demand for building materials such as cement and timber in addition to steel, plastics, copper, asphalt, and other materials (partly dependent on the nature of the building in the society). Peacetime will likely see a return to projects aimed at longer-term goals, and this leads to a different set of material demands. For example, in the wake of the war in Ukraine, we may see renewed vigor in many societies, especially in Europe, to develop alternative energy production including wind and solar power ventures. Subsequently, these projects may be sufficiently large to increase demand and drive prices for related materials upward.

In thinking about wars from a macroeconomic perspective, they are perhaps best viewed as a set of market distortions both in the present tense and prospectively. The distortions include disruptions to normal economic activity of various sorts. In very large wars, governments increase spending dramatically, leading to increased demand for resources, stress on supplies, and upward pressure on prices, especially in the case of widespread and/or systemic wars. In modern commodity markets, wars lead to increased speculative buying and selling behavior, especially when the wars seem likely to affect the extraction, export, and/or flow of commodities. Shifts in labor availability can disrupt such inputs into commodity extraction, driving up labor costs and increasing the negotiating position of workers, all things being equal.

While the cases of World War II and the Russian invasion of Ukraine offer lessons for large-scale disruptions to commodities and other materials, most cases of political violence, including terrorism, interstate wars, and civil wars, result in far more localized effects, especially in the long term. In most cases, disruptions will tend to be relatively short term, and global commodity markets and globalized supplies adjust to meet demand relatively effectively before long. Therefore the impacts of most modern conflicts are more limited than we might initially expect.

References

Aldagbashy, A., 2019. Yemen's Forests Another Casualty of War Amid Fuel Crisis. Science and Development Network. https://www.scidev.net/global/news/yemen-s-forests-another-casualty-of-war-amid-fuel-crisis/.

Asenov, G., 2022. Decline of Russian Steel in US Negates Need for Sanctions. Fastmarkets. https://www.fastmarkets.com/insights/decline-of-russian-steel-in-us-negates-need-for-sanctions.

Baffes, J., Nagle, P., 2022. Commodity Prices Surge Due to the War in Ukraine. World Bank Blog. https://blogs.worldbank.org/developmenttalk/commodity-prices-surge-due-war-ukraine.

Berman, N., Siripurapu, A., 2023. One Year of War in Ukraine: Are Sanctions Against Russia Making a Difference? Council on Foreign Relations. https://www.cfr.org/in-brief/one-year-war-ukraine-are-sanctions-against-russia-making-difference.

Casey, J.P., 2023. One Year On: Confusion and Conclusions from the Russian Invasion. Mining Technology. https://www.mining-technology.com/features/russian-invasion-war-mineral-exports-ukraine/.

Center for Preventive Action, 2023. Instability in the Democratic Republic of Congo. Council on Foreign Relations Global Conflict Tracker. https://www.cfr.org/global-conflict-tracker/conflict/violence-democratic-republic-congo.

Cheng, I.-H., Xiong, W., 2014. Financialization of commodity markets. Annu. Rev. Financ. Econ. 6, 419–441.

Collier, P., Hoeffler, A., 2004. Greed and grievance in civil war. Oxf. Econ. Pap. 56, 563–595.

Critical Mineral Commodities in Renewable Energy, 2019. United States Geological Survey. https://www.usgs.gov/media/images/critical-mineral-commodities-renewable-energy.

Depledge, D., 2023. Low-carbon warfare: climate change, net zero and military operations. Int. Aff. 9 (2), 667–685.

Dreher, A., Kreibaum, M., 2016. Weapons of choice: the effect of natural resources on terror and insurgencies. J. Peace Res. 55 (4), 539–555.

Extractive Industries and Conflict: Toolkit and Guidance for Preventing and Managing Land and Natural Resources Conflict, 2012. The United Nations Interagency Framework for Preventive Action. https://www.un.org/en/land-natural-resources-conflict/pdfs/GN_Extractive.pdf.

Findlay, R., O'Rourke, K., 2010. War, trade, and natural resources: a historical perspective. In: Yale-Princeton Conference of Trade and War. https://sites.socsci.uci.edu/~mrgarfin/OUP/papers/Findlay.pdf.

Golden, J., 2022. Agreements, aggression, and embargoes: parallels from the past to Russia and Ukraine. Columbia J. Int. Aff.

Grima, N., Singh, S.J., 2019. How does the end of armed conflicts influence forest cover and subsequently ecosystem services provision? An analysis of four case studies in biodiversity hotspots. Land Use Policy 81, 267–275.

Haas, F., 2021. Insurgency and ivory: the territorial origins of illicit resource extraction in civil conflicts. Comp. Polit. Stud. 54 (8), 1327–1495.

Halle, S. (Ed.), 2009. From Conflict to Peacebuilding: The Role of Natural Resources and the Environment. United Nations Environment Programme. https://www.iisd.org/publications/conflict-peacebuilding-role-natural-resources-and-environment.

Harding, B., Pohle-Anderson, C., 2022. The Next Five Years are Crucial for Bougainville's Independence Bid. United States Institute for Peace. https://www.usip.org/publications/2022/08/next-five-years-are-crucial-bougainvilles-independence-bid.

Hayes, A., 2021. Commodity market: definition, types, example, and how it works. Investopedia. https://www.investopedia.com/terms/c/commodity-market.asp#toc-history-of-commodity-markets.

Helbling, T., 2023. Opening Remarks for the Press Briefing of the 2023 China Article IV Staff Report. International Monetary Fund. https://www.imf.org/en/News/Articles/2023/02/01/sp-china-aiv-press-briefing-opening-remarks.

How Rare-Gas Supply Adapted to Russia's War, 2023. De Economist.

Klare, M.T., 2001. Resource Wars: The New Landscape of Conflict. MacMillan Publishing, New York.

Kratz, J., 2018. You Can't Dig Coal with Bayonets. National Archives, Pieces of History. https://prologue.blogs.archives.gov/2018/07/11/you-cant-dig-coal-with-bayonets/.

Lassoued, T., Hamida, A., Hadhek, Z., 2016. Terrorism and economic growth. Int. J. Econ. Financ. Issues 8 (1), 175–178.

Leruth, L., Mazarei, A., 2022. Who Controls the world's Minerals Needed for Green Energy? Peterson Institute for International Economics. Retrieved from: https://www.piie.com/blogs/realtime-economic-issues-watch/who-controls-worlds-minerals-needed-green-energy.

Lujala, P., Gleditsch, N.P., Gilmore, E., 2005. A diamond curse? Civil war and a Lootable resource. J. Confl. Resolut. 49 (4), 538–562.

Ma'oz, M., 2005. Can Israel and Syria Reach Peace? Obstacles, Lessons, and Prospects. The James A. Baker III Institute for Public Policy. https://www.bakerinstitute.org/sites/default/files/2013-08/import/wp_israelsyria.pdf.

Martin, J., 2021. The global crisis of commodity glut during the second world war. Int. Hist. Rev. 43 (6), 1273–1290.

Mulder, N., 2022. The Economic Weapon: The Rise of Sanctions as a Tool of Modern Warfare. Yale University Press, New Haven.

Owda, R., 2023. How Israeli Settlements Impede a Two-State Solution. Carnegie Endowment for International Peace. https://carnegieendowment.org/sada/89215.

Peake, G., Pohle-Anderson, C., 2023. What Does U.S. Reengagement in Papua New Guinea Mean for Bouganville? United States Institute of Peace. https://www.usip.

org/publications/2023/03/what-does-us-reengagement-papua-new-guinea-mean-bougainville.

Russia Exports, 2023. Trading economics. https://tradingeconomics.com/russia/exports.

Russia's War on Ukraine, 2023. International energy agency. https://www.iea.org/topics/russias-war-on-ukraine.

Saefong, M., 2023. Russia's War Set Off a Commodity Scare. A Year Later, the Fright is Gone. Barron's. https://www.barrons.com/articles/russia-ukraine-war-crude-oil-palladium-coal-commodity-prices-86a90625.

Siberfein, M., 2004. The geopolitics of conflict and diamonds in Sierra Leone. 9 (1), 213–241.

Stokstad, E., 2021. Civil war drove these elephants to lose their tusks – through evolution. Science. https://www.science.org/content/article/civil-war-drove-these-elephants-lose-their-tusks-through-evolution.

Weir, D., 2020. How Does War Damage the Environment? Conflict and Environment Observatory. https://ceobs.org/how-does-war-damage-the-environment/.

Wilson, C., 2022. Bouganville Starts Process to Restart Controversial Panguna Mine. Al Jazeera. https://www.aljazeera.com/news/2022/5/6/holdbougainvillestartsprocessto-reopen-controversial-panguna-mine.

CHAPTER 9

Conclusion

This book has explained how a variety of markets affect and are effected by international war, civil war, terrorism, and other forms of conflict. We have seen that market forces can cause conflict and that conflict can warp market forces. This knowledge is essential to empower investors, firms, and governments to make rational economic decisions in times of conflict, ranging from trade wars to terrorist attacks, to full-scale war, with a primary focus on the latter.

Sadly, our current reality includes all too many examples of armed conflict. An international war between Russia and Ukraine has raged for nearly 2 years, and Hamas' deadly attack against the state of Israel has resulted in a massive response that looks like it will have devastating consequences throughout the region long into the future. The consequences of conflict, and especially armed conflict, are devastating. The worst of these consequences are death, grave bodily injury, and secondary harm that people suffer, but the economic consequences can also be devastating and enduring. Understanding those consequences, and how to best prepare for and possibly avoid them, has been among the primary purposes of this book. The effects are not unidirectional, however. Conflicts affect markets, but market dynamics also affect conflict. How markets may exacerbate, motivate, or even cause conflict was also a major focus of this book. By understanding one potential cause of conflict, we have a better chance of avoiding it all together.

This final chapter summarizes the main findings of the book. In Chapter 2, we discussed equity markets. This chapter provided a broad overview of equity markets and conflict, noting that price volatility is a common reaction at the onset of conflict. No simple pattern emerges from the historical record that can be unfailingly applied, but broader lessons are obtainable. This chapter delved into three case studies, World Wars I and II and the Iraq War, and instances of terrorism, to uncover some of those lessons, which we apply to provide strategies for preparing for conflict.

Through examination of statistical research and a thorough analysis of the historical record, this chapter demonstrated that the two biggest threats to

Markets and Conflict
https://doi.org/10.1016/B978-0-323-85525-9.00010-6

investors are lack of preparedness and irrational panic. Though conflict often negatively impacts markets, thoughtful preparation and the deliberate management of investments can reduce risks and generate opportunities. A variety of strategies, such as diversification, well-timed buying and selling, and switching to other forms of investment, may limit losses and even generate gains.

In Chapter 3, we examined energy markets, with a major focus on oil. Energy commodities, and oil especially, drive economic growth and are at the heart of the global economy. Without oil or other forms of energy, much of the global economy would grind to a halt. Modern militaries are also dependent on oil. The importance of oil, both economically and militarily, makes it worth fighting for and has sometimes fueled conflict as well as vehicles. Oil is also important in relation to conflict because the revenues derived from its production and sale can be used to fund armies, rebellions, and terrorist attacks alike. Oil revenues can also inflame ethnic or group jealousies if divided unevenly, benefiting some sectors of society but not others. This can lead to social fracturing and ultimately internal civil conflict.

In order to provide a framework of understanding, in this chapter we provided sections on the basic workings of energy markets as well as a discussion of production and distribution logistics. The importance of the Organization of the Petroleum Exporting Countries (OPEC) was described along with differences in market structure between oil, which is an international market, and natural gas, which is generally sold on more regional markets. Once these basics were established, the chapter moved on to discuss how energy markets affect and are affected by criminality, terrorism, and civil wars before moving on to international conflicts.

The potential vulnerabilities generated by oil scarcity and price fluctuation have led some states, particularly the United States, to seek greater energy independence. Increased production in the U.S. has offset or at least limited some disruptions in the Middle East and other oil-producing regions. This fundamentally changed the balance between suppliers and consumers in the larger international market and had significant repercussions for other large producers, such as Russia and OPEC countries, which suddenly found themselves with additional competition and a United States that was less reliant upon them. Nonetheless, these changes have only gone so far, and the Middle East and other high-production states remain significant, and even dominant, in global energy markets.

Petrostates—states which generate a substantial proportion of their GDP from oil production—remain critical to world oil markets and are therefore discussed. The most important of these are Russia, Saudi Arabia, Iran, Venezuela, and various Gulf states. The wealth these countries derive from oil revenues has bolstered their domestic strength and international influence. Reliance on oil production has also, however, made these states remarkably vulnerable to reductions in price. Lower prices on international markets have had major repercussions for the economy of Venezuela, and international sanctions against oil production in Russia and Iran have similarly affected those countries' broader economies.

The broad conclusions of Chapter 3 were that while energy resources have the potential to drive conflict, conflict also affects markets. Conflict, especially in energy-producing countries, can cause panic in markets and subsequent volatility in prices, usually manifesting in higher prices. Since energy is at the base of much of the larger economy, increased prices can result in widespread inflation throughout the economy. Certain elements of energy market volatility, such as the magnitude of the effect and how long the effects are likely to last, vary by circumstance and are important considerations for both investors and policymakers.

Agricultural markets were the topic of Chapter 4. Agricultural lands and production have been a target of warfare for millennia. Their destruction has been seen as a way to deprive the enemy of a critical resource, and their seizure has been seen as an opportunity to sustain one's own military forces. While conflict can of course have devastating consequences for farmers whose land is targeted and destroyed directly, for those lucky enough not to have their lands and produce destroyed, war can be a boon as prices are nearly certain to rise. Consumers, on the other hand, will just as certainly experience shortages and price increases. This is sometimes enough to create widespread famine, malnutrition, and death. Due to the international nature of today's agricultural markets, these effects can be felt far beyond the borders of the combatants themselves.

Chapter 4 started by detailing how agricultural markets work and looked at the three fundamental elements of agricultural production: land, labor, and capital. This section detailed how a variety of factors, such as the overall development level of a country, transportation infrastructure, global value chains, and trade agreements, impinge upon agricultural markets. Also discussed were basic economic principles, such as supply and demand, and futures markets, and how they apply specifically to agricultural markets.

After providing these basics, the chapter moved on to discuss how conflict affects agricultural markets generally before delving into specific case studies in subsequent sections. These sections included discussions of the ancient world, the American Civil War, and World War II. The continuing postconflict effects of war were also discussed. The effects of violent conflict on agricultural markets can be long lasting, sometimes taking years or even decades to overcome.

As with other types of markets, agricultural markets can present both danger and opportunity in times of conflict. Because of the likely increased price of produce, investors in agricultural markets may find opportunities for profit. Consumers, however, are likely to suffer from these higher prices, and governments and policymakers are likely to seek ways to circumvent increased costs, either through price controls, subsidization, direct food assistance, or other policy interventions. The effects of conflict may be long lasting even after its cessation. Loss of labor and human resources, the destruction of infrastructure, and altered production practices may not normalize immediately.

Chapter 5 examined industrial markets. Conflict potentially disrupts industrial production in several different ways. Armed conflict can destroy infrastructure and fixed capital assets that are critical to industrial production. Supply chain disruption caused by violence similarly impact industrial production capacity for finished products when raw materials become scarce. Conflict also alters production priorities, with the government incentivizing the production of war material, including armaments and military vehicles. In large-scale wars, this leads to a reduction or cessation of production of ordinary but nonessential industrial goods. Labor shortages, created in circumstances of large-scale military mobilization, also reduce industrial production as workers are diverted into fighting.

The distortions created in industrial markets can be more easily dealt with, or even profited from, with proper planning. Supply chain diversification and altering investment strategies based upon likely changes in supply and demand brought about by the conflict can reduce losses and increase the potential for financial gains. New opportunities may abound in the aftermath of conflicts as demand rebounds for consumer goods that were unavailable during the conflict and reconstruction drives demands as houses, infrastructure, and societies are rebuilt. Because supply chains, infrastructure, and labor shortages may take a long time to resolve, businesses that foresee those challenges and find ways to resolve them may reap substantial rewards in an era of rebounding demand but limited supply.

In Chapter 6, we discussed how violent conflict is both affected by and itself affects international trade. While it's true that trade can create tensions between countries, its benefits create powerful incentives for peace since violence would threaten the prosperity generated by trade. Both internal and international wars tend to reduce overall trade levels, which is bound to have negative economic consequences for all involved, and even for many neutral parties.

Wars also increase volatility in international exchange rates. The currencies of combatant countries tend to decrease in value. This effect is most pronounced for currencies that are not major reserve currencies and of countries where fighting takes place. Currency speculators and those seeking to protect the value of their holdings are likely to switch to more stable currencies or other commodities, such as gold. Governments involved in the conflict must be cognizant of the impact it is likely to have in devaluing its currency and take countervailing actions, such as the imposition of capital controls.

This chapter also focuses on a nonviolent form of conflict that has profound repercussions on markets. . Trade wars have become less common with the modern international monetary and trade structure created by such institutions as the World Trade Organization (WTO) which set the rules for international trade and allow for mediation of conflicting interpretations of those rules. Despite the existence of these institutions, trade wars do still happen. The primary example in recent times is that between the United States and China. Even in this case, however, both sides have shown considerable restraint when compared to past trade wars, and the economic consequences, while serious, have been limited.

In Chapter 7, we delved into the world of military contracting. Contractors play a large role in modern conflicts, up to and including war. Many states use contractors to supplement, or in some cases even replace, their militaries' roles in weapons development and production, support services such as food preparation and laundry, equipment maintenance, training, security, and even fighting. Defense contracting has become a business that exists even when conflict is at an ebb.

The use of contractors has become so pervasive that it might be seen as its own type of market. Of course, the contractors themselves, along with their investors, have the most directly at stake financially. Their company values of the most established and best-placed companies often rise substantially at the onset of conflicts, but the longevity of that initial spike often fades. Once the shape of conflicts becomes clearer, so do profit forecasts for companies as contracts are signed and profits are realized. Despite these enhanced wartime profits, many defense corporations are more dependent on long-term contracts for service provision and weapons development and production during peacetime. Therefore they profit more reliably from the shadows of war than from the wars themselves.

Though states hope that military contractors will ultimately save them money and provide needed services more efficiently than the state itself can produce, overreliance on contractors can erode the ability of the state military to perform crucial functions over time and can also reduce the government's overall control over military activities and undermine its agency and legitimacy. Contractors are not always financially cheaper in the long run and often come at great cost in terms of human rights accountability and long-term readiness. The use of military contractors can create difficult problems for states as contractors might have incentives to engage in behaviors that run counter to state interest, whether through seeking to inflate profits or prioritizing short-term company interests over long-term state priorities. Due to these challenges, states and societies must carefully consider accountability and regulation of military contractors.

Finally, in Chapter 8, we explored resource management. Waging wars requires substantial resources. Steel, copper, other metals, cement, plastics, rubber, and a long list of other resources are necessary to successfully prosecute a war. Governments may therefore find it necessary to direct resource usage into directions and channels that they wouldn't naturally flow under peaceful conditions. Certain businesses may find their access to resources limited if their product is not considered to be essential to the war effort while those companies producing war material will find themselves in a favored position. Those firms that see far enough ahead that there may be reduced access to certain critical raw materials in the future can seek to mitigate that possibility by diversification of their supply chain or through stockpiling of those materials before the onset of increased scarcity.

Both companies and governments must also keep in mind that not only are there likely to be changes in access to resources during wars, but in their aftermath as well. The cessation of conflict often leads to a revival of demand for housing, transportation infrastructure, and ordinary consumer goods. Businesses and investors who can most quickly readjust to this demand may find themselves in an advantageous position. It is important to remember that wars and other types of conflict do not last forever. In most cases, conflicts and their concomitant financial disruptions will be relatively short-lived after which markets will gradually revert to more typical conditions, though some areas may never fully recover and others may experience a resurgence greater than obtained during preconflict conditions.

Global commodity markets and supply chains will likely adjust to post-conflict conditions fairly rapidly. Those who adjust the most quickly are likely to prosper while those who fail to do so may find themselves left behind. From an overall picture, the speed of economic recovery and market adjustment after conflict typically means that the long-term impacts of conflict on commodity markets are not as extensive as many might fear. Keeping that long view in mind is perhaps the most important lesson of all.

This book has demonstrated how variety of markets are affected differently by conflict and by different types of conflict. There is no one-size-fits-all approach to markets and conflict. It is impossible, therefore, to draw broad lessons that are applicable to all forms of economic markets. If there is one such lesson, however, it is that foreknowledge is our best hope of avoiding the worst economic outcomes of conflict. We hope that this book constitutes one step toward that goal.

Index

Note: Page numbers followed by *f* indicate figures and *t* indicate tables.

Printed and bound by CPI Group (UK) Ltd, Croydon, CR0 4YY

08/05/2025

01864775-0001